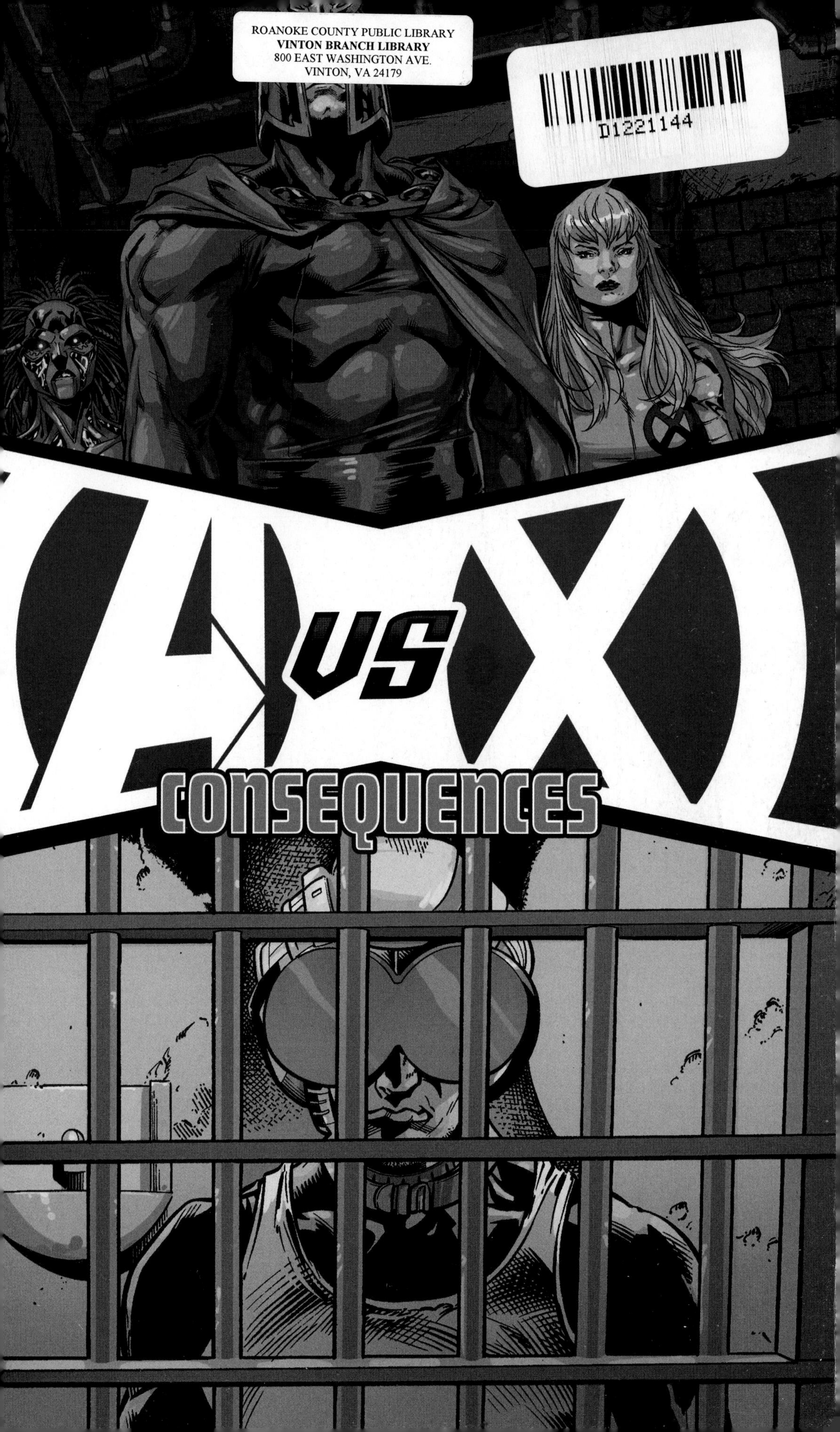
A VS X
CONSEQUENCES

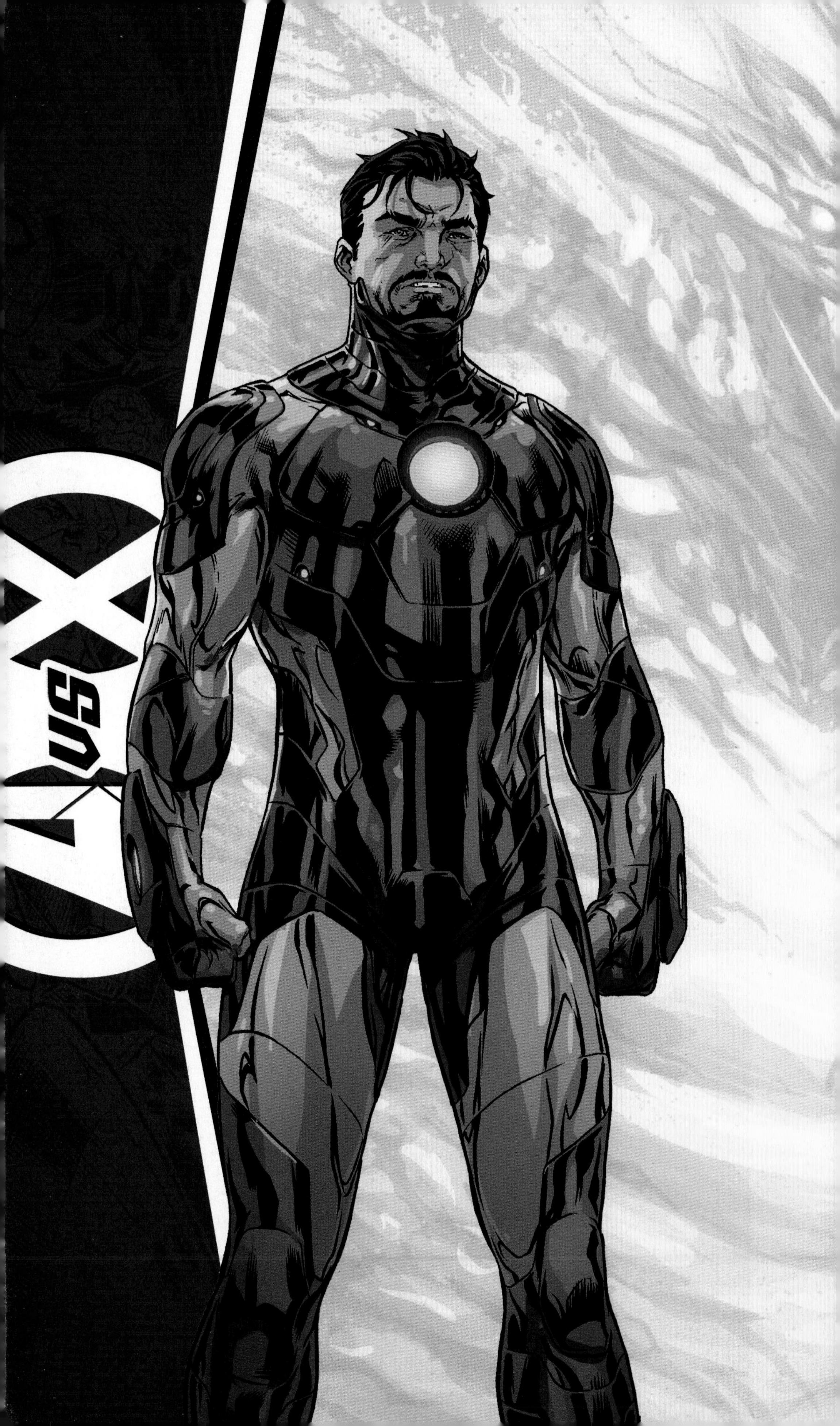

CONSEQUENCES

WRITER: **KIERON GILLEN**

PENCILERS: **TOM RANEY** (#1), **STEVE KURTH** (#2),
SCOT EATON (#3), **MARK BROOKS** (#4)
& **GABRIEL HERNANDEZ WALTA** (#5)

INKERS: **TOM RANEY** (#1), **ALLEN MARTINEZ** (#2),
ANDREW HENNESSY (#3-4), **MARK BROOKS** (#4)
& **GABRIEL HERNANDEZ WALTA** (#5)

COLORIST: **JIM CHARALAMPIDIS**

LETTERER: **VC'S CLAYTON COWLES**

COVER ARTISTS: **PATRICK ZIRCHER**
WITH **DOMMO SANCHEZ AYMARA** (#1),
RON GARNEY WITH **JASON KEITH** (#2-3)
& **SALVADOR LARROCA** WITH **DAVID CURIEL** (#4-5)

ASSISTANT EDITOR: **JORDAN D. WHITE**

EDITOR: **NICK LOWE**

COLLECTION EDITOR: **CORY LEVINE**
ASSISTANT EDITORS: **ALEX STARBUCK** & **NELSON RIBEIRO**
EDITORS, SPECIAL PROJECTS: **JENNIFER GRÜNWALD** & **MARK D. BEAZLEY**
SENIOR EDITOR, SPECIAL PROJECTS: **JEFF YOUNGQUIST**
SENIOR VICE PRESIDENT OF SALES: **DAVID GABRIEL**
BOOK DESIGN: **JEFF POWELL**

EDITOR IN CHIEF: **AXEL ALONSO** CHIEF CREATIVE OFFICER: **JOE QUESADA**
PUBLISHER: **DAN BUCKLEY** EXECUTIVE PRODUCER: **ALAN FINE**

VENGERS VS. X-MEN: CONSEQUENCES. Contains material originally published in magazine form as AVX: CONSEQUENCES #1-5. First printing
013. ISBN# 978-0-7851-6646-7. Published by MARVEL WORLDWIDE, INC., a subsidiary of MARVEL ENTERTAINMENT, LLC. OFFICE OF PUBLICA-
ON: 135 West 50th Street, New York, NY 10020. Copyright © 2012 and 2013 Marvel Characters, Inc. All rights reserved. All characters featured in
nis issue and the distinctive names and likenesses thereof, and all related indicia are trademarks of Marvel Characters, Inc. No similarity between
ny of the names, characters, persons, and/or institutions in this magazine with those of any living or dead person or institution is intended, and any
uch similarity which may exist is purely coincidental. **Printed in the U.S.A.** ALAN FINE, EVP - Office of the President, Marvel Worldwide, Inc. and
VP & CMO Marvel Characters B.V.; DAN BUCKLEY, Publisher & President - Print, Animation & Digital Divisions; JOE QUESADA, Chief Creative Officer;
OM BREVOORT, SVP of Publishing; DAVID BOGART, SVP of Operations & Procurement, Publishing; RUWAN JAYATILLEKE, SVP & Associate Publisher,
ublishing; C.B. CEBULSKI, SVP of Creator & Content Development; DAVID GABRIEL, SVP of Publishing Sales & Circulation; JIM O'KEEFE, VP of Opera-
ons & Logistics; DAN CARR, Executive Director of Publishing Technology; SUSAN CRESPI, Editorial Operations Manager; ALEX MORALES, Publishing
perations Manager; STAN LEE, Chairman Emeritus. For information regarding advertising in Marvel Comics or on Marvel.com, please contact Niza
isla, Director of Marvel Partnerships, at ndisla@marvel.com. For Marvel subscription inquiries, please call 800-217-9158. **Manufactured between
2/13/2012 and 1/15/2013 by QUAD/GRAPHICS, DUBUQUE, IA, USA.**

0987654321

AvsX

CONSEQUENCES

HOPE SUMMERS WAS DESTINED TO HOST THE PHOENIX FORCE. H[ER]
IMPENDING POSSESSION PITTED WOLVERINE AND THE AVENGERS AGAIN[ST]
UTOPIA'S MUTANT RESIDENTS. MANY FEARED THE PHOENIX'S ARRIVAL WOU[LD]
SPELL DISASTER. CYCLOPS BELIEVED IT WOULD BE HIS PEOPLE'S REBIRT[H.]

THE AVENGERS FRAGMENTED THE PHOENIX FORCE, UNINTENTIONAL[LY]
SPLITTING AND DIVERTING IT INTO CYCLOPS, EMMA FROST, COLOSSUS, MAG[IK]
AND NAMOR. ITS POWER SOON CORRUPTED THE FIVE AS THEY BEG[AN]
REMAKING THE WORLD IN THEIR IMAGE. EVENTUALLY, THE PHOENIX W[AS]
EXCISED FROM ALL BUT CYCLOPS, GRANTING HIM TOTAL CONTROL OF [ITS]
LIMITLESS POWER. PROFESSOR XAVIER WAS KILLED BY CYCLOPS AS [HE]
ATTEMPTED TO STOP HIS FORMER PUPIL.

AS THE COMBINED FORCES OF THE AVENGERS AND X-MEN DROVE T[HE]
PHOENIX OUT OF CYCLOPS, HOPE FULFILLED HER DESTINY BY BECOMING O[NE]
WITH THE COSMIC ENTITY. SHE AND THE SCARLET WITCH DISPERSED [ITS]
POWER ACROSS THE GLOBE, SPARKING THE AWAKENING OF A N[EW]
GENERATION OF MUTANTS.

HUMAN AND MUTANTKIND HAVE BEEN SAVED, BUT NOT WITHOUT GRE[AT]
CONSEQUENCES. CYCLOPS HAS BEEN IMPRISONED, MANY REMAIN FUGITIV[ES]
AND ENTIRE NATIONS LIE IN RUIN...

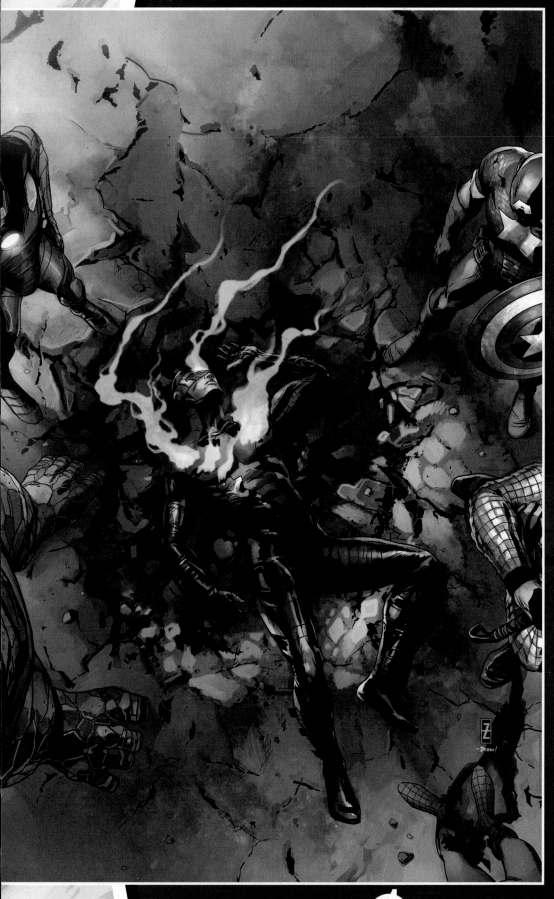

ISSUE #1

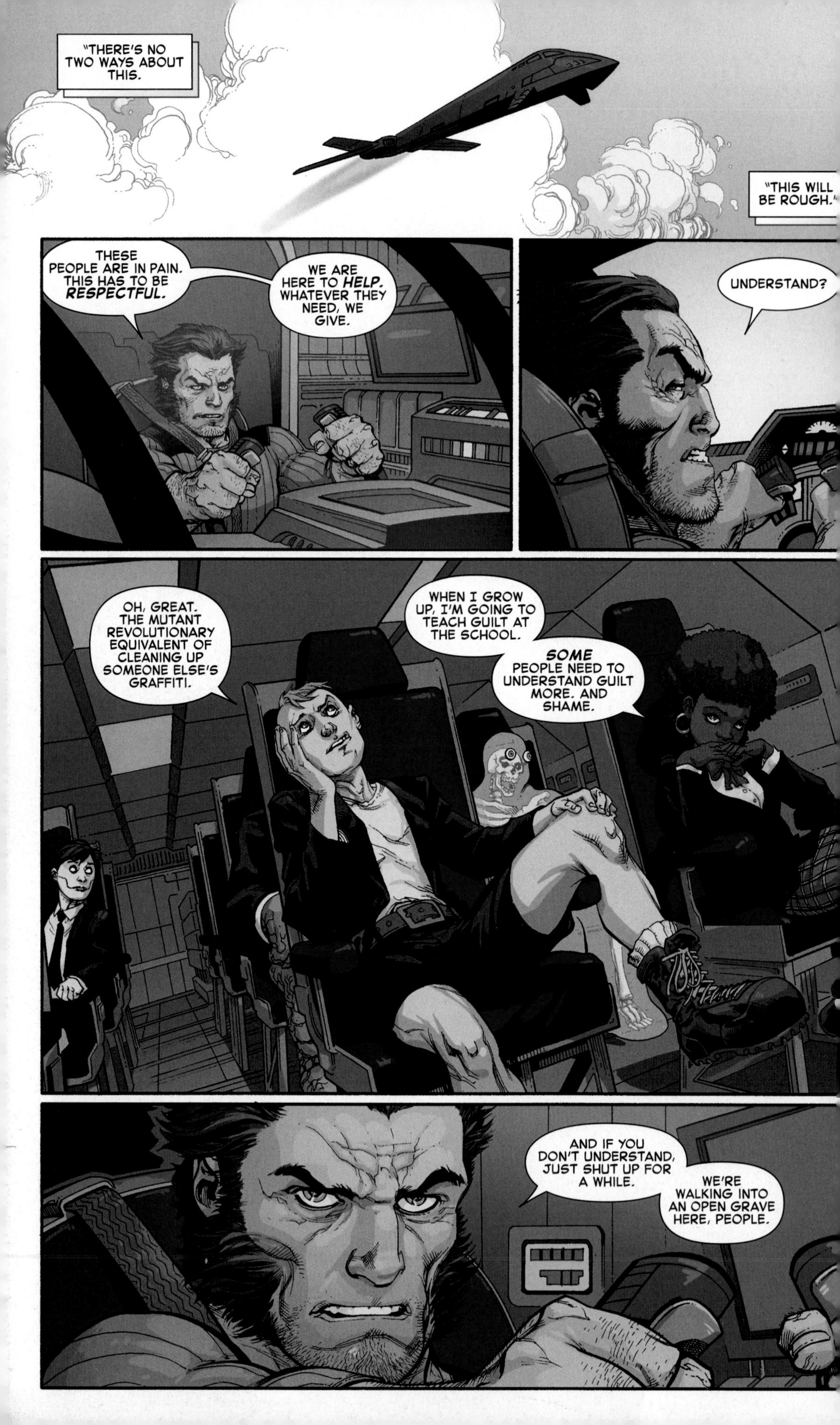
"THERE'S NO TWO WAYS ABOUT THIS.
"THIS WILL BE ROUGH."
THESE PEOPLE ARE IN PAIN. THIS HAS TO BE RESPECTFUL.
WE ARE HERE TO HELP. WHATEVER THEY NEED, WE GIVE.
UNDERSTAND?
OH, GREAT. THE MUTANT REVOLUTIONARY EQUIVALENT OF CLEANING UP SOMEONE ELSE'S GRAFFITI.
WHEN I GROW UP, I'M GOING TO TEACH GUILT AT THE SCHOOL.
SOME PEOPLE NEED TO UNDERSTAND GUILT MORE. AND SHAME.
AND IF YOU DON'T UNDERSTAND, JUST SHUT UP FOR A WHILE.
WE'RE WALKING INTO AN OPEN GRAVE HERE, PEOPLE.

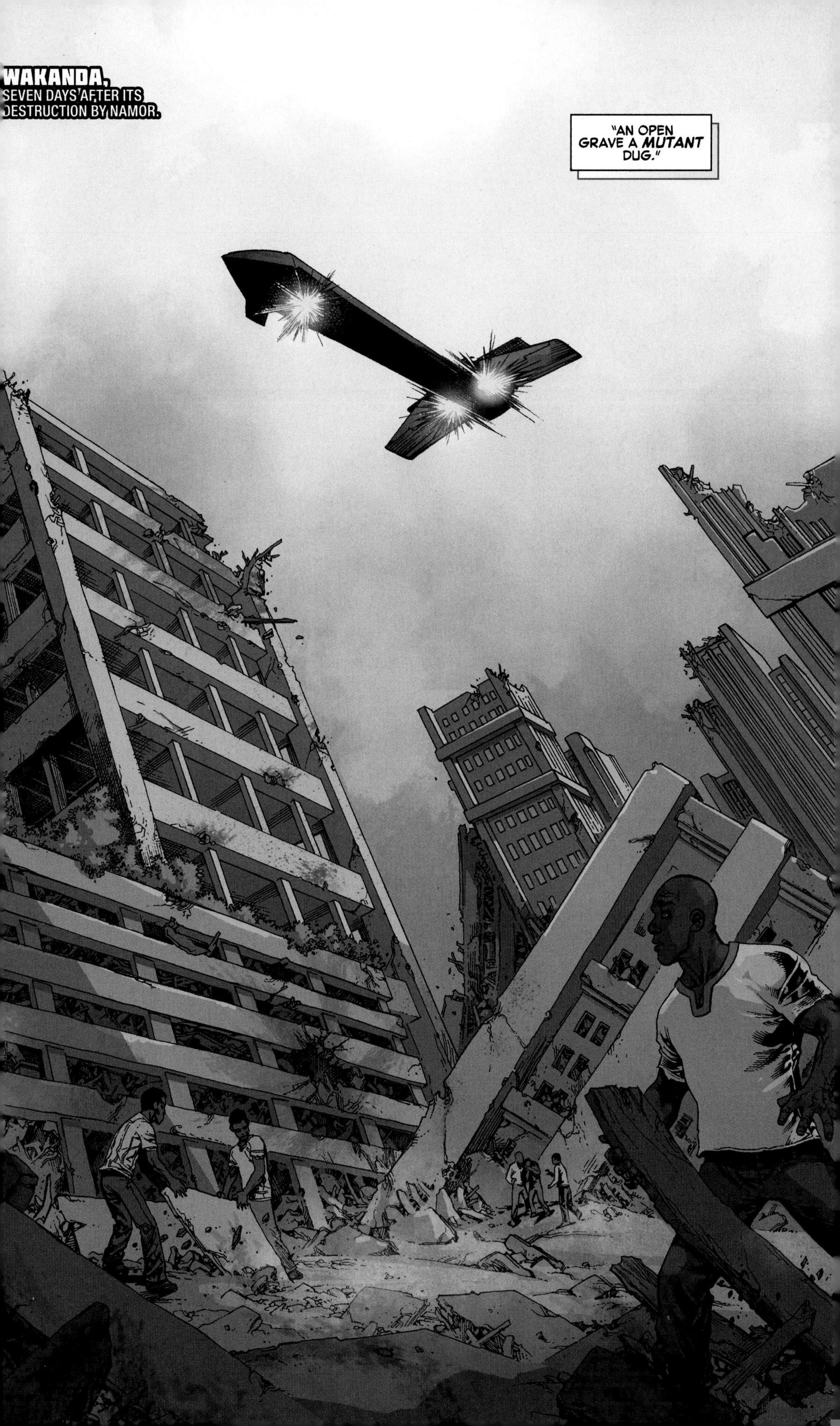
WAKANDA,
SEVEN DAYS AFTER ITS
DESTRUCTION BY NAMOR.
"AN OPEN GRAVE A *MUTANT* DUG."

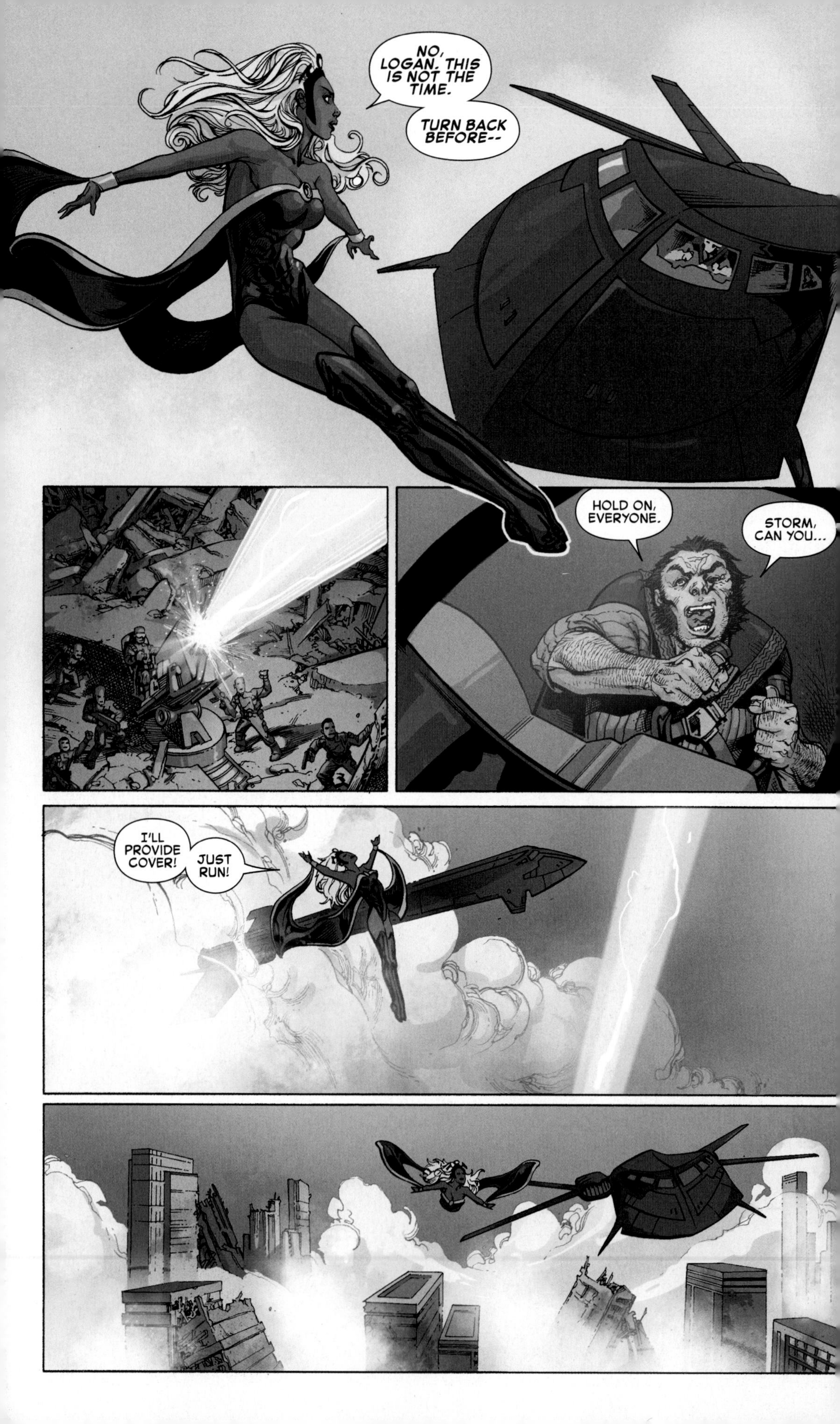
NO, LOGAN. THIS IS NOT THE TIME.
TURN BACK BEFORE--
HOLD ON, EVERYONE.
STORM, CAN YOU...
I'LL PROVIDE COVER!
JUST RUN!

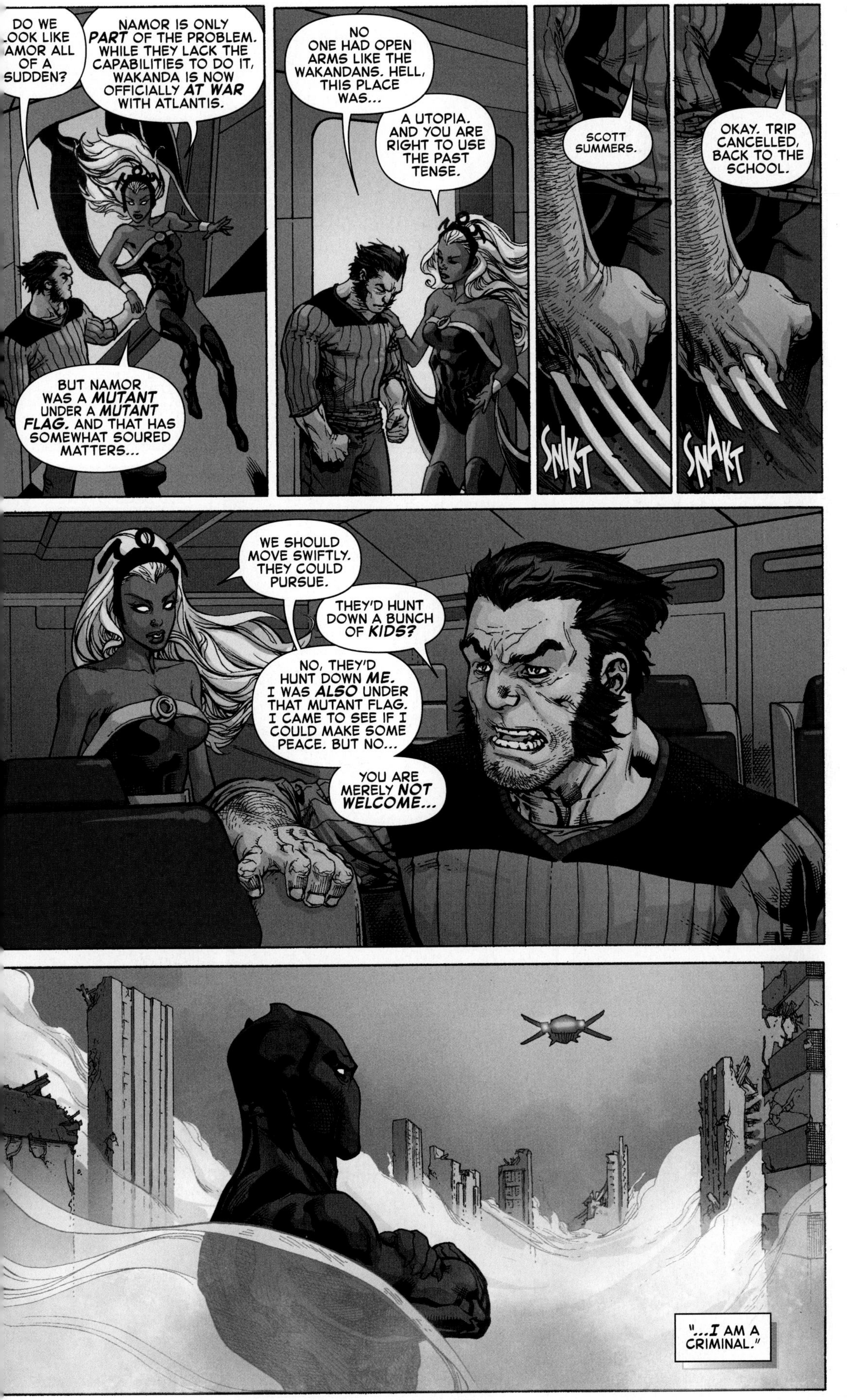

DO WE LOOK LIKE NAMOR ALL OF A SUDDEN?
NAMOR IS ONLY PART OF THE PROBLEM. WHILE THEY LACK THE CAPABILITIES TO DO IT, WAKANDA IS NOW OFFICIALLY AT WAR WITH ATLANTIS.
BUT NAMOR WAS A MUTANT UNDER A MUTANT FLAG. AND THAT HAS SOMEWHAT SOURED MATTERS...
NO ONE HAD OPEN ARMS LIKE THE WAKANDANS. HELL, THIS PLACE WAS...
A UTOPIA. AND YOU ARE RIGHT TO USE THE PAST TENSE.
SCOTT SUMMERS.
SNIKT
OKAY. TRIP CANCELLED, BACK TO THE SCHOOL.
SNAKT
WE SHOULD MOVE SWIFTLY. THEY COULD PURSUE.
THEY'D HUNT DOWN A BUNCH OF KIDS?
NO, THEY'D HUNT DOWN ME. I WAS ALSO UNDER THAT MUTANT FLAG. I CAME TO SEE IF I COULD MAKE SOME PEACE. BUT NO...
YOU ARE MERELY NOT WELCOME...
"...I AM A CRIMINAL."

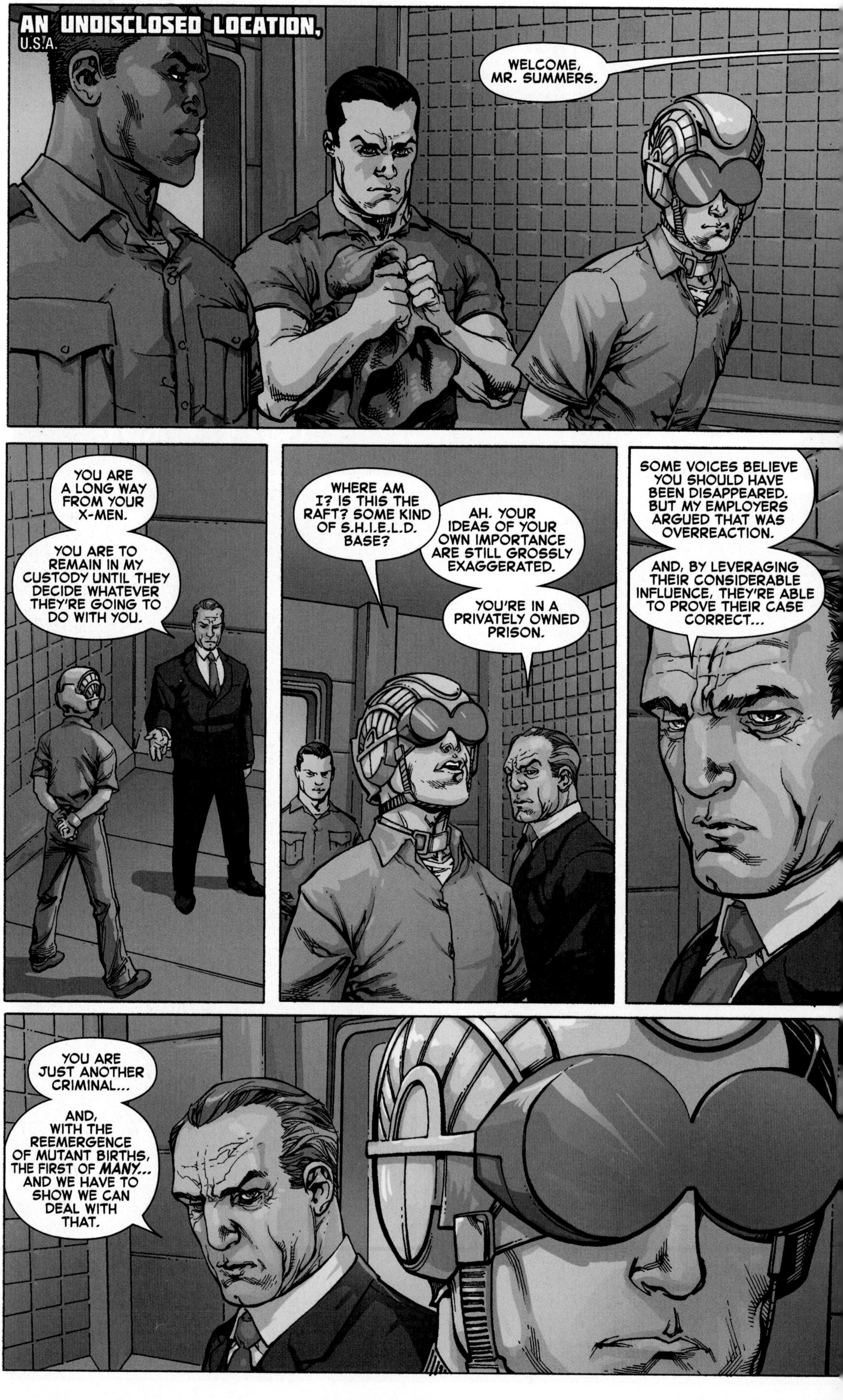
AN UNDISCLOSED LOCATION,
U.S.A.
WELCOME, MR. SUMMERS.
YOU ARE A LONG WAY FROM YOUR X-MEN.
YOU ARE TO REMAIN IN MY CUSTODY UNTIL THEY DECIDE WHATEVER THEY'RE GOING TO DO WITH YOU.
WHERE AM I? IS THIS THE RAFT? SOME KIND OF S.H.I.E.L.D. BASE?
AH. YOUR IDEAS OF YOUR OWN IMPORTANCE ARE STILL GROSSLY EXAGGERATED.
YOU'RE IN A PRIVATELY OWNED PRISON.
SOME VOICES BELIEVE YOU SHOULD HAVE BEEN DISAPPEARED. BUT MY EMPLOYERS ARGUED THAT WAS OVERREACTION.
AND, BY LEVERAGING THEIR CONSIDERABLE INFLUENCE, THEY'RE ABLE TO PROVE THEIR CASE CORRECT...
YOU ARE JUST ANOTHER CRIMINAL...
AND, WITH THE REEMERGENCE OF MUTANT BIRTHS, THE FIRST OF MANY... AND WE HAVE TO SHOW WE CAN DEAL WITH THAT.

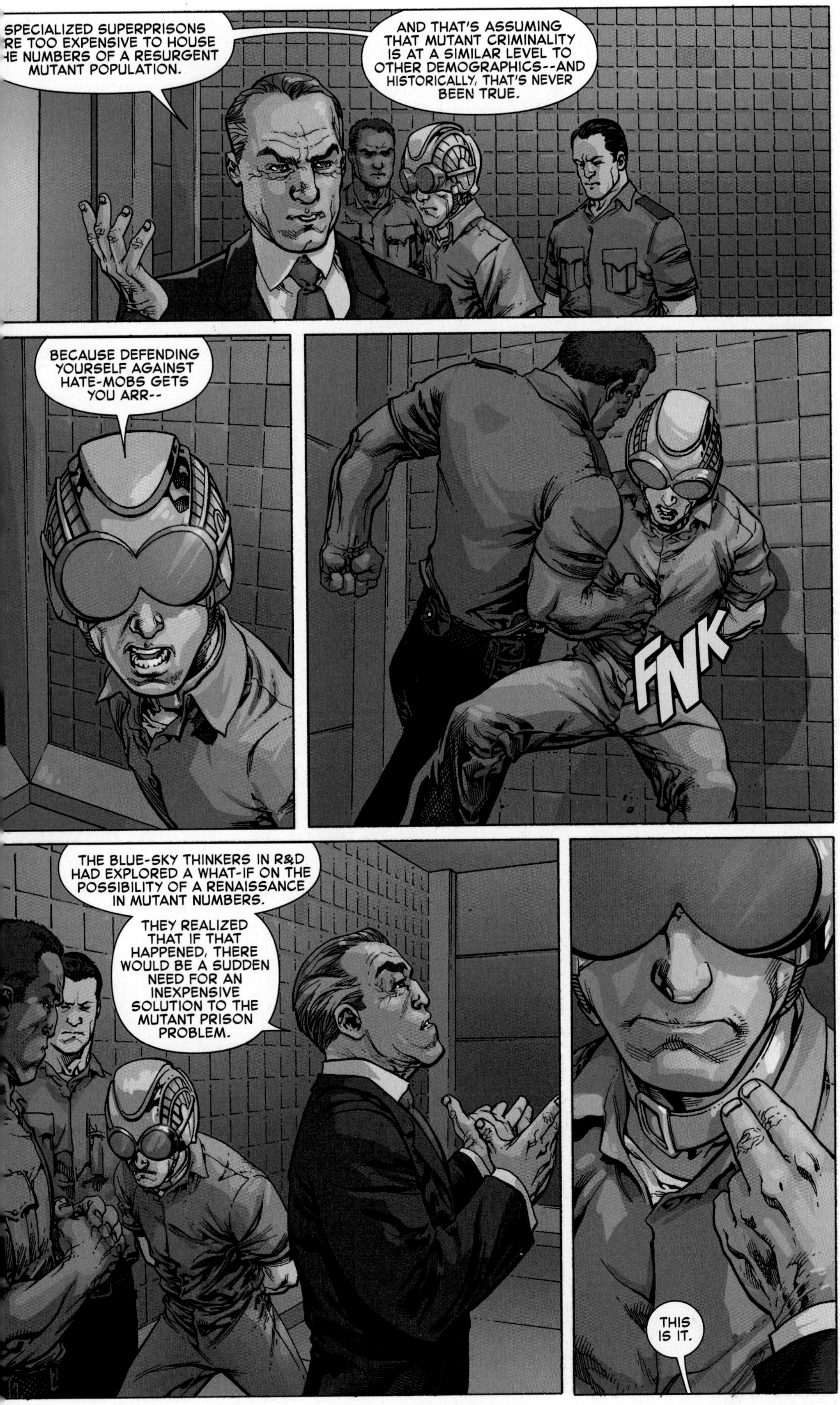
SPECIALIZED SUPERPRISONS RE TOO EXPENSIVE TO HOUSE HE NUMBERS OF A RESURGENT MUTANT POPULATION.
AND THAT'S ASSUMING THAT MUTANT CRIMINALITY IS AT A SIMILAR LEVEL TO OTHER DEMOGRAPHICS--AND HISTORICALLY, THAT'S NEVER BEEN TRUE.
BECAUSE DEFENDING YOURSELF AGAINST HATE-MOBS GETS YOU ARR--
FNK
THE BLUE-SKY THINKERS IN R&D HAD EXPLORED A WHAT-IF ON THE POSSIBILITY OF A RENAISSANCE IN MUTANT NUMBERS.
THEY REALIZED THAT IF THAT HAPPENED, THERE WOULD BE A SUDDEN NEED FOR AN INEXPENSIVE SOLUTION TO THE MUTANT PRISON PROBLEM.
THIS IS IT.

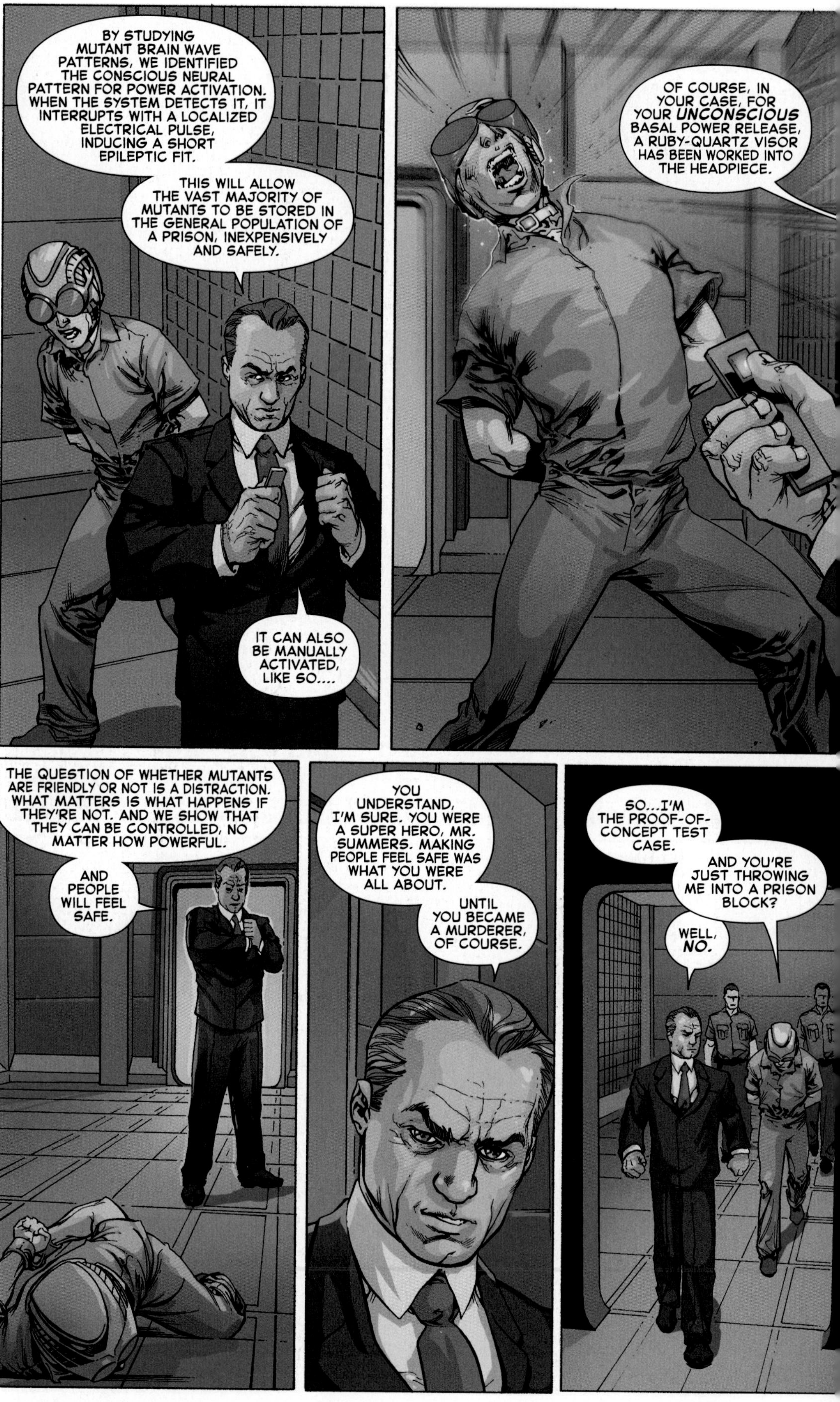

BY STUDYING MUTANT BRAIN WAVE PATTERNS, WE IDENTIFIED THE CONSCIOUS NEURAL PATTERN FOR POWER ACTIVATION. WHEN THE SYSTEM DETECTS IT, IT INTERRUPTS WITH A LOCALIZED ELECTRICAL PULSE, INDUCING A SHORT EPILEPTIC FIT.
THIS WILL ALLOW THE VAST MAJORITY OF MUTANTS TO BE STORED IN THE GENERAL POPULATION OF A PRISON, INEXPENSIVELY AND SAFELY.
IT CAN ALSO BE MANUALLY ACTIVATED, LIKE SO....
OF COURSE, IN YOUR CASE, FOR YOUR UNCONSCIOUS BASAL POWER RELEASE, A RUBY-QUARTZ VISOR HAS BEEN WORKED INTO THE HEADPIECE.
THE QUESTION OF WHETHER MUTANTS ARE FRIENDLY OR NOT IS A DISTRACTION. WHAT MATTERS IS WHAT HAPPENS IF THEY'RE NOT. AND WE SHOW THAT THEY CAN BE CONTROLLED, NO MATTER HOW POWERFUL.
AND PEOPLE WILL FEEL SAFE.
YOU UNDERSTAND, I'M SURE. YOU WERE A SUPER HERO, MR. SUMMERS. MAKING PEOPLE FEEL SAFE WAS WHAT YOU WERE ALL ABOUT.
UNTIL YOU BECAME A MURDERER, OF COURSE.
SO...I'M THE PROOF-OF-CONCEPT TEST CASE.
AND YOU'RE JUST THROWING ME INTO A PRISON BLOCK?
WELL, NO.

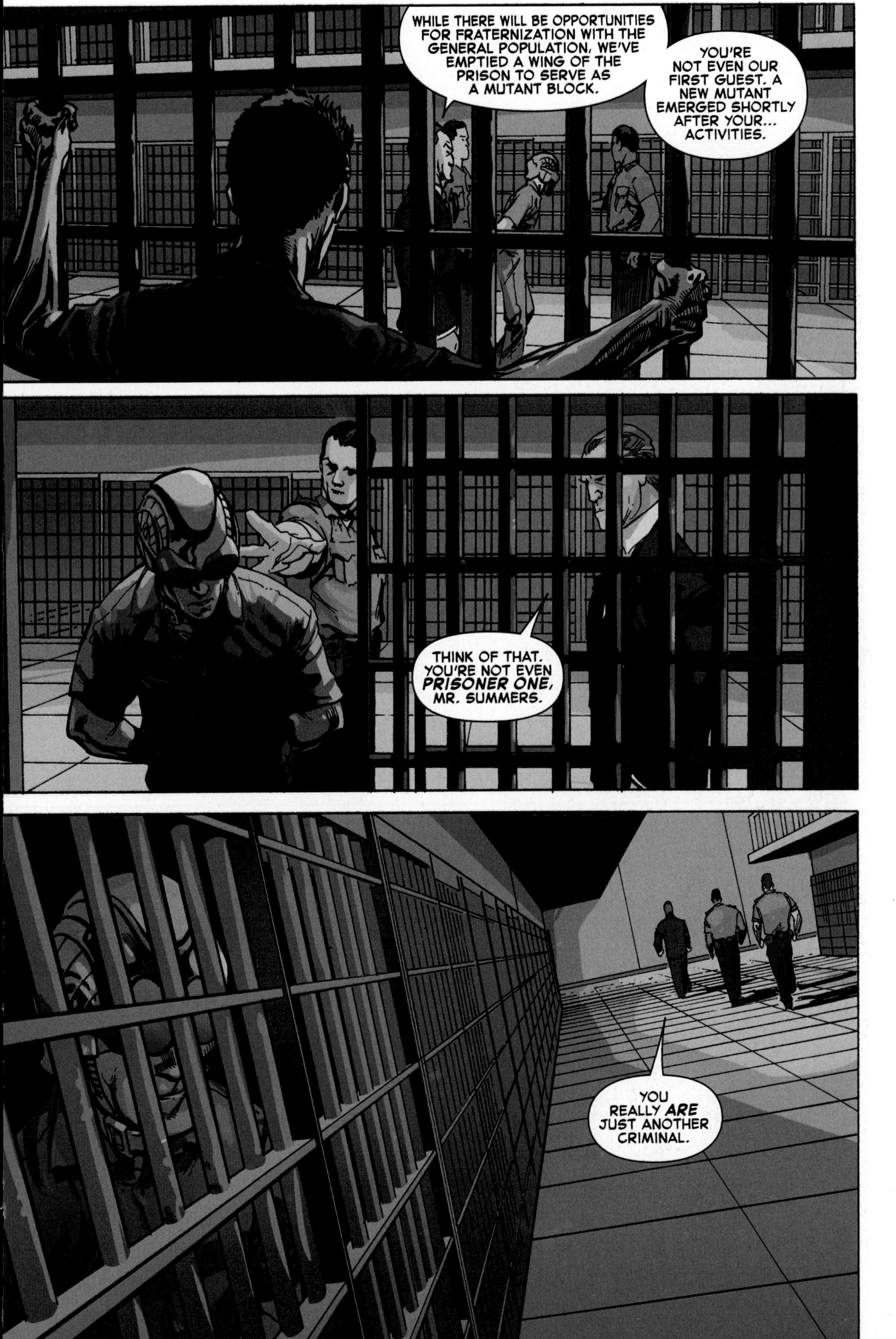
WHILE THERE WILL BE OPPORTUNITIES FOR FRATERNIZATION WITH THE GENERAL POPULATION, WE'VE EMPTIED A WING OF THE PRISON TO SERVE AS A MUTANT BLOCK.
YOU'RE NOT EVEN OUR FIRST GUEST. A NEW MUTANT EMERGED SHORTLY AFTER YOUR... ACTIVITIES.
THINK OF THAT. YOU'RE NOT EVEN PRISONER ONE, MR. SUMMERS.
YOU REALLY ARE JUST ANOTHER CRIMINAL.

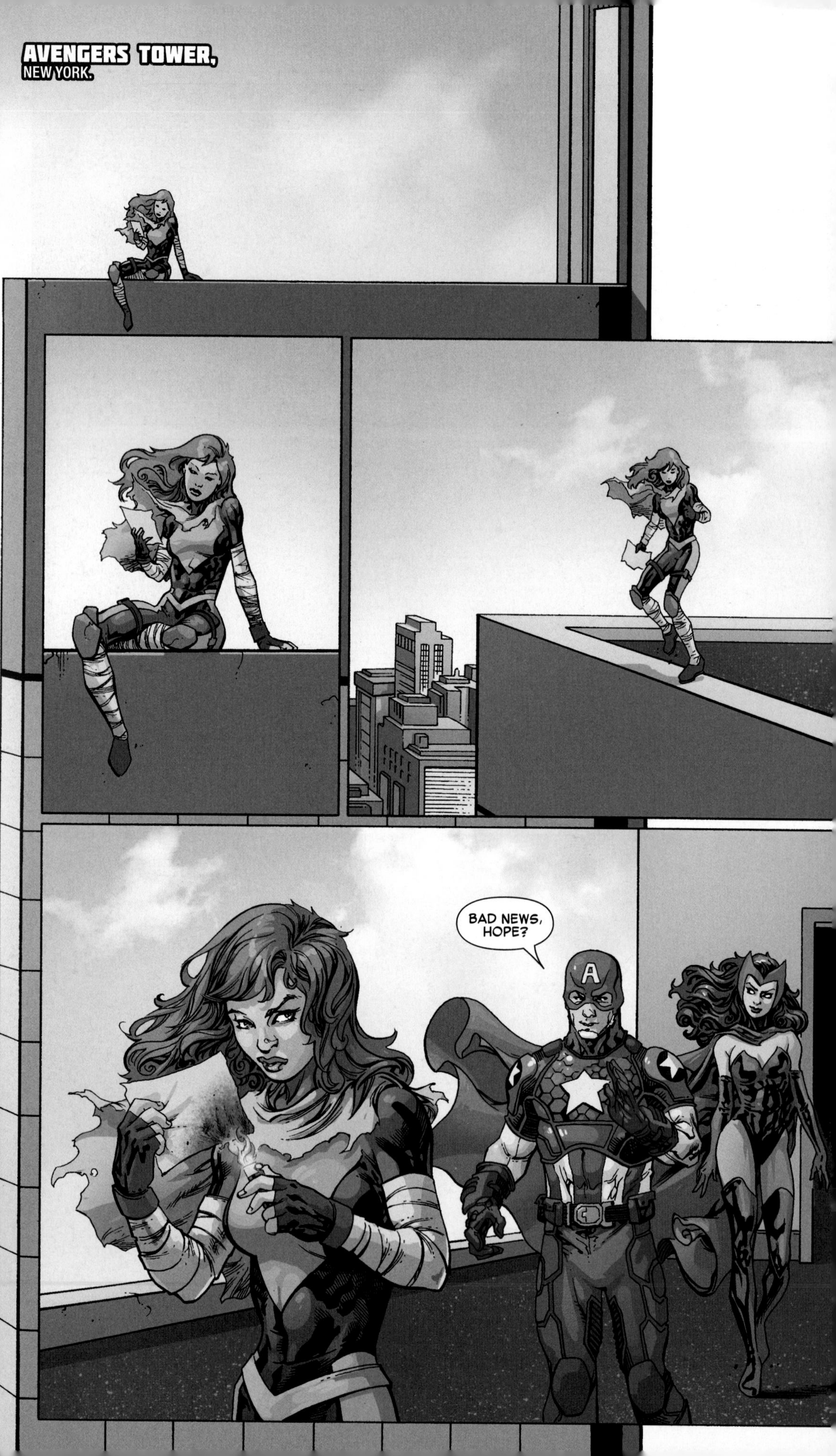
AVENGERS TOWER,
NEW YORK.
BAD NEWS, HOPE?

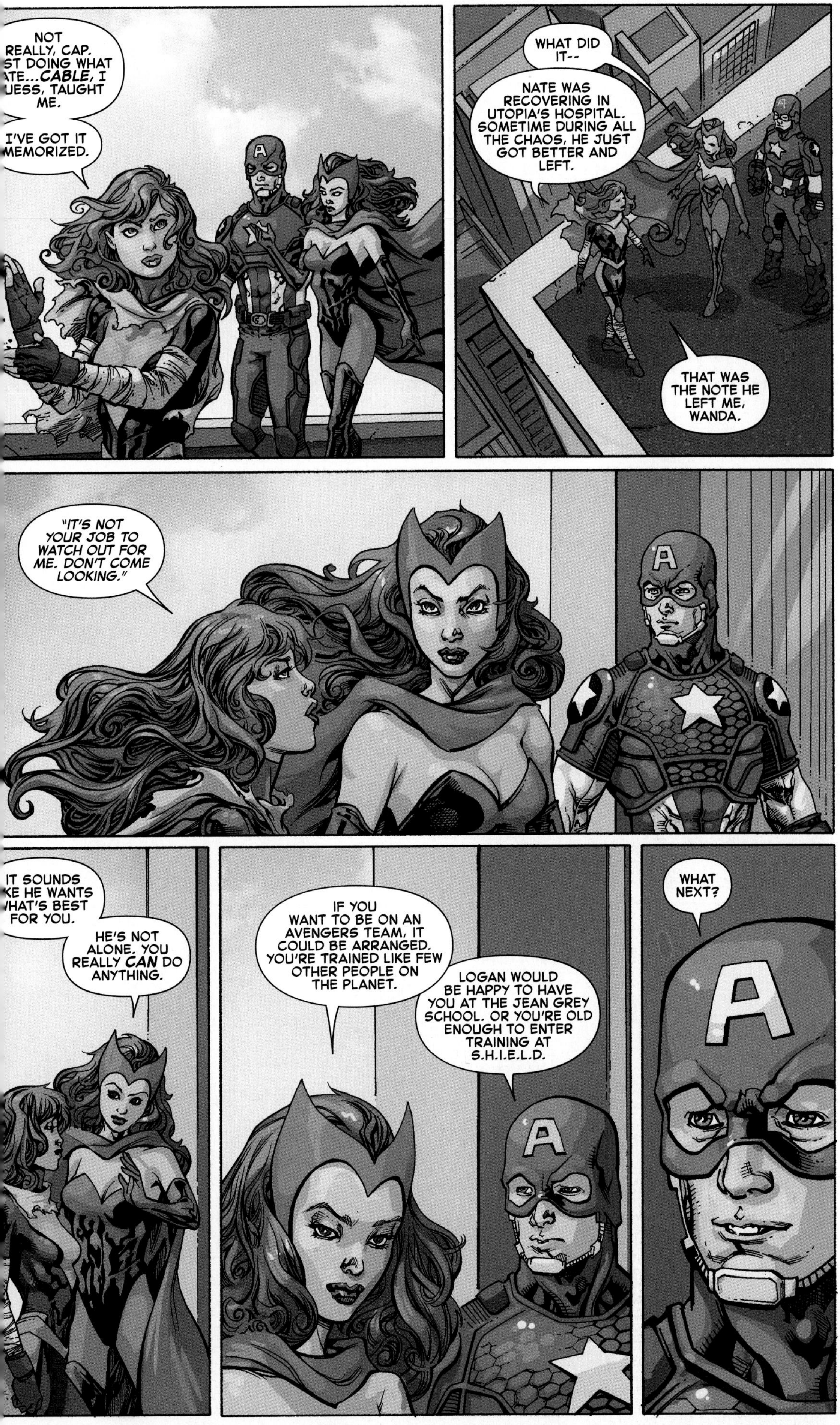

NOT REALLY, CAP. ST DOING WHAT ATE...*CABLE*, I UESS, TAUGHT ME.
I'VE GOT IT MEMORIZED.
WHAT DID IT--
NATE WAS RECOVERING IN UTOPIA'S HOSPITAL. SOMETIME DURING ALL THE CHAOS, HE JUST GOT BETTER AND LEFT.
THAT WAS THE NOTE HE LEFT ME, WANDA.
"IT'S NOT YOUR JOB TO WATCH OUT FOR ME. DON'T COME LOOKING."
IT SOUNDS KE HE WANTS HAT'S BEST FOR YOU.
HE'S NOT ALONE. YOU REALLY **CAN** DO ANYTHING.
IF YOU WANT TO BE ON AN AVENGERS TEAM, IT COULD BE ARRANGED. YOU'RE TRAINED LIKE FEW OTHER PEOPLE ON THE PLANET.
LOGAN WOULD BE HAPPY TO HAVE YOU AT THE JEAN GREY SCHOOL. OR YOU'RE OLD ENOUGH TO ENTER TRAINING AT S.H.I.E.L.D.
WHAT NEXT?

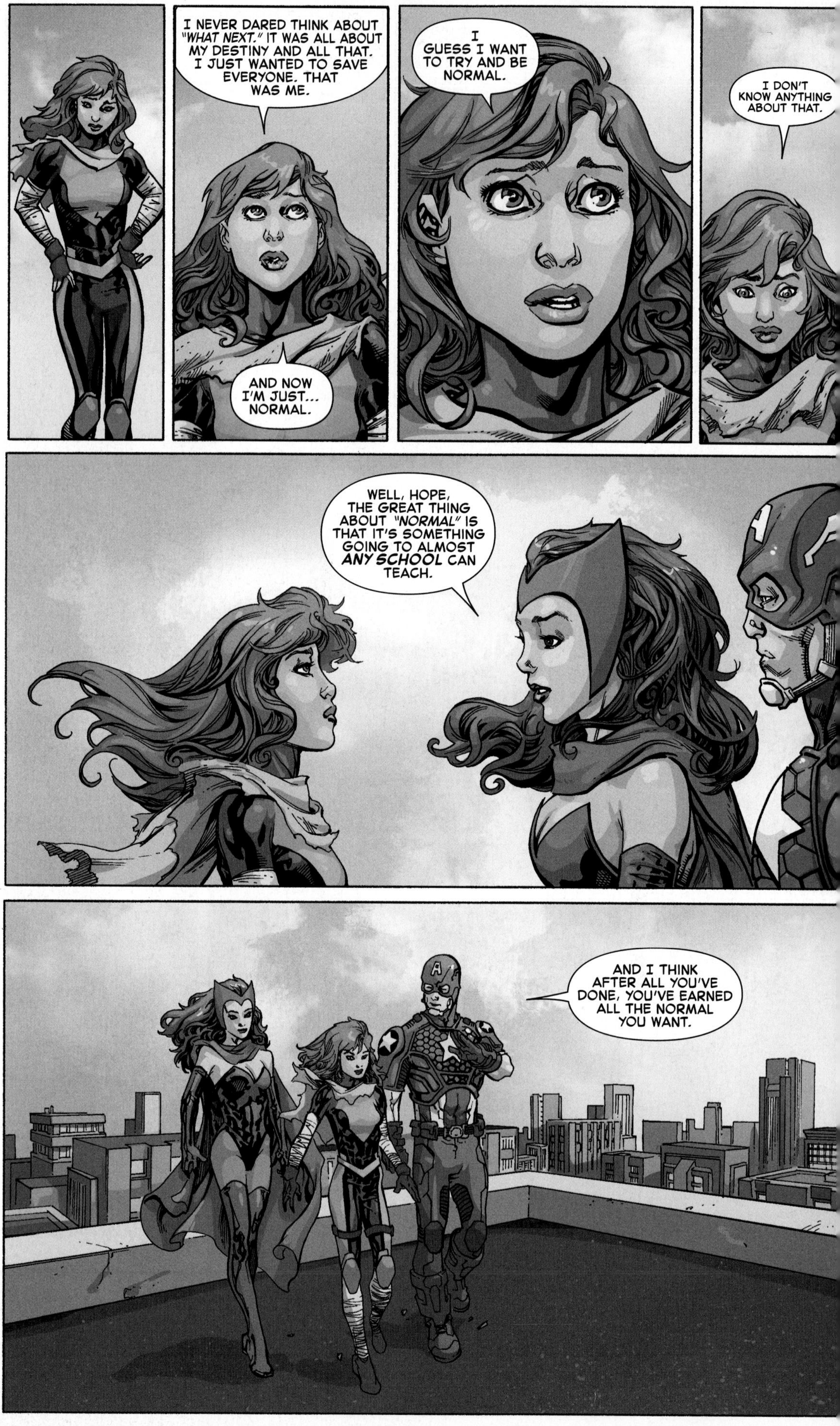
I NEVER DARED THINK ABOUT "WHAT NEXT." IT WAS ALL ABOUT MY DESTINY AND ALL THAT. I JUST WANTED TO SAVE EVERYONE. THAT WAS ME.
AND NOW I'M JUST... NORMAL.
I GUESS I WANT TO TRY AND BE NORMAL.
I DON'T KNOW ANYTHING ABOUT THAT.
WELL, HOPE, THE GREAT THING ABOUT "NORMAL" IS THAT IT'S SOMETHING GOING TO ALMOST ANY SCHOOL CAN TEACH.
AND I THINK AFTER ALL YOU'VE DONE, YOU'VE EARNED ALL THE NORMAL YOU WANT.

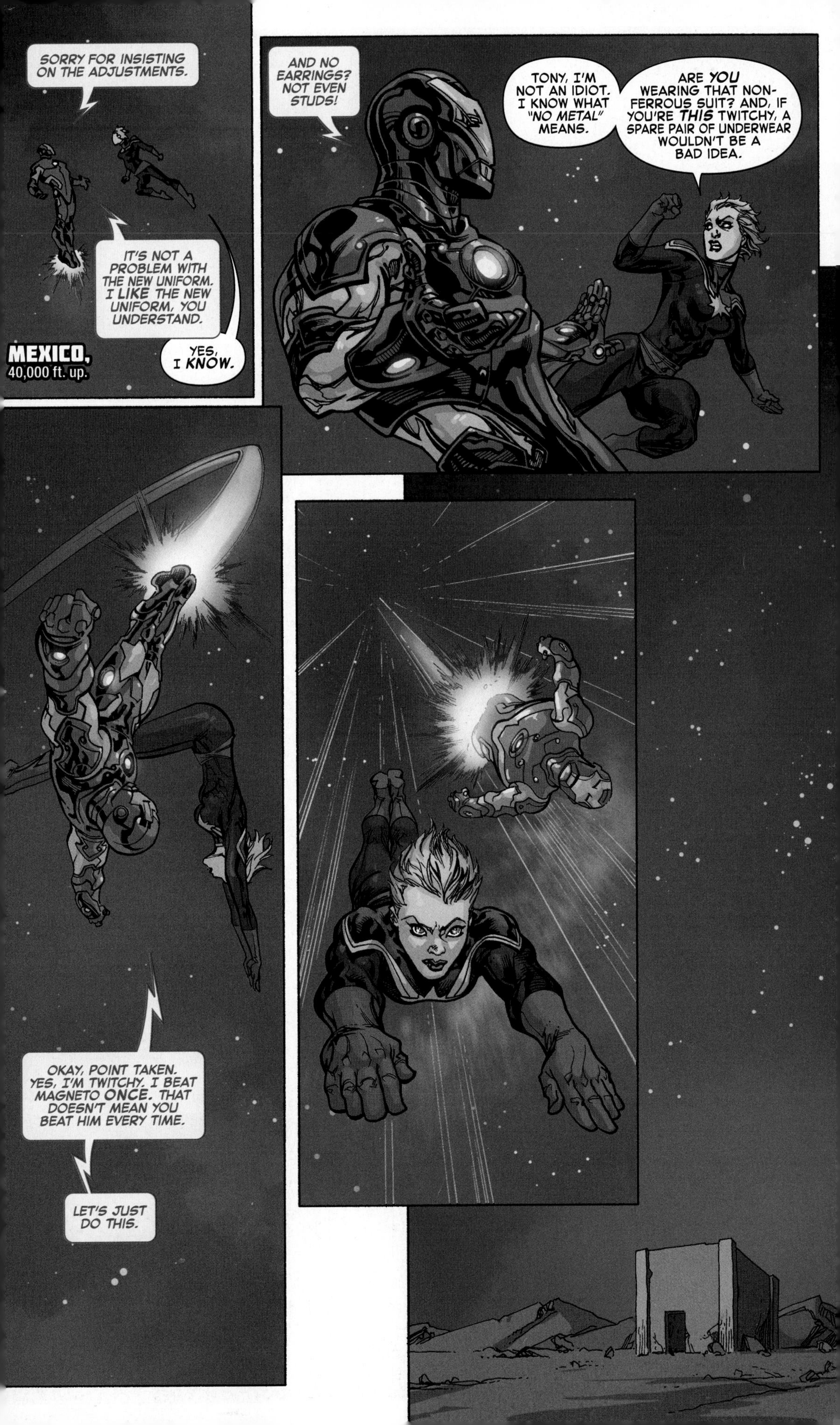

SORRY FOR INSISTING ON THE ADJUSTMENTS.
IT'S NOT A PROBLEM WITH THE NEW UNIFORM. I LIKE THE NEW UNIFORM, YOU UNDERSTAND.
YES, I KNOW.
MEXICO, 40,000 ft. up.
AND NO EARRINGS? NOT EVEN STUDS!
TONY, I'M NOT AN IDIOT. I KNOW WHAT "NO METAL" MEANS.
ARE YOU WEARING THAT NON-FERROUS SUIT? AND, IF YOU'RE THIS TWITCHY, A SPARE PAIR OF UNDERWEAR WOULDN'T BE A BAD IDEA.
OKAY, POINT TAKEN. YES, I'M TWITCHY. I BEAT MAGNETO ONCE. THAT DOESN'T MEAN YOU BEAT HIM EVERY TIME.
LET'S JUST DO THIS.

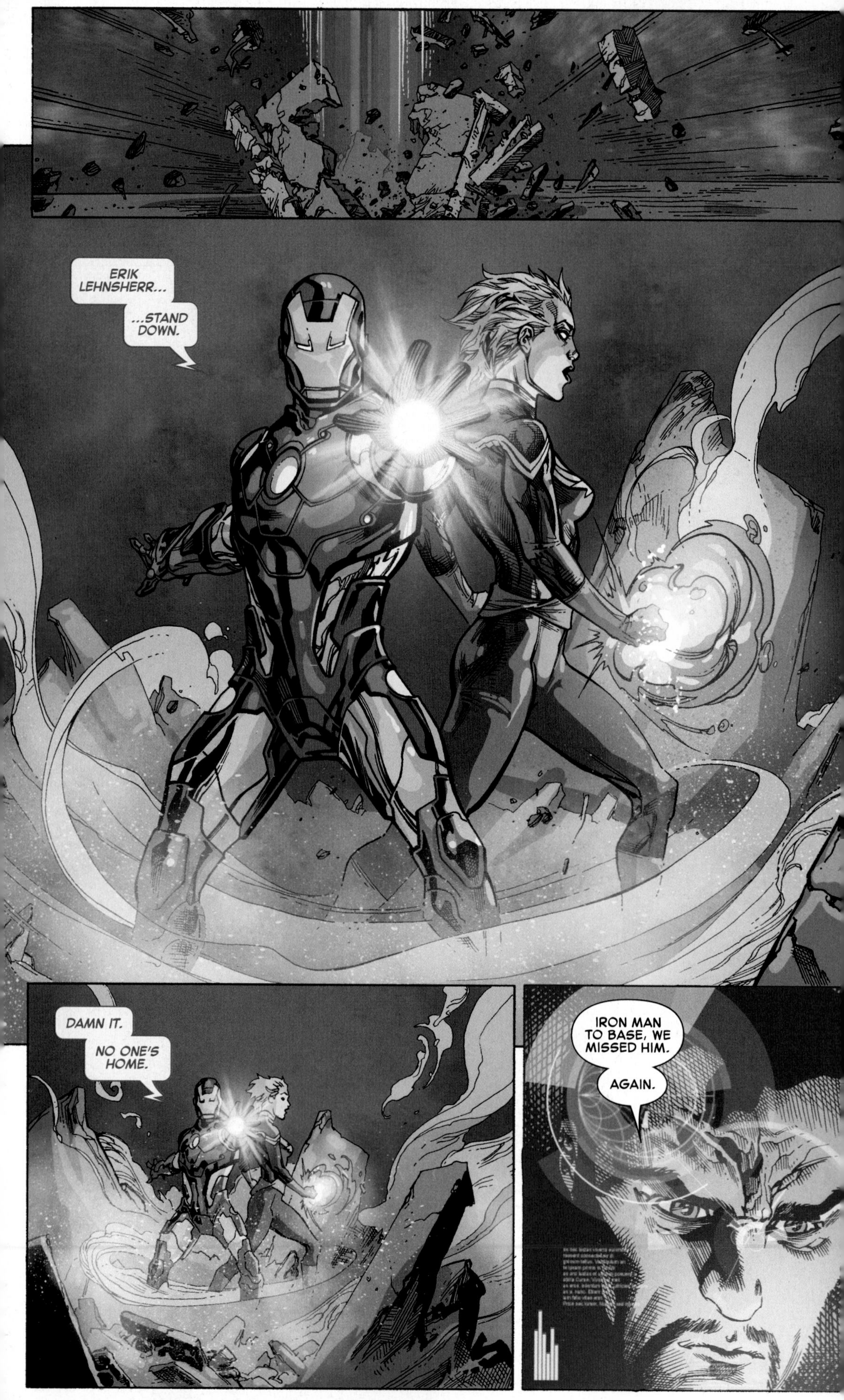
ERIK LEHNSHERR...
...STAND DOWN.
DAMN IT.
NO ONE'S HOME.
IRON MAN TO BASE, WE MISSED HIM.
AGAIN.

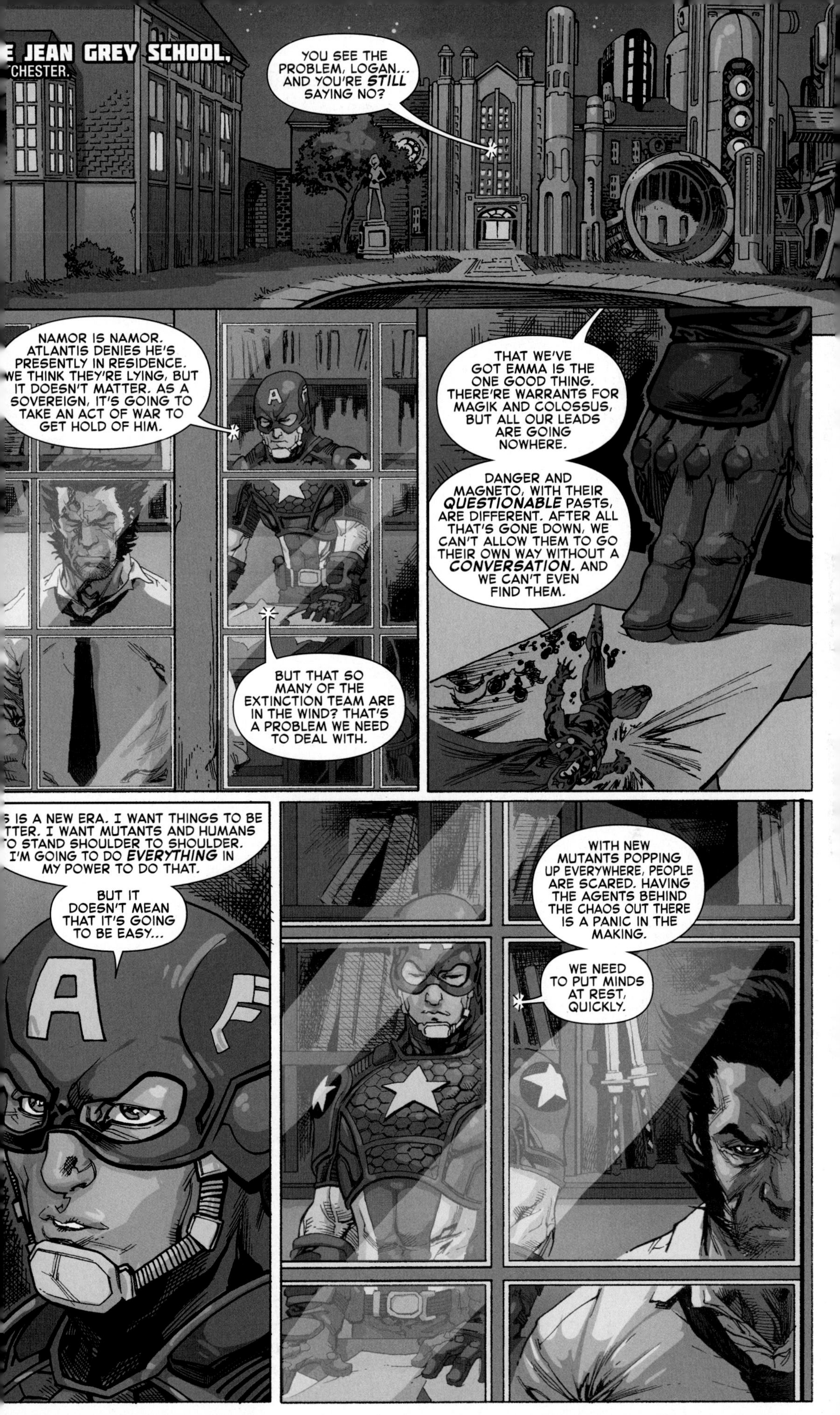

E JEAN GREY SCHOOL,
CHESTER.
YOU SEE THE PROBLEM, LOGAN... AND YOU'RE STILL SAYING NO?
NAMOR IS NAMOR. ATLANTIS DENIES HE'S PRESENTLY IN RESIDENCE. WE THINK THEY'RE LYING, BUT IT DOESN'T MATTER. AS A SOVEREIGN, IT'S GOING TO TAKE AN ACT OF WAR TO GET HOLD OF HIM.
BUT THAT SO MANY OF THE EXTINCTION TEAM ARE IN THE WIND? THAT'S A PROBLEM WE NEED TO DEAL WITH.
THAT WE'VE GOT EMMA IS THE ONE GOOD THING. THERE'RE WARRANTS FOR MAGIK AND COLOSSUS, BUT ALL OUR LEADS ARE GOING NOWHERE.
DANGER AND MAGNETO, WITH THEIR QUESTIONABLE PASTS, ARE DIFFERENT. AFTER ALL THAT'S GONE DOWN, WE CAN'T ALLOW THEM TO GO THEIR OWN WAY WITHOUT A CONVERSATION. AND WE CAN'T EVEN FIND THEM.
S IS A NEW ERA. I WANT THINGS TO BE TTER. I WANT MUTANTS AND HUMANS O STAND SHOULDER TO SHOULDER. I'M GOING TO DO EVERYTHING IN MY POWER TO DO THAT.
BUT IT DOESN'T MEAN THAT IT'S GOING TO BE EASY...
WITH NEW MUTANTS POPPING UP EVERYWHERE, PEOPLE ARE SCARED. HAVING THE AGENTS BEHIND THE CHAOS OUT THERE IS A PANIC IN THE MAKING.
WE NEED TO PUT MINDS AT REST, QUICKLY.

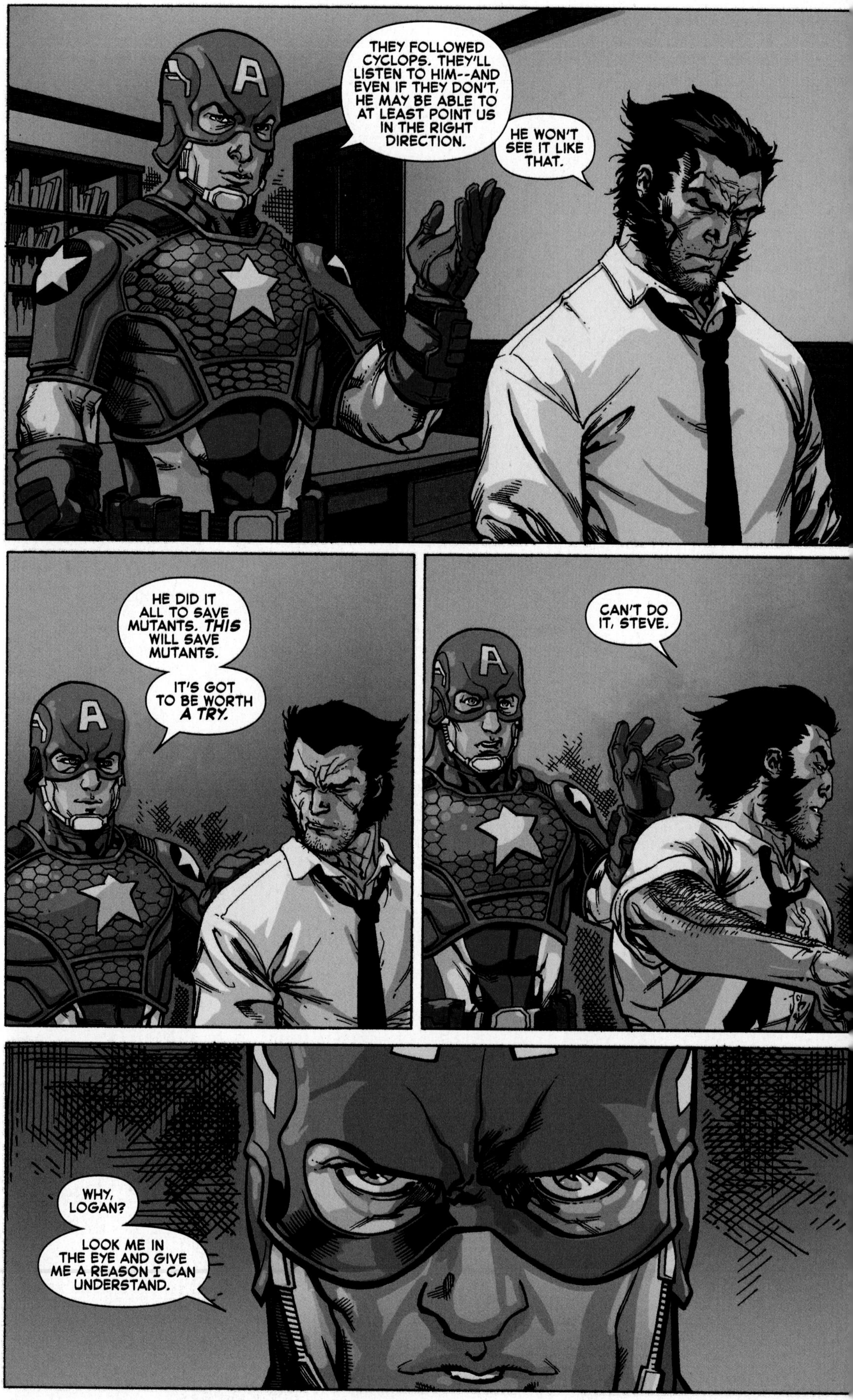
THEY FOLLOWED CYCLOPS. THEY'LL LISTEN TO HIM--AND EVEN IF THEY DON'T, HE MAY BE ABLE TO AT LEAST POINT US IN THE RIGHT DIRECTION.
HE WON'T SEE IT LIKE THAT.
HE DID IT ALL TO SAVE MUTANTS. *THIS* WILL SAVE MUTANTS.
IT'S GOT TO BE WORTH *A TRY.*
CAN'T DO IT, STEVE.
WHY, LOGAN?
LOOK ME IN THE EYE AND GIVE ME A REASON I CAN UNDERSTAND.

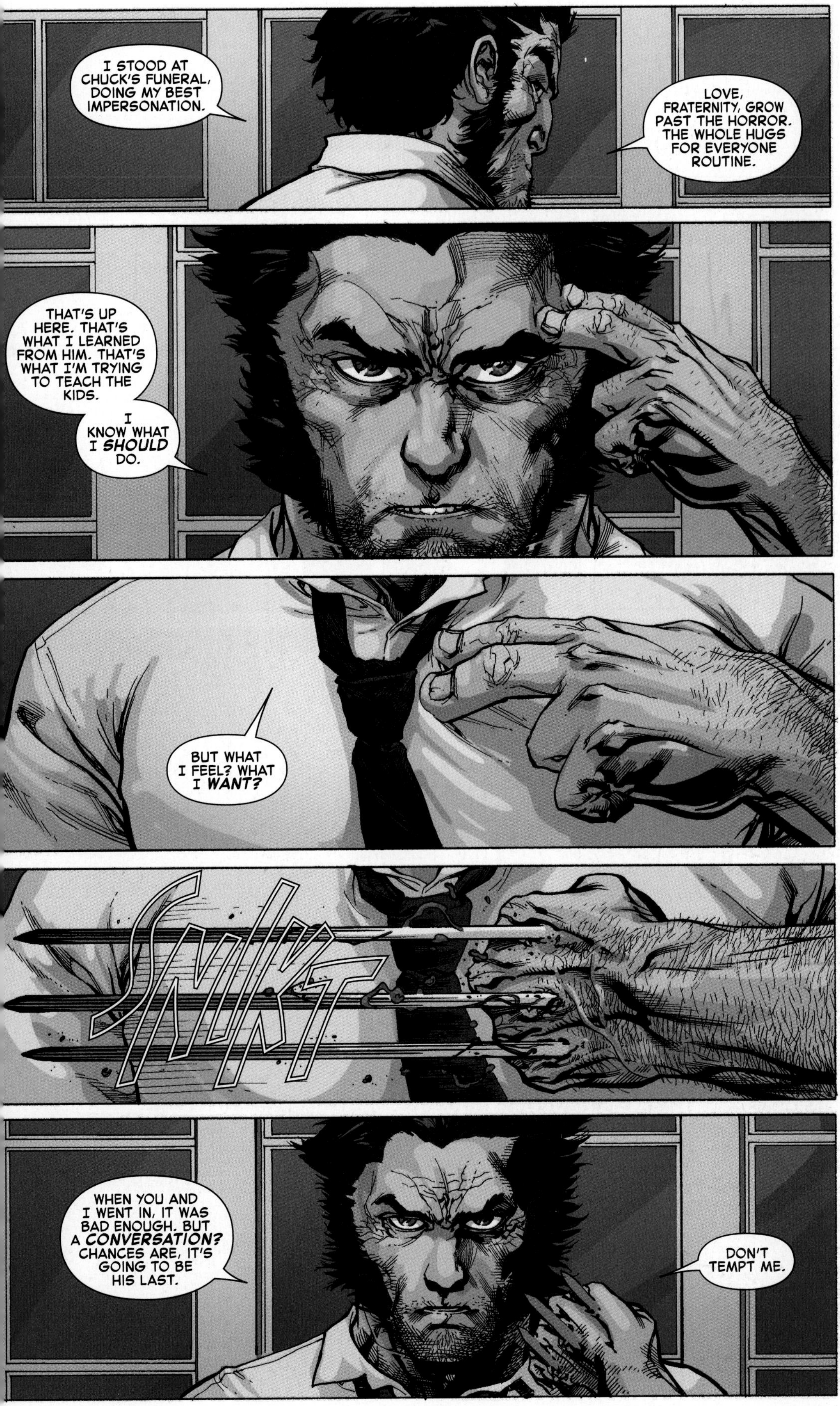
I STOOD AT CHUCK'S FUNERAL, DOING MY BEST IMPERSONATION.
LOVE, FRATERNITY, GROW PAST THE HORROR. THE WHOLE HUGS FOR EVERYONE ROUTINE.
THAT'S UP HERE. THAT'S WHAT I LEARNED FROM HIM. THAT'S WHAT I'M TRYING TO TEACH THE KIDS.
I KNOW WHAT I *SHOULD* DO.
BUT WHAT I FEEL? WHAT I *WANT?*
SNIKT
WHEN YOU AND I WENT IN, IT WAS BAD ENOUGH. BUT A *CONVERSATION?* CHANCES ARE, IT'S GOING TO BE HIS LAST.
DON'T TEMPT ME.

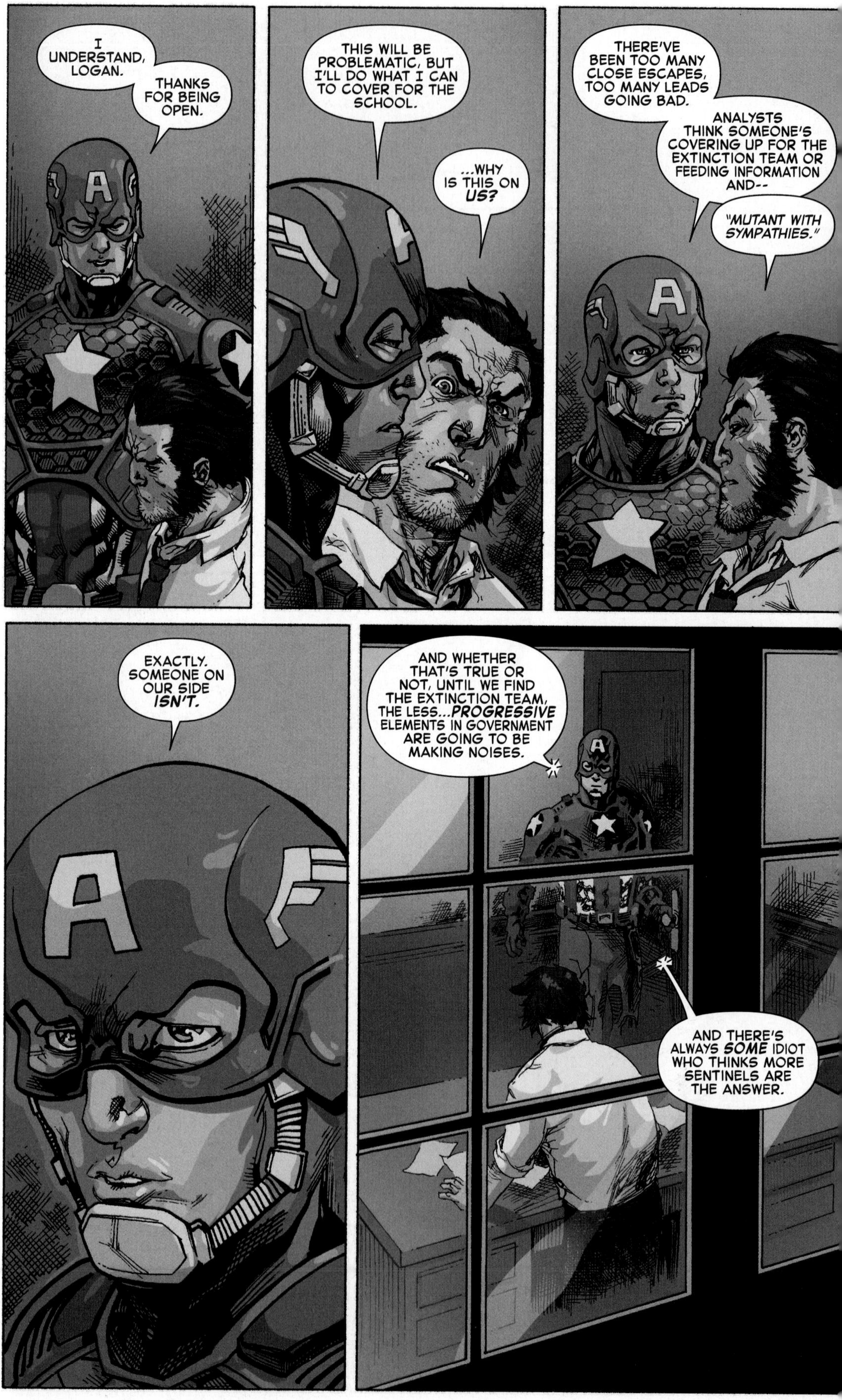
I UNDERSTAND, LOGAN.
THANKS FOR BEING OPEN.
THIS WILL BE PROBLEMATIC, BUT I'LL DO WHAT I CAN TO COVER FOR THE SCHOOL.
...WHY IS THIS ON *US?*
THERE'VE BEEN TOO MANY CLOSE ESCAPES, TOO MANY LEADS GOING BAD.
ANALYSTS THINK SOMEONE'S COVERING UP FOR THE EXTINCTION TEAM OR FEEDING INFORMATION AND--
"MUTANT WITH SYMPATHIES."
EXACTLY. SOMEONE ON OUR SIDE *ISN'T.*
AND WHETHER THAT'S TRUE OR NOT, UNTIL WE FIND THE EXTINCTION TEAM, THE LESS...*PROGRESSIVE* ELEMENTS IN GOVERNMENT ARE GOING TO BE MAKING NOISES.
AND THERE'S ALWAYS *SOME* IDIOT WHO THINKS MORE SENTINELS ARE THE ANSWER.

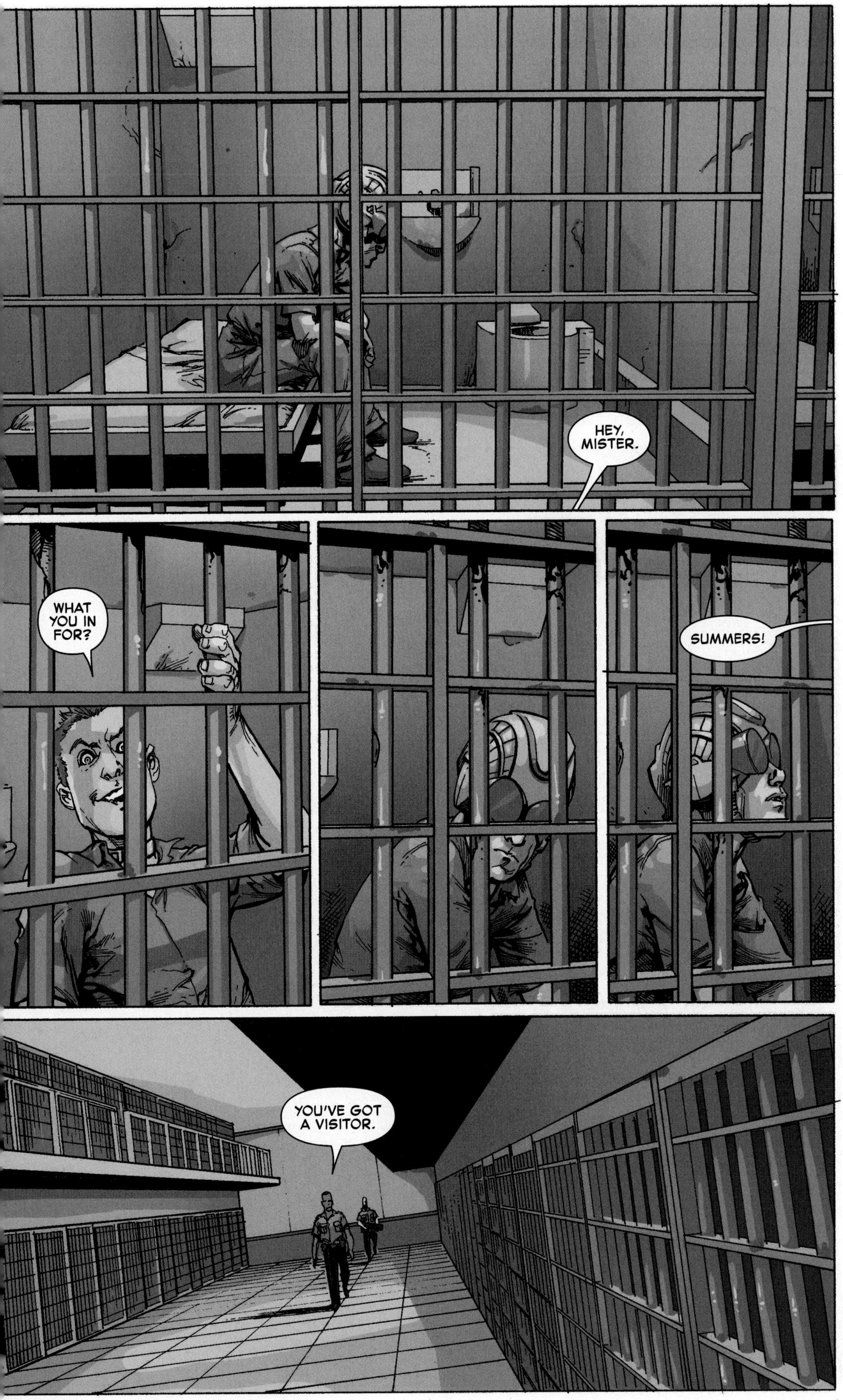
HEY, MISTER.
WHAT YOU IN FOR?
SUMMERS!
YOU'VE GOT A VISITOR.

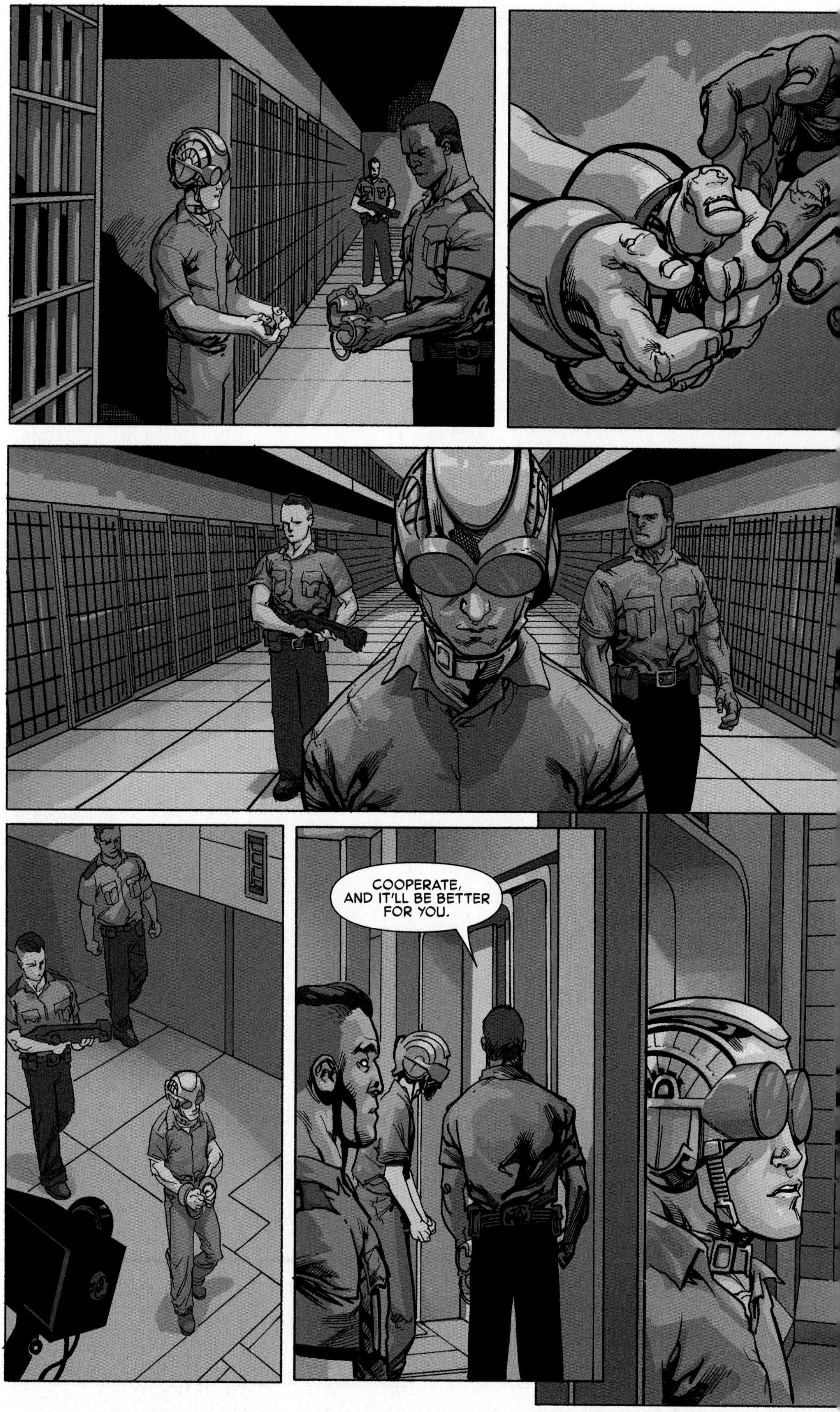
COOPERATE, AND IT'LL BE BETTER FOR YOU.

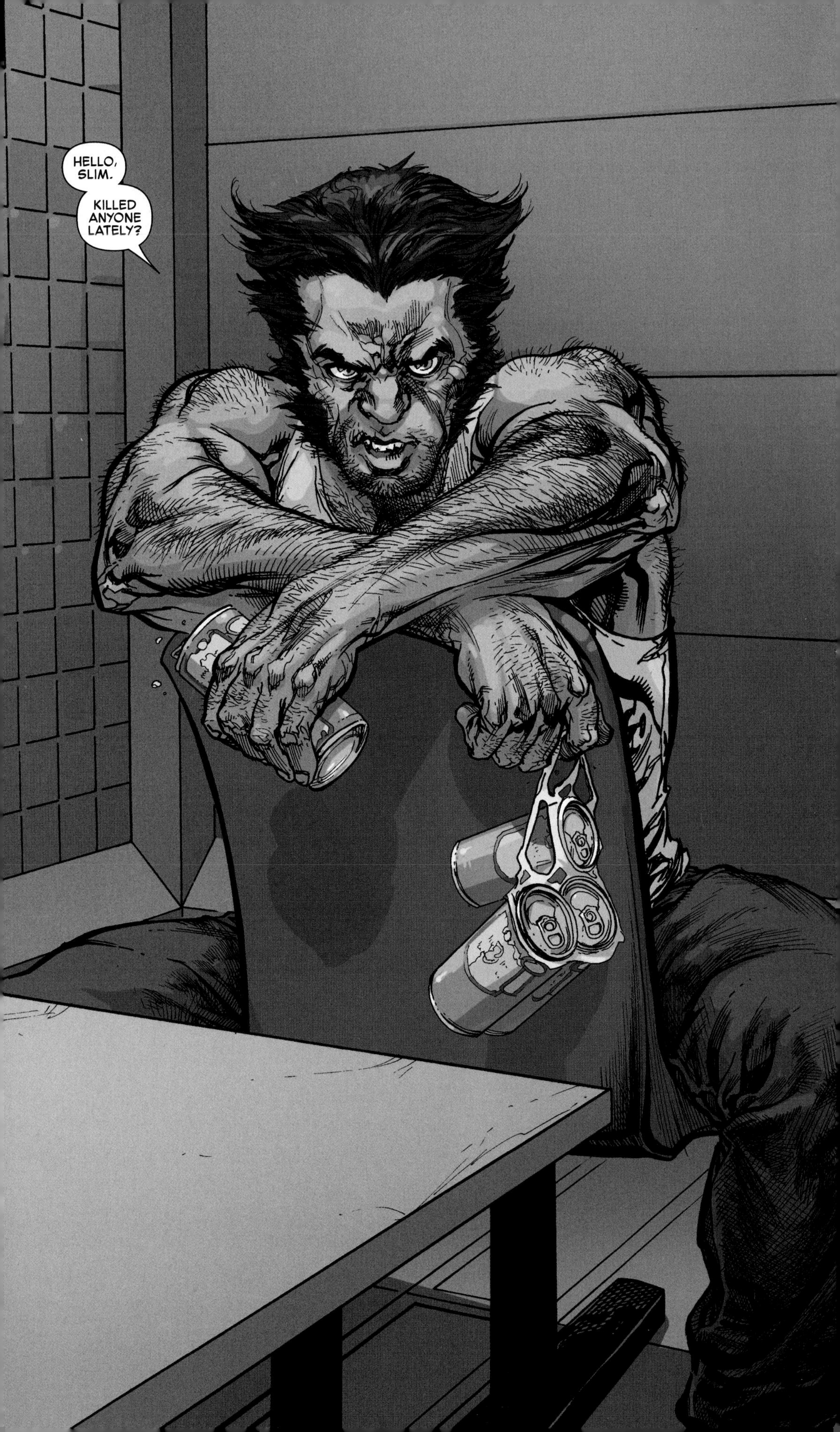
HELLO, SLIM.
KILLED ANYONE LATELY?

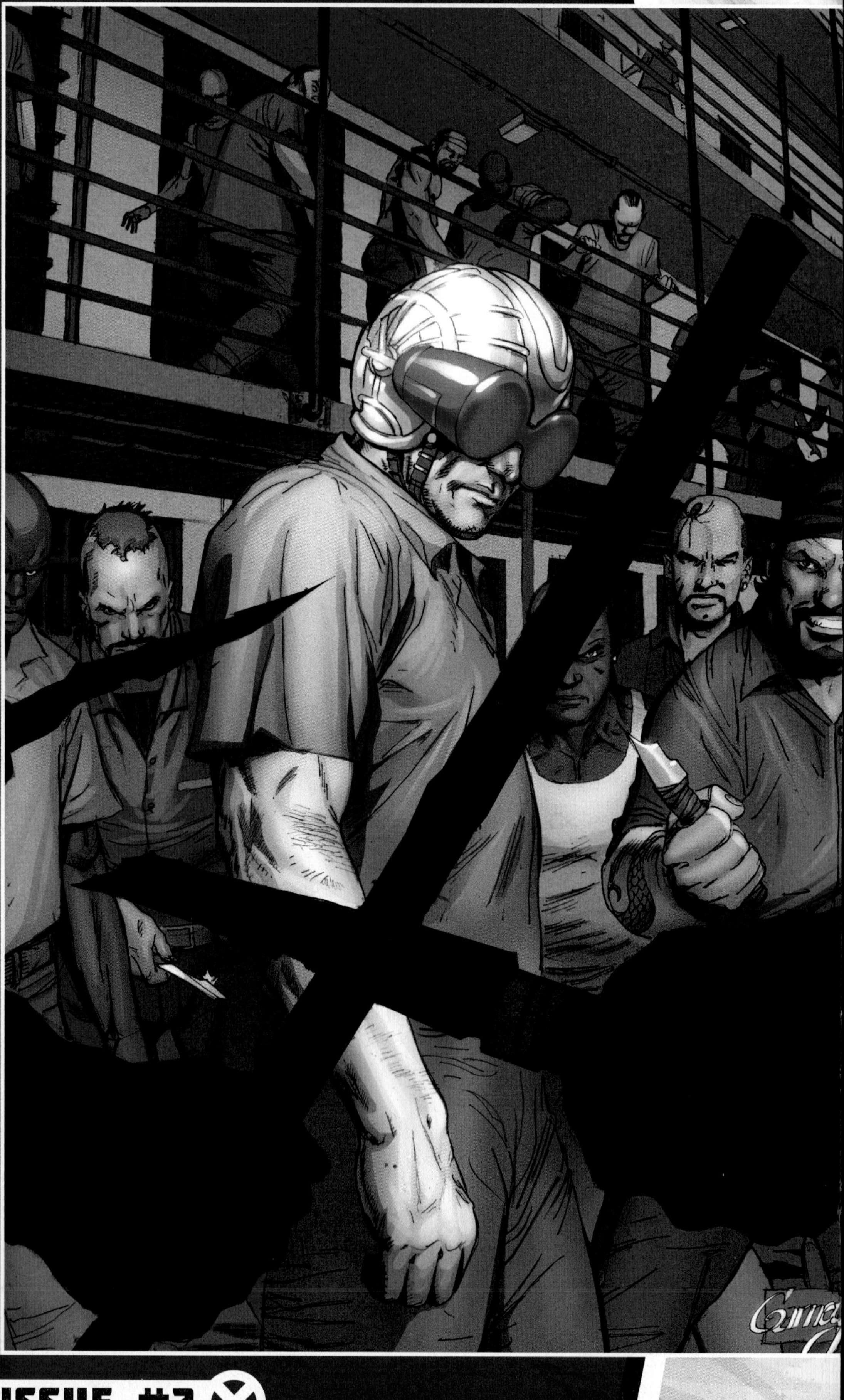

ISSUE #2

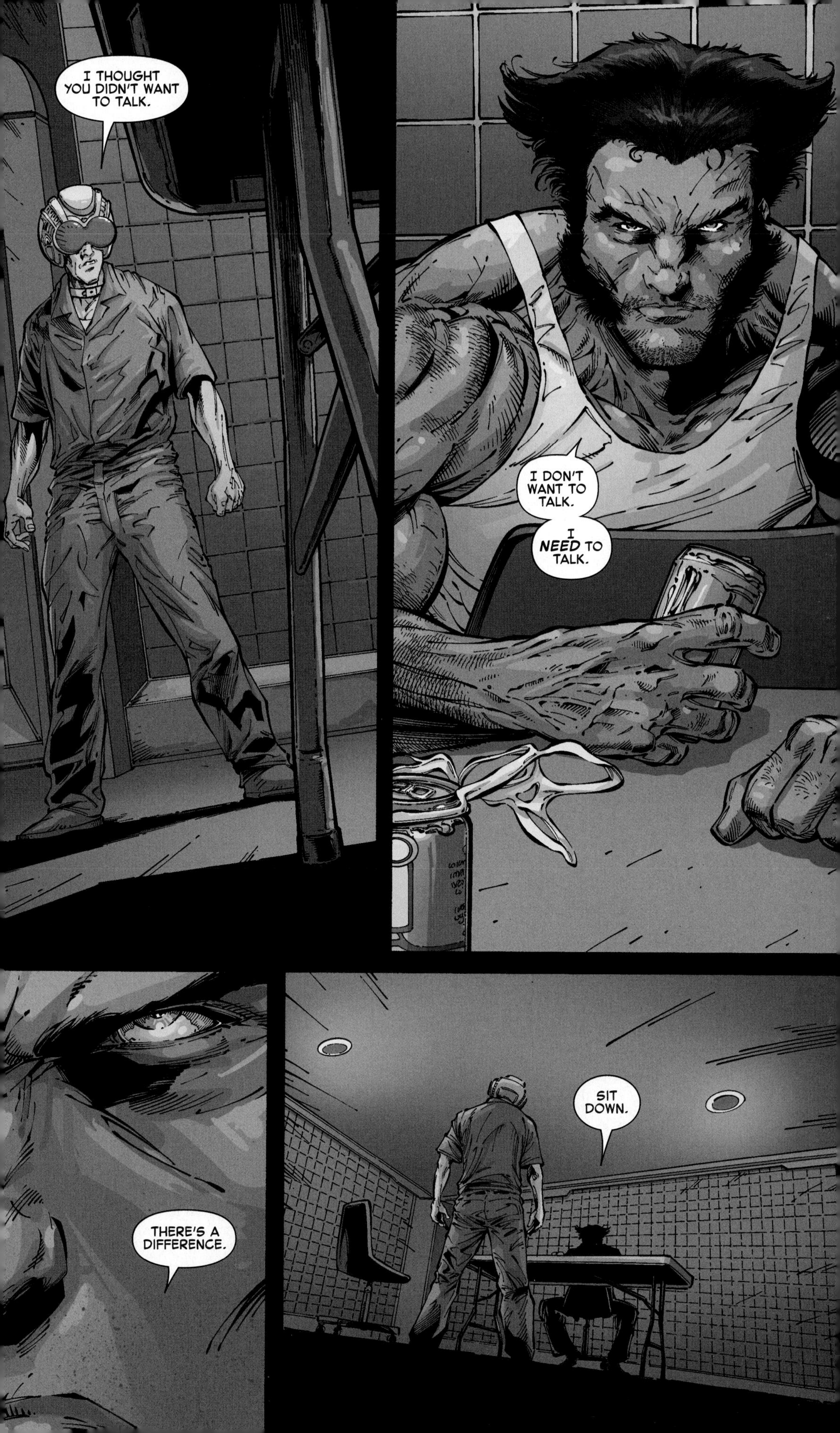
I THOUGHT YOU DIDN'T WANT TO TALK.
I DON'T WANT TO TALK.
I *NEED* TO TALK.
THERE'S A DIFFERENCE.
SIT DOWN.

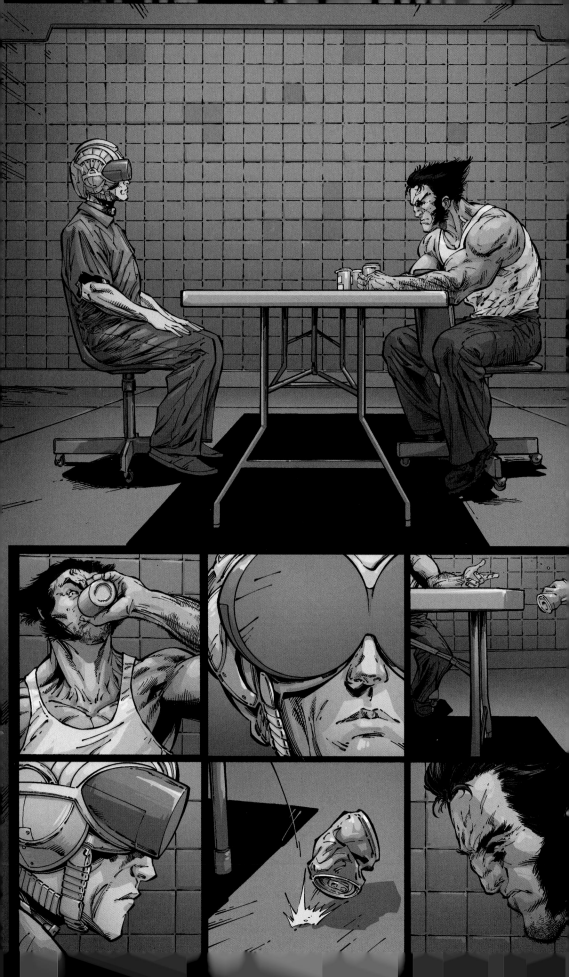

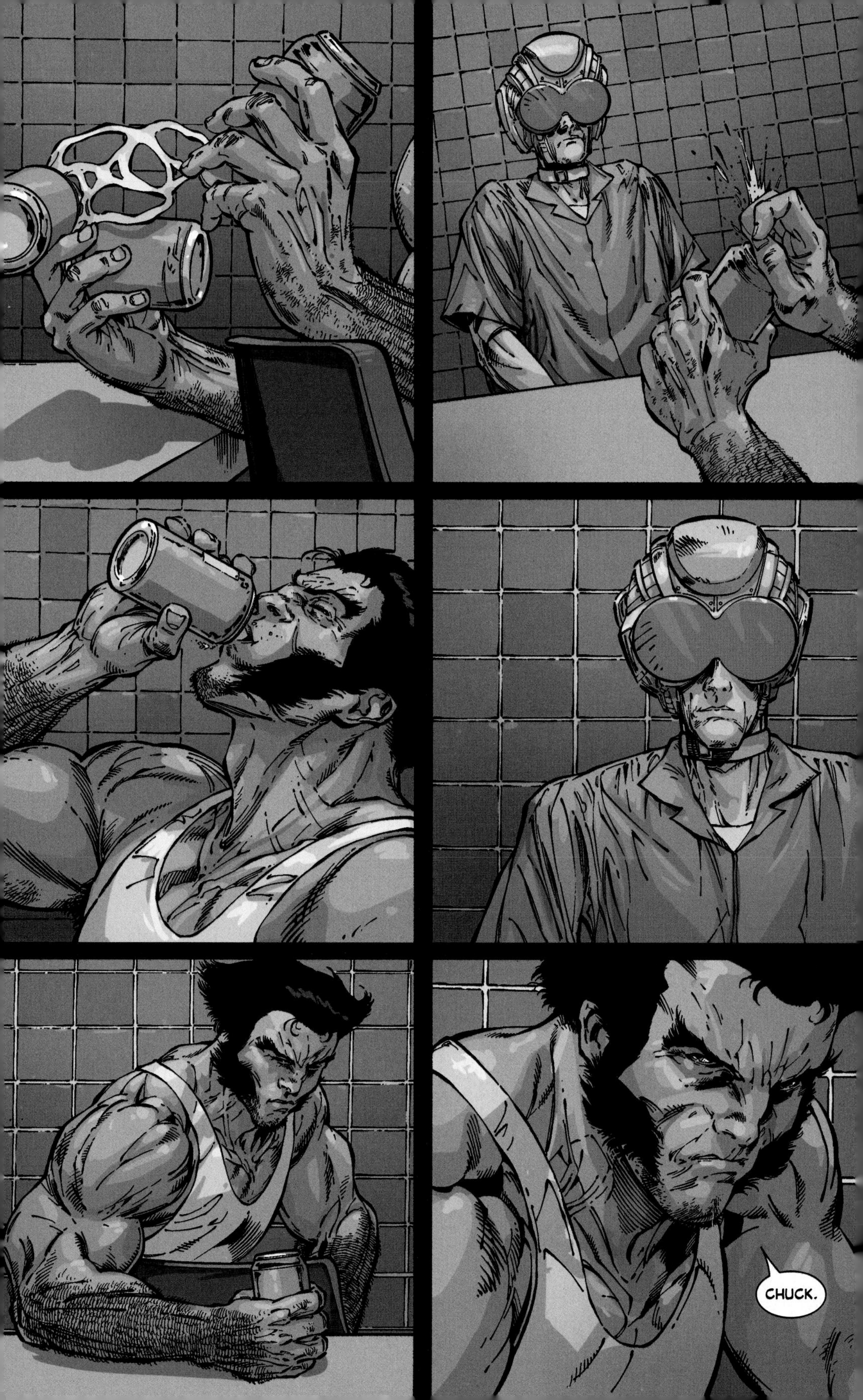
CHUCK.

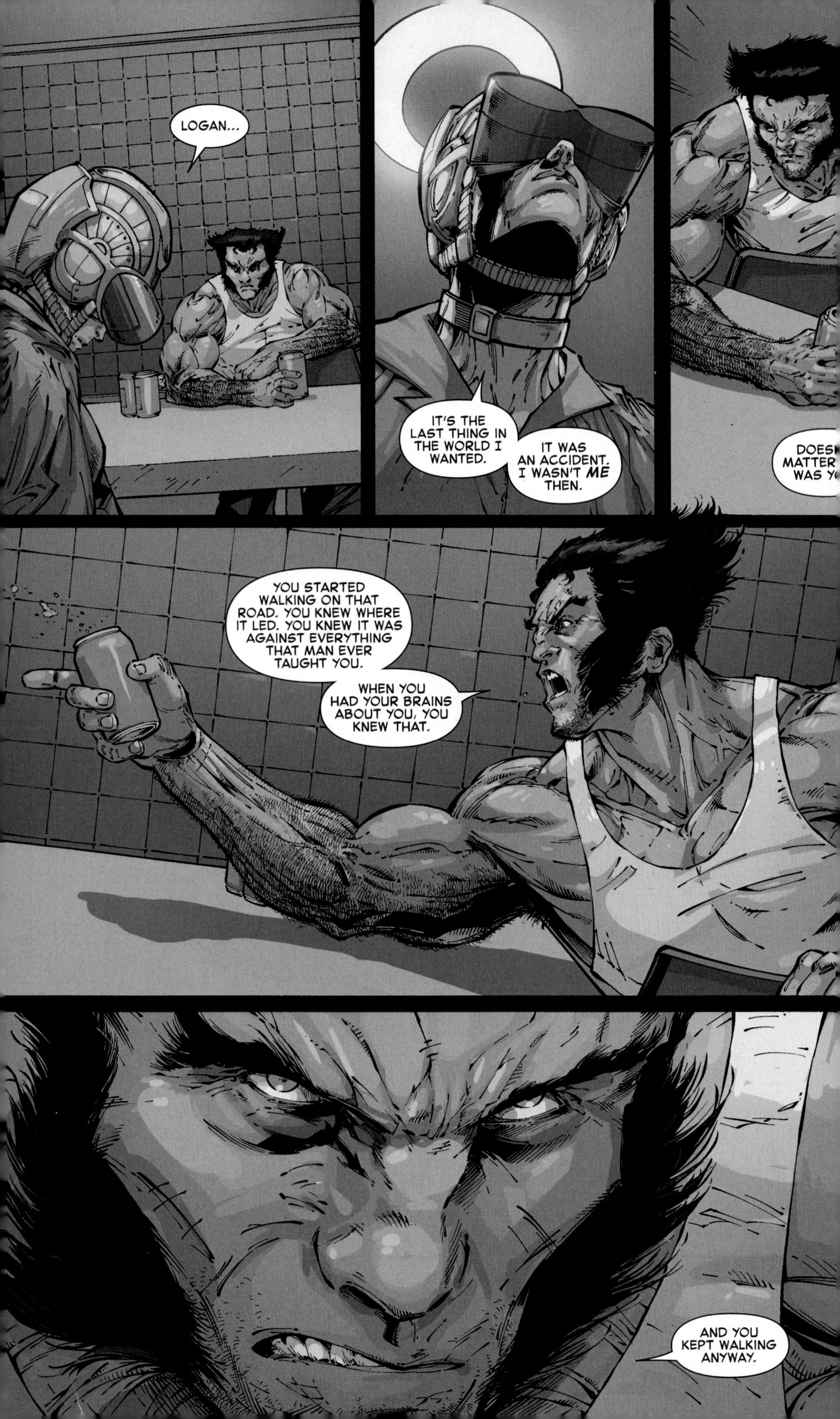
LOGAN...
IT'S THE LAST THING IN THE WORLD I WANTED.
IT WAS AN ACCIDENT. I WASN'T *ME* THEN.
YOU STARTED WALKING ON THAT ROAD. YOU KNEW WHERE IT LED. YOU KNEW IT WAS AGAINST EVERYTHING THAT MAN EVER TAUGHT YOU.
WHEN YOU HAD YOUR BRAINS ABOUT YOU, YOU KNEW THAT.
AND YOU KEPT WALKING ANYWAY.

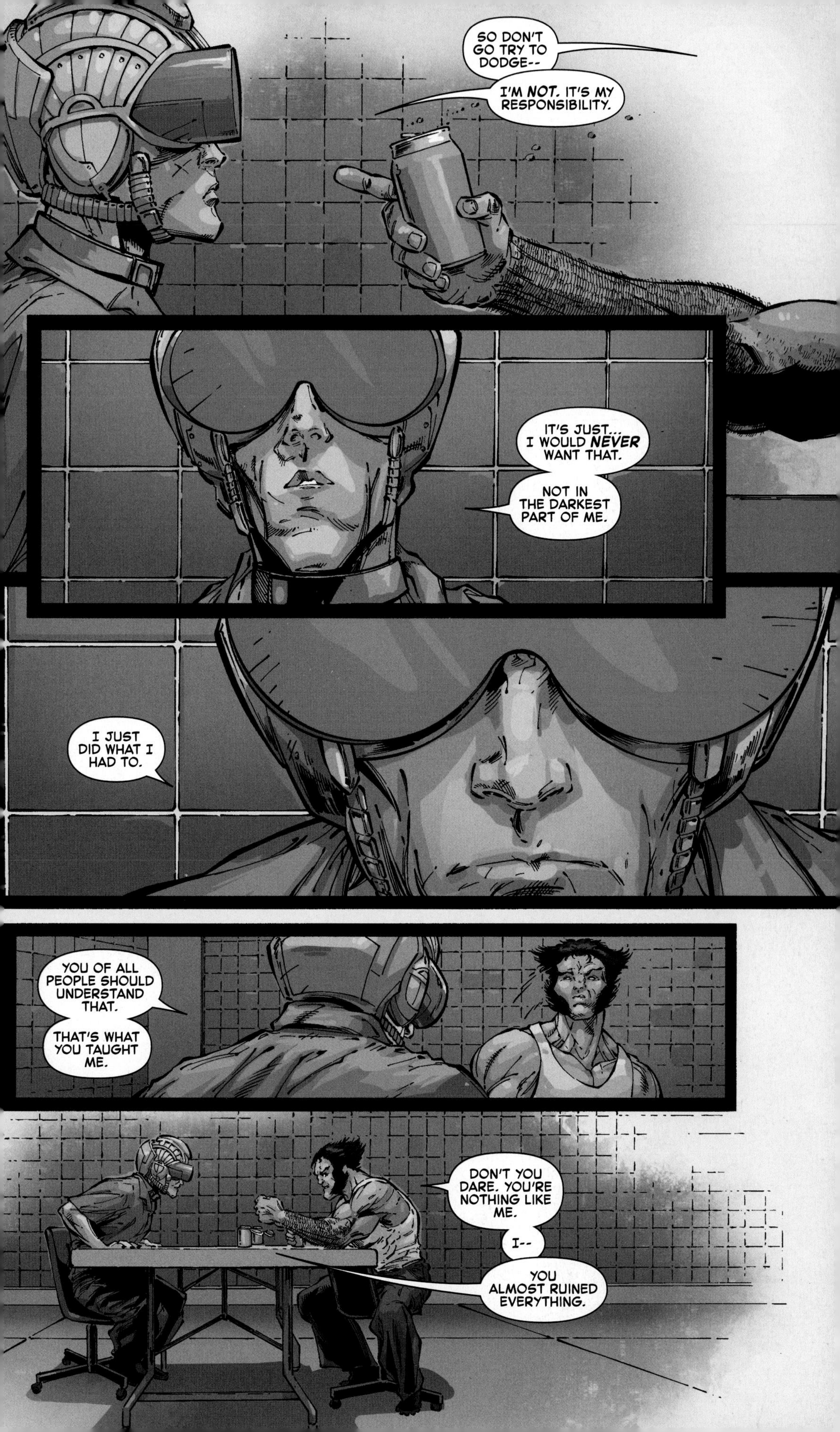
SO DON'T GO TRY TO DODGE--
I'M *NOT.* IT'S MY RESPONSIBILITY.
IT'S JUST... I WOULD *NEVER* WANT THAT.
NOT IN THE DARKEST PART OF ME.
I JUST DID WHAT I HAD TO.
YOU OF ALL PEOPLE SHOULD UNDERSTAND THAT.
THAT'S WHAT YOU TAUGHT ME.
DON'T YOU DARE. YOU'RE NOTHING LIKE ME.
I--
YOU ALMOST RUINED EVERYTHING.

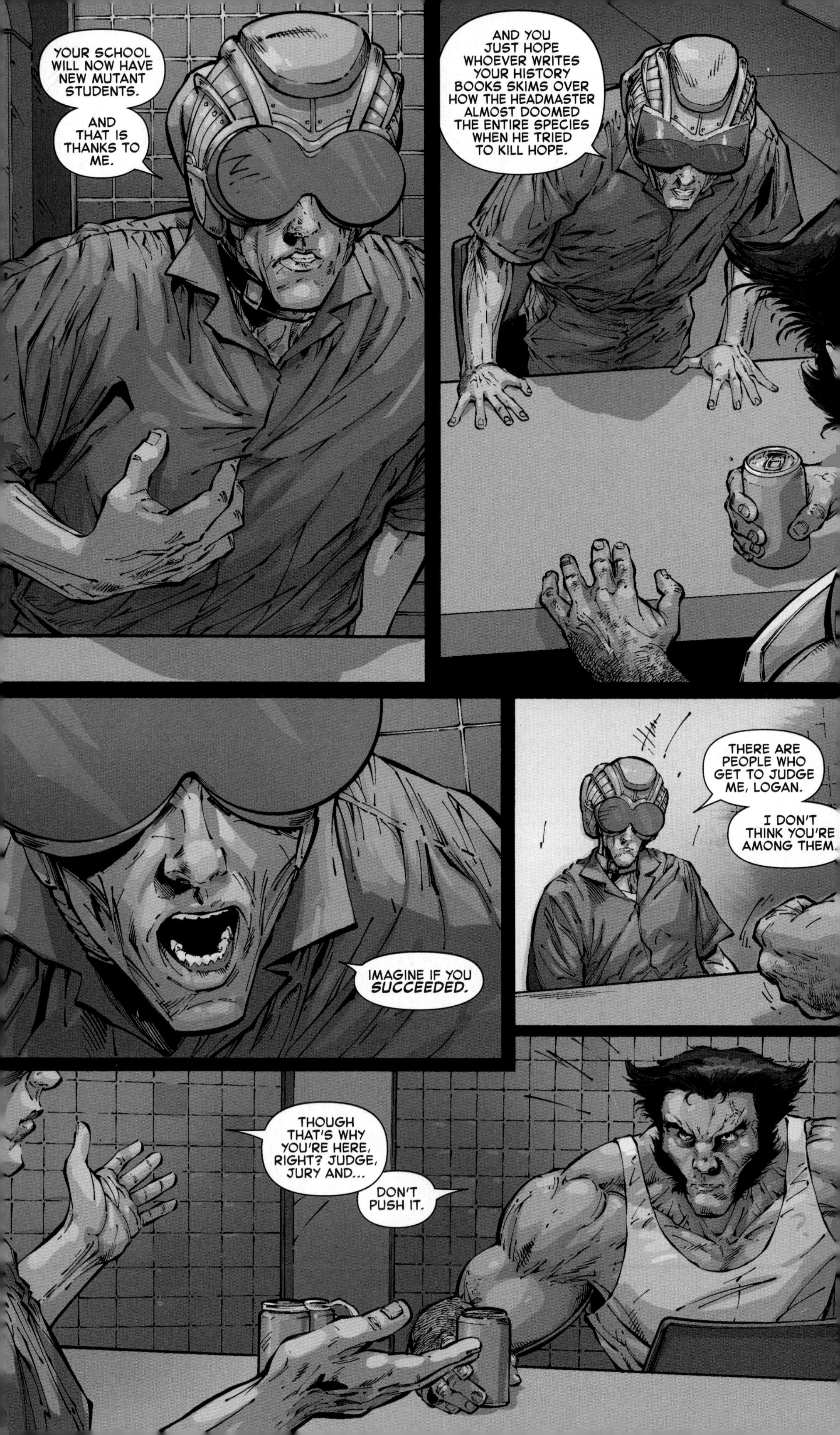
YOUR SCHOOL WILL NOW HAVE NEW MUTANT STUDENTS.
AND THAT IS THANKS TO ME.
AND YOU JUST HOPE WHOEVER WRITES YOUR HISTORY BOOKS SKIMS OVER HOW THE HEADMASTER ALMOST DOOMED THE ENTIRE SPECIES WHEN HE TRIED TO KILL HOPE.
IMAGINE IF YOU *SUCCEEDED.*
THERE ARE PEOPLE WHO GET TO JUDGE ME, LOGAN.
I DON'T THINK YOU'RE AMONG THEM.
THOUGH THAT'S WHY YOU'RE HERE, RIGHT? JUDGE, JURY AND...
DON'T PUSH IT.

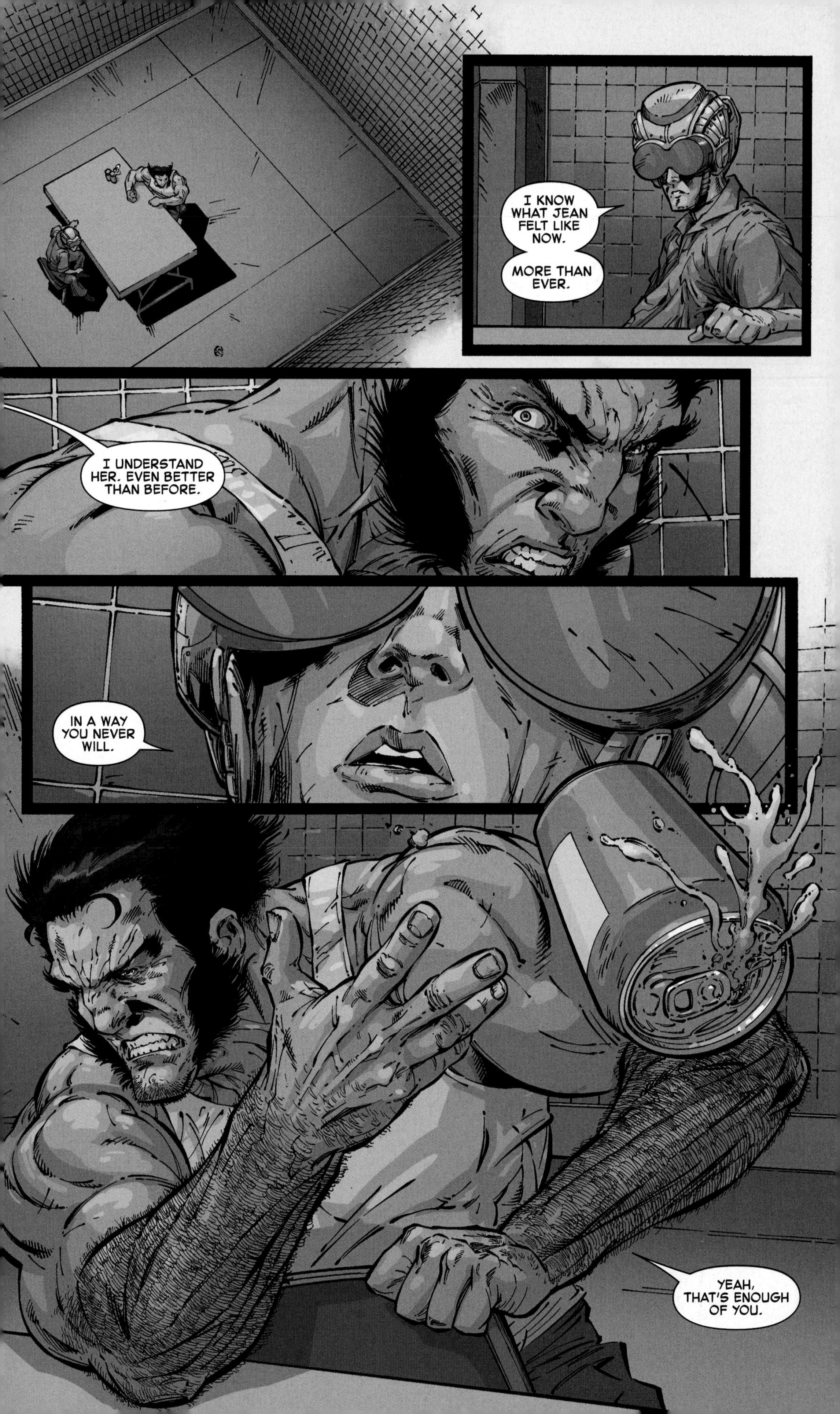
I KNOW WHAT JEAN FELT LIKE NOW.
MORE THAN EVER.
I UNDERSTAND HER. EVEN BETTER THAN BEFORE.
IN A WAY YOU NEVER WILL.
YEAH, THAT'S ENOUGH OF YOU.

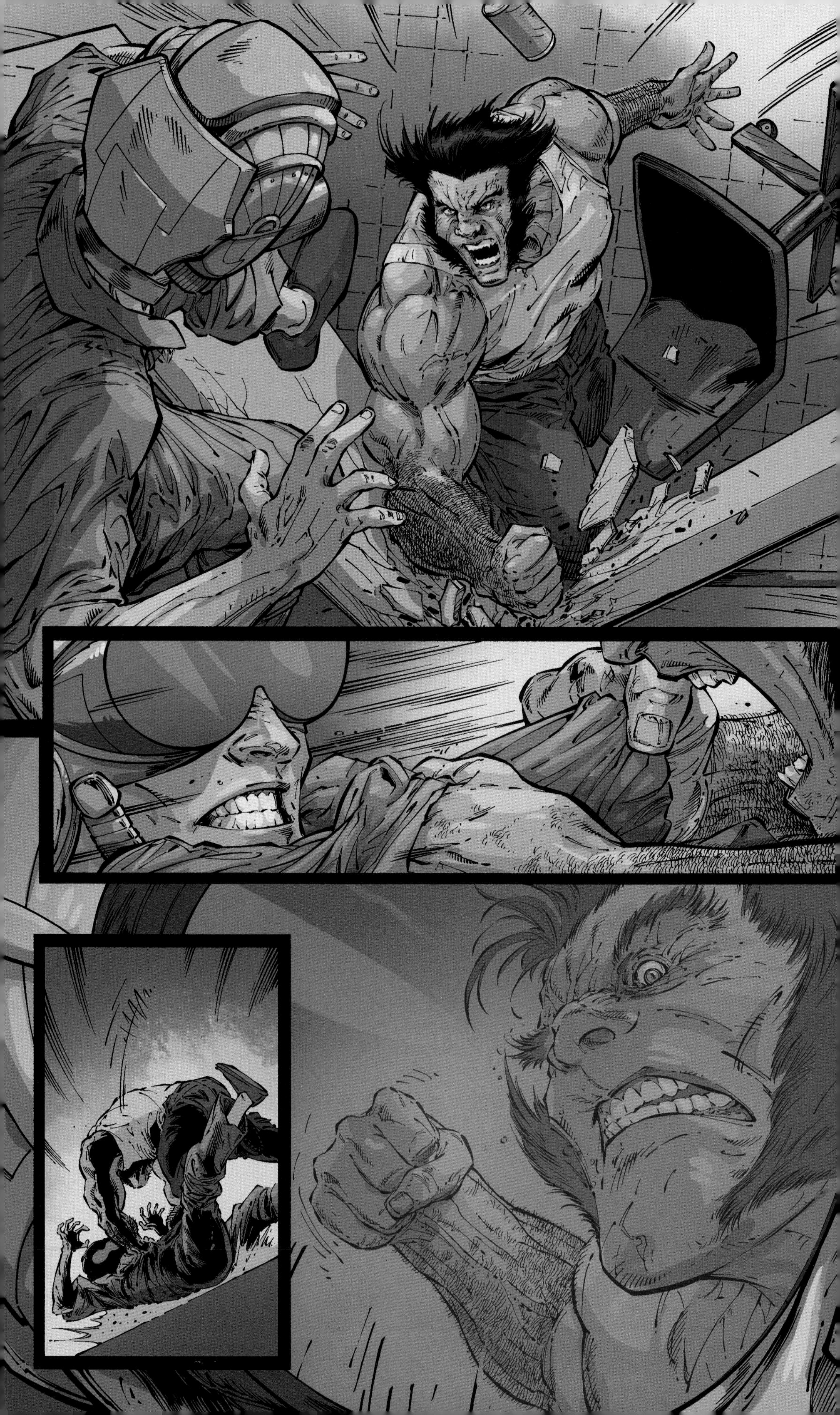

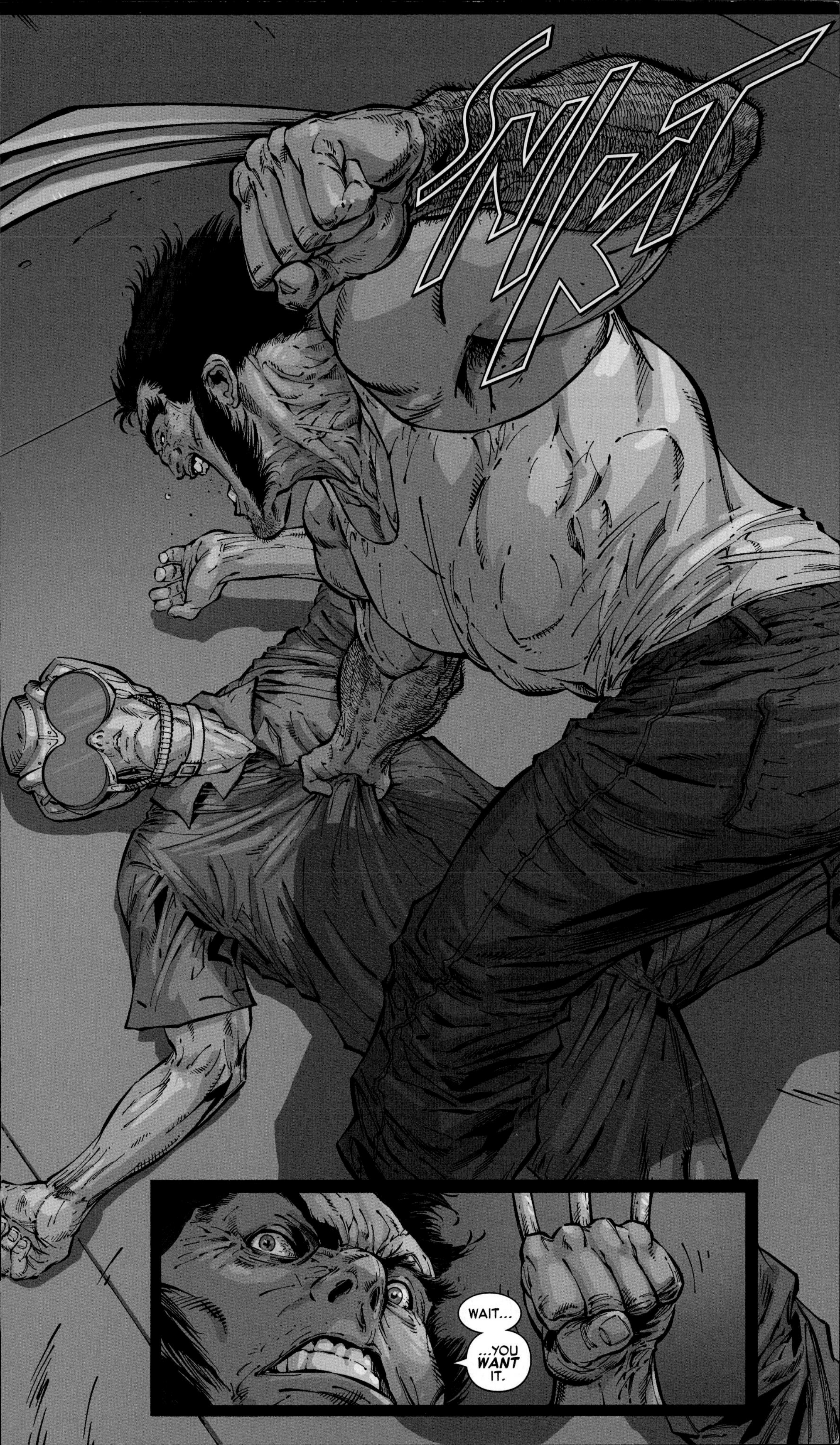
SNIKT
WAIT...
...YOU WANT IT.

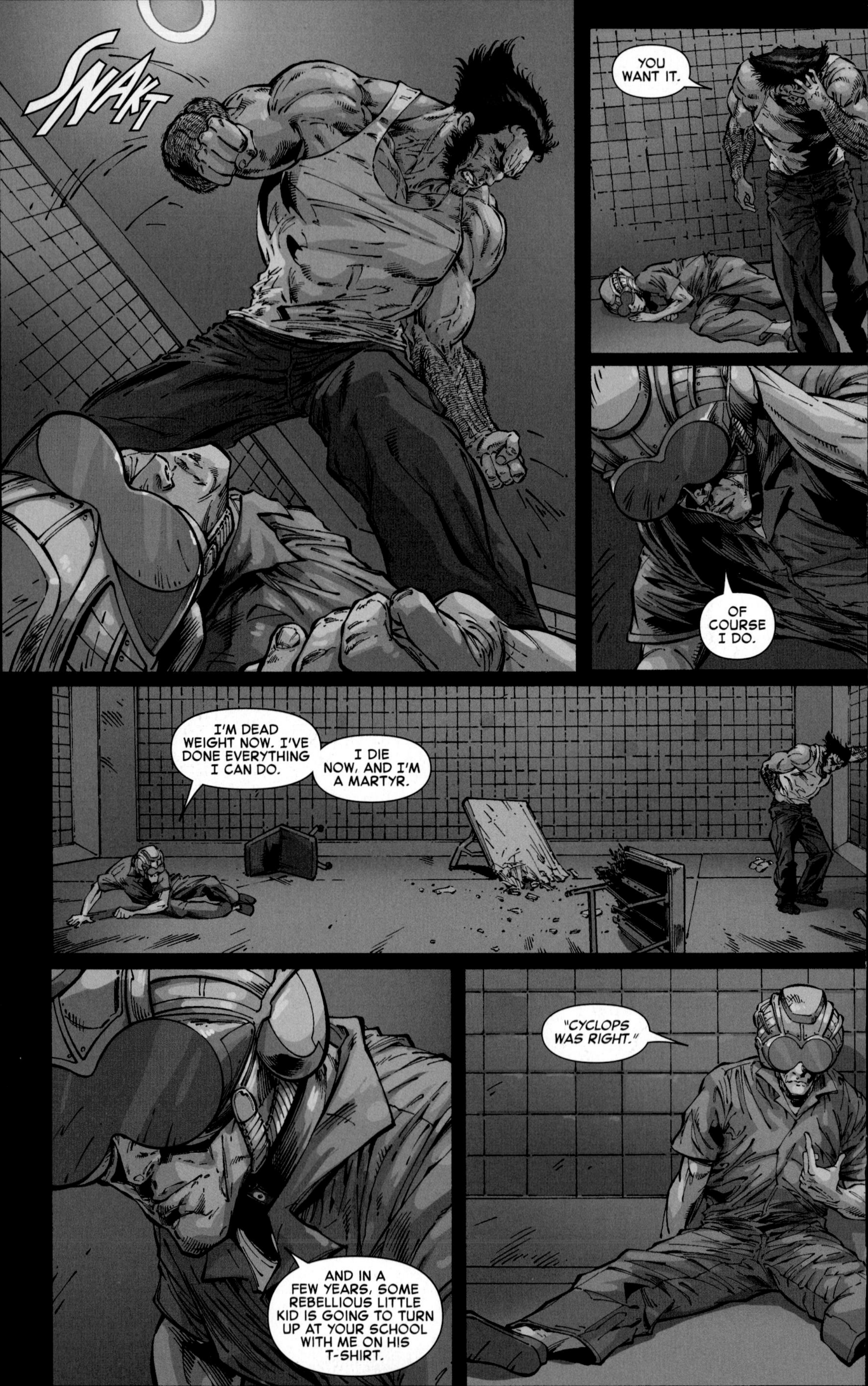
SNAKT
YOU WANT IT.
OF COURSE I DO.
I'M DEAD WEIGHT NOW. I'VE DONE EVERYTHING I CAN DO.
I DIE NOW, AND I'M A MARTYR.
AND IN A FEW YEARS, SOME REBELLIOUS LITTLE KID IS GOING TO TURN UP AT YOUR SCHOOL WITH ME ON HIS T-SHIRT.
"CYCLOPS WAS RIGHT."

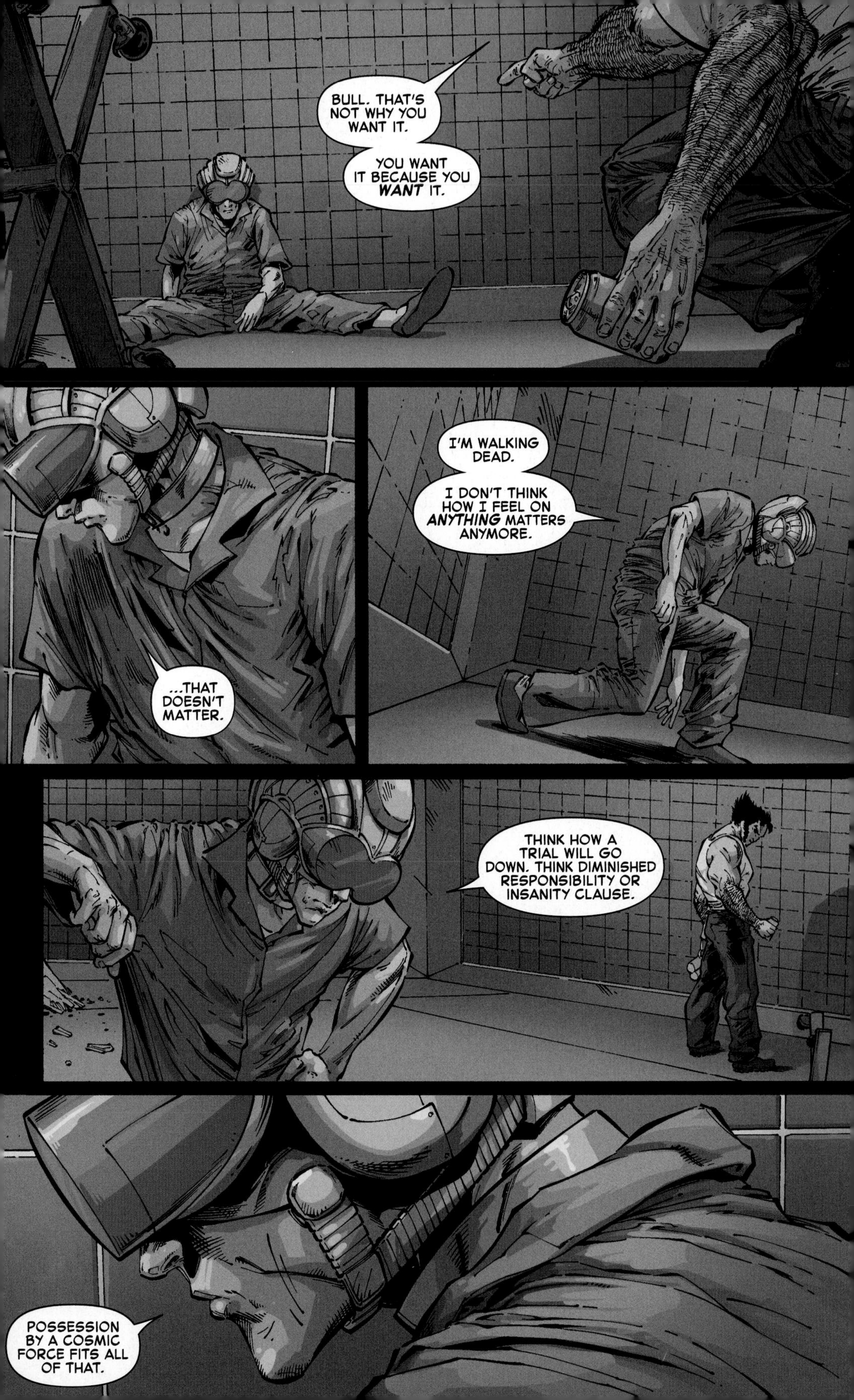
BULL. THAT'S NOT WHY YOU WANT IT.
YOU WANT IT BECAUSE YOU *WANT* IT.
...THAT DOESN'T MATTER.
I'M WALKING DEAD.
I DON'T THINK HOW I FEEL ON *ANYTHING* MATTERS ANYMORE.
THINK HOW A TRIAL WILL GO DOWN. THINK DIMINISHED RESPONSIBILITY OR INSANITY CLAUSE.
POSSESSION BY A COSMIC FORCE FITS ALL OF THAT.

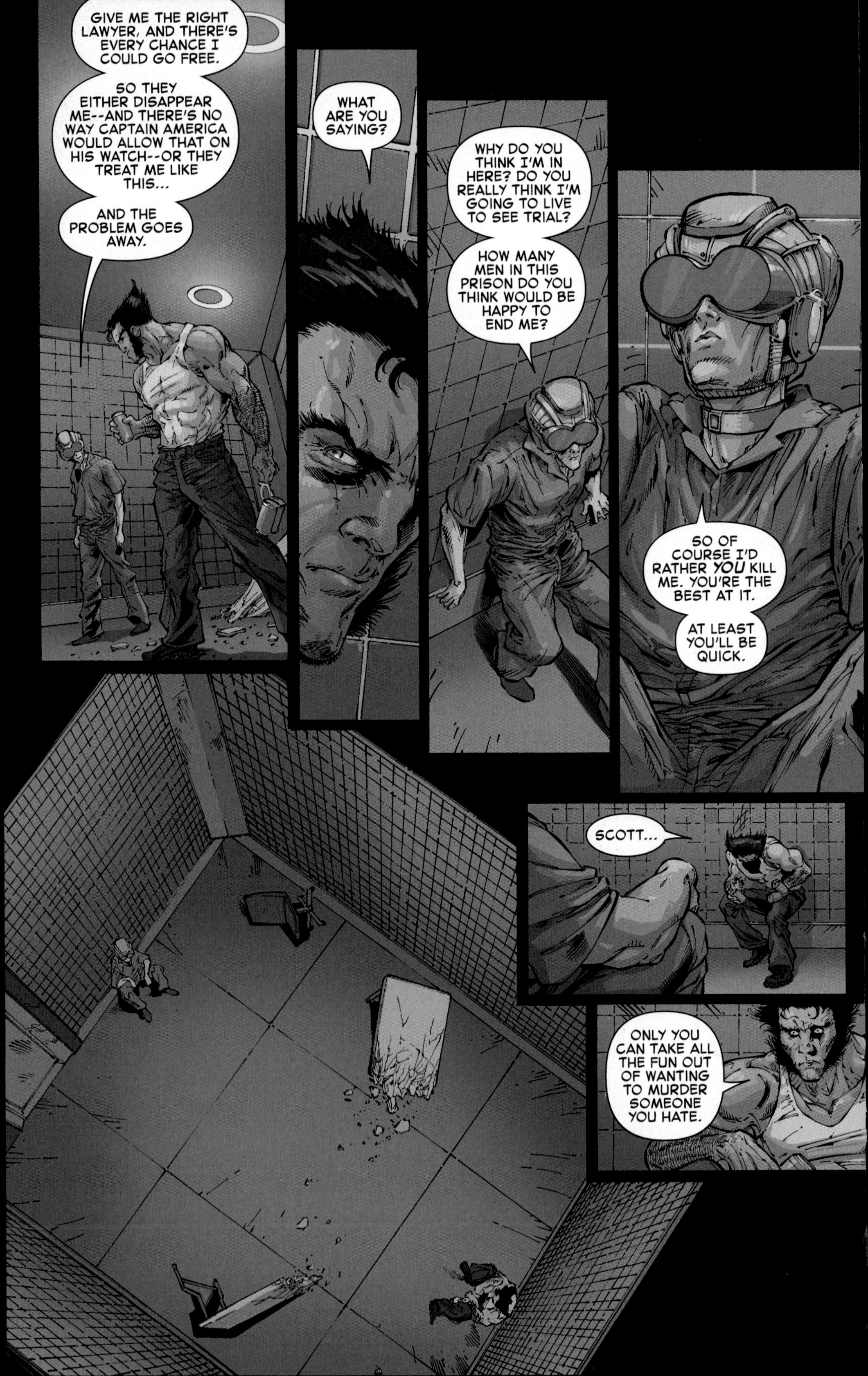
GIVE ME THE RIGHT LAWYER, AND THERE'S EVERY CHANCE I COULD GO FREE.
SO THEY EITHER DISAPPEAR ME--AND THERE'S NO WAY CAPTAIN AMERICA WOULD ALLOW THAT ON HIS WATCH--OR THEY TREAT ME LIKE THIS...
AND THE PROBLEM GOES AWAY.
WHAT ARE YOU SAYING?
WHY DO YOU THINK I'M IN HERE? DO YOU REALLY THINK I'M GOING TO LIVE TO SEE TRIAL?
HOW MANY MEN IN THIS PRISON DO YOU THINK WOULD BE HAPPY TO END ME?
SO OF COURSE I'D RATHER YOU KILL ME. YOU'RE THE BEST AT IT.
AT LEAST YOU'LL BE QUICK.
SCOTT...
ONLY YOU CAN TAKE ALL THE FUN OUT OF WANTING TO MURDER SOMEONE YOU HATE.

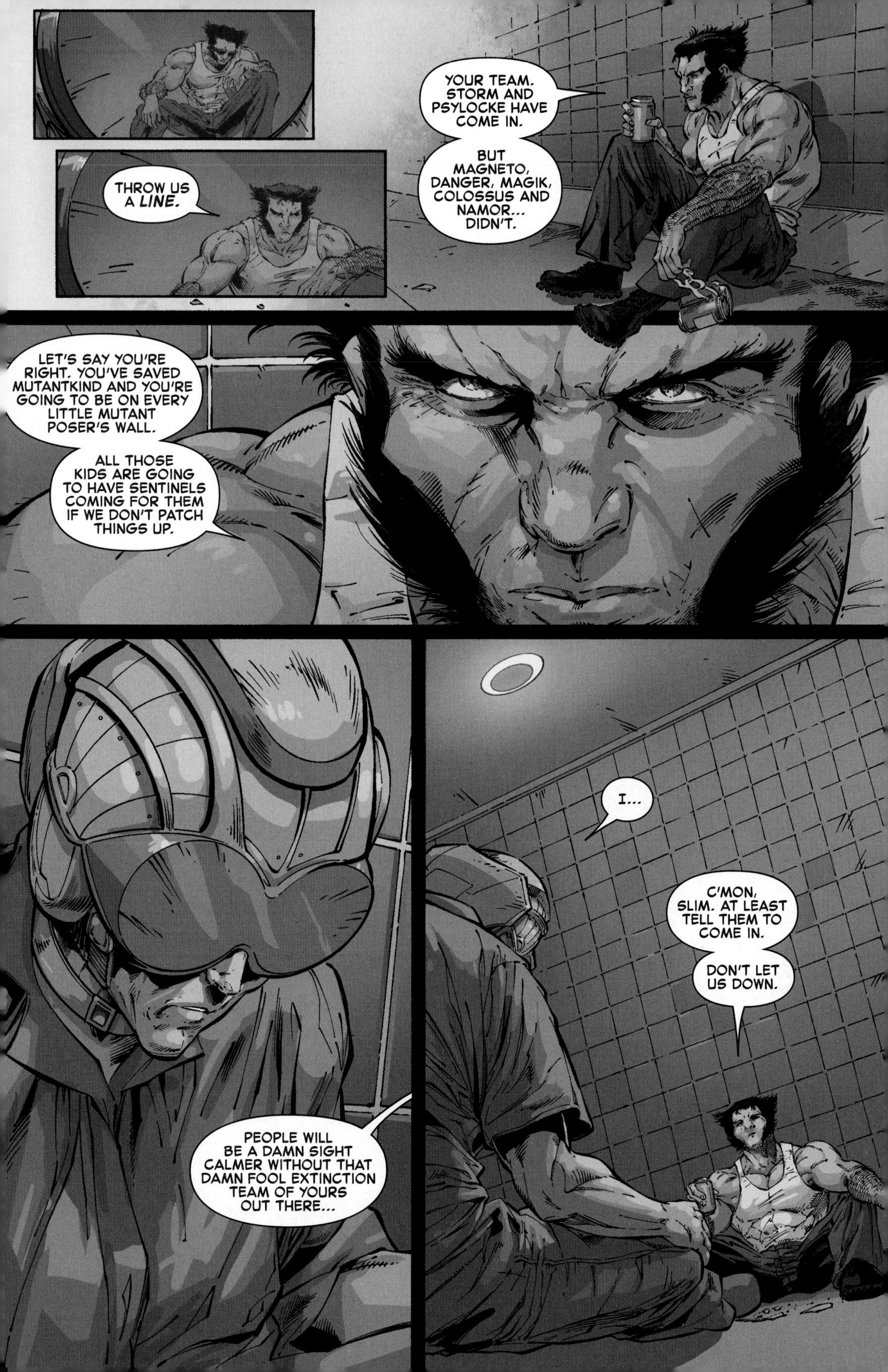
YOUR TEAM. STORM AND PSYLOCKE HAVE COME IN.
BUT MAGNETO, DANGER, MAGIK, COLOSSUS AND NAMOR... DIDN'T.
THROW US A *LINE*.
LET'S SAY YOU'RE RIGHT. YOU'VE SAVED MUTANTKIND AND YOU'RE GOING TO BE ON EVERY LITTLE MUTANT POSER'S WALL.
ALL THOSE KIDS ARE GOING TO HAVE SENTINELS COMING FOR THEM IF WE DON'T PATCH THINGS UP.
PEOPLE WILL BE A DAMN SIGHT CALMER WITHOUT THAT DAMN FOOL EXTINCTION TEAM OF YOURS OUT THERE...
I...
C'MON, SLIM. AT LEAST TELL THEM TO COME IN.
DON'T LET US DOWN.

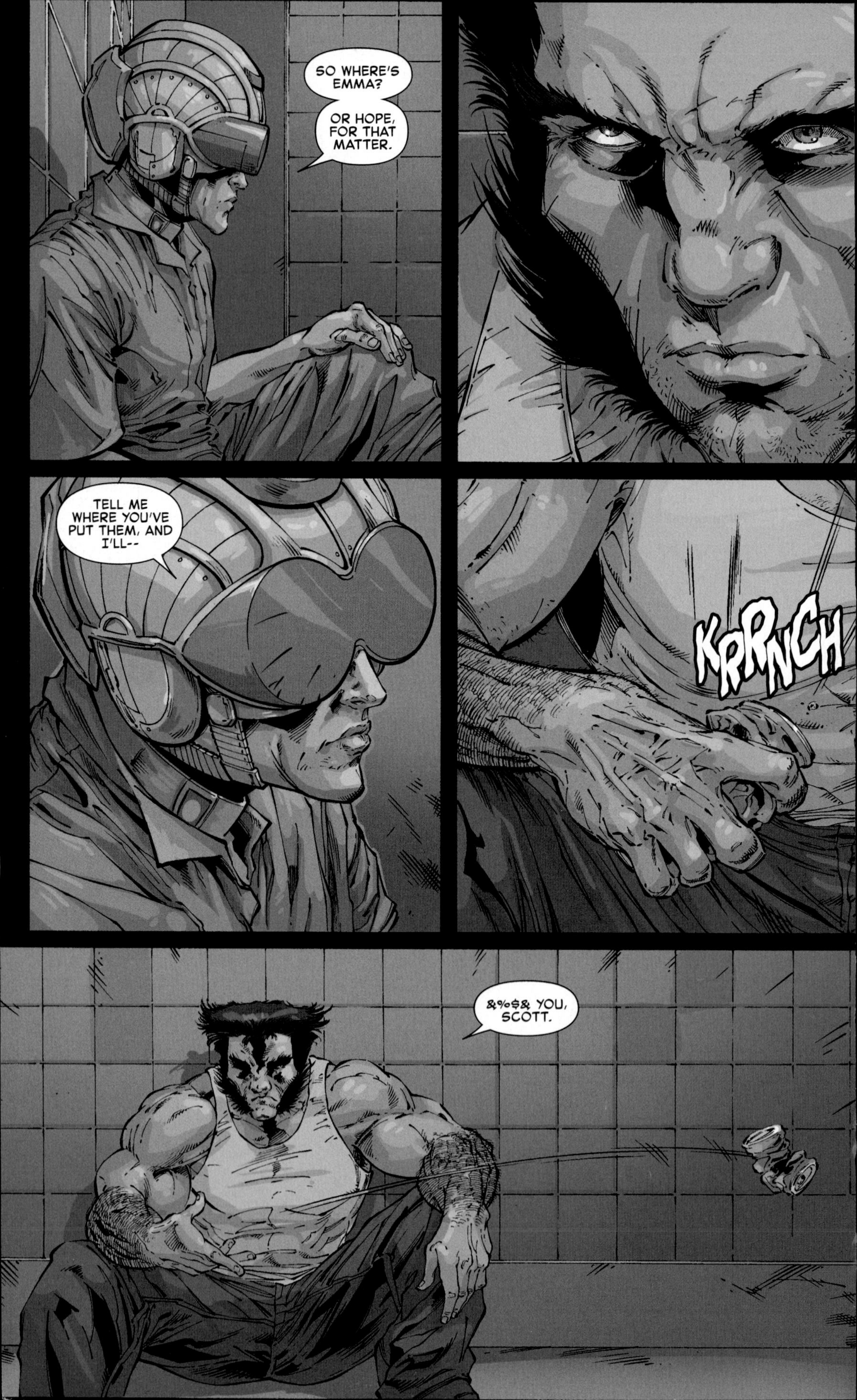
SO WHERE'S EMMA?
OR HOPE, FOR THAT MATTER.
TELL ME WHERE YOU'VE PUT THEM, AND I'LL--
KRRNCH
&%$& YOU, SCOTT.

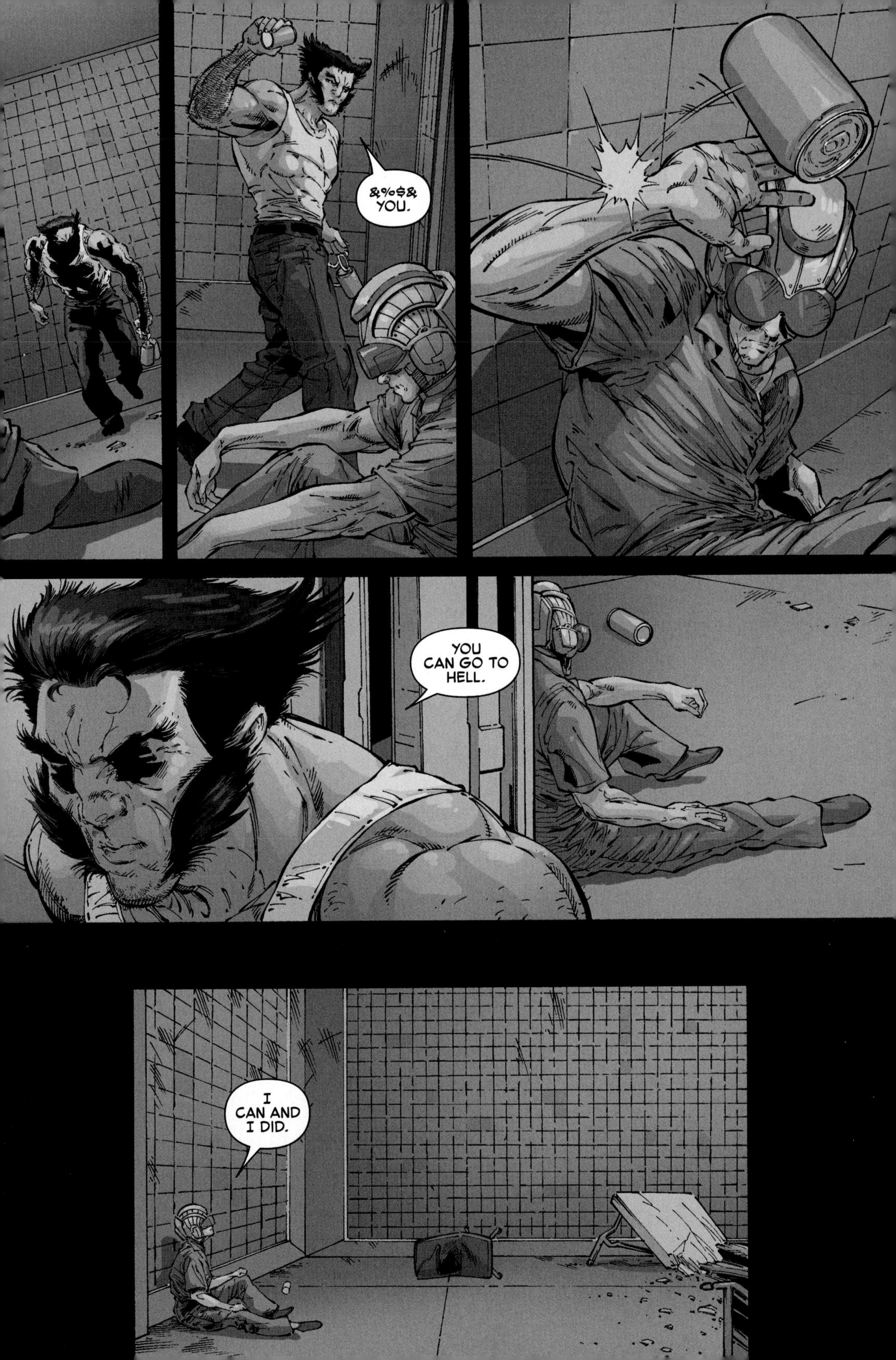
&%$& YOU.
YOU CAN GO TO HELL.
I CAN AND I DID.

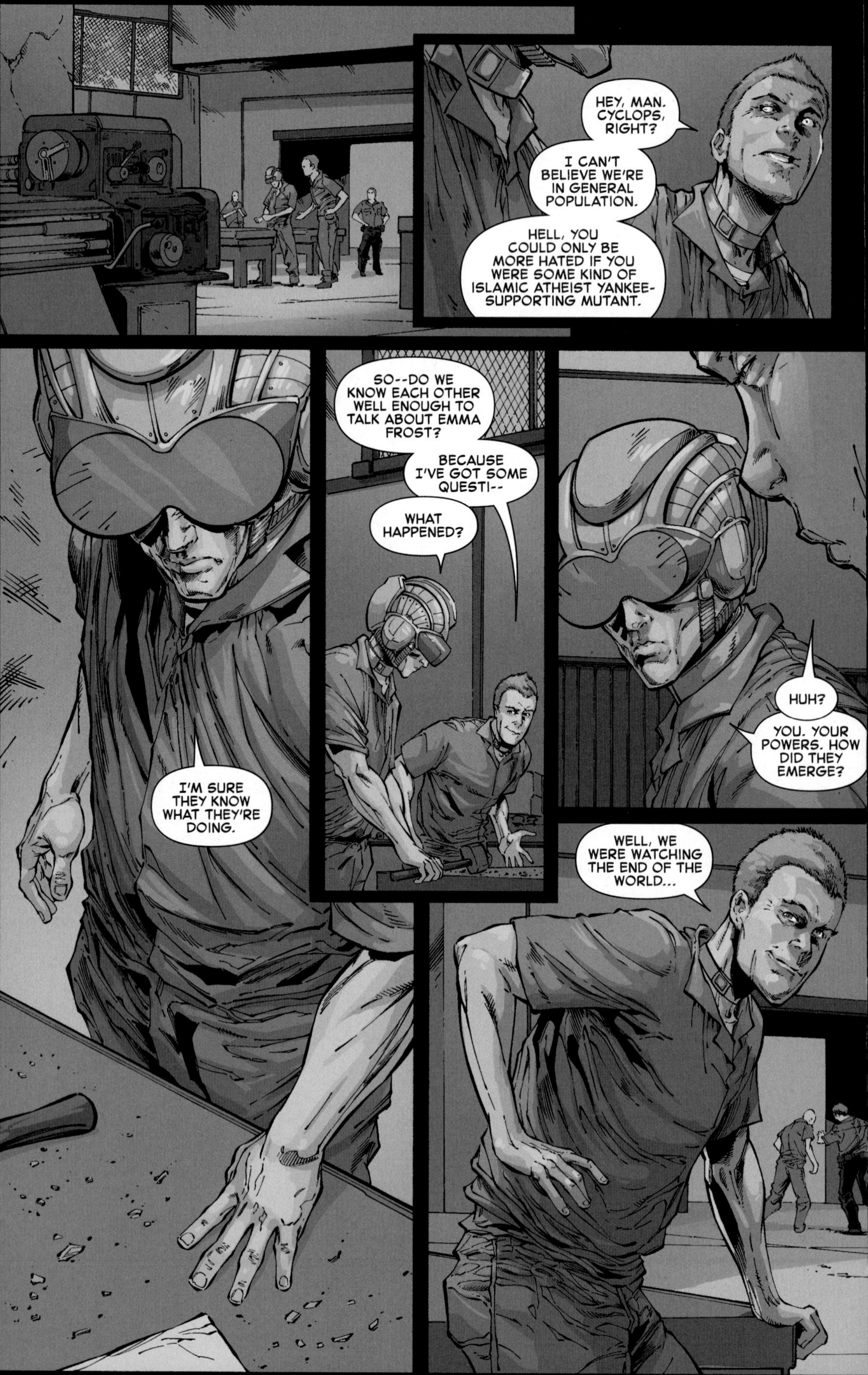
HEY, MAN. CYCLOPS, RIGHT?
I CAN'T BELIEVE WE'RE IN GENERAL POPULATION.
HELL, YOU COULD ONLY BE MORE HATED IF YOU WERE SOME KIND OF ISLAMIC ATHEIST YANKEE-SUPPORTING MUTANT.
SO--DO WE KNOW EACH OTHER WELL ENOUGH TO TALK ABOUT EMMA FROST?
BECAUSE I'VE GOT SOME QUESTI--
WHAT HAPPENED?
I'M SURE THEY KNOW WHAT THEY'RE DOING.
HUH?
YOU. YOUR POWERS. HOW DID THEY EMERGE?
WELL, WE WERE WATCHING THE END OF THE WORLD...

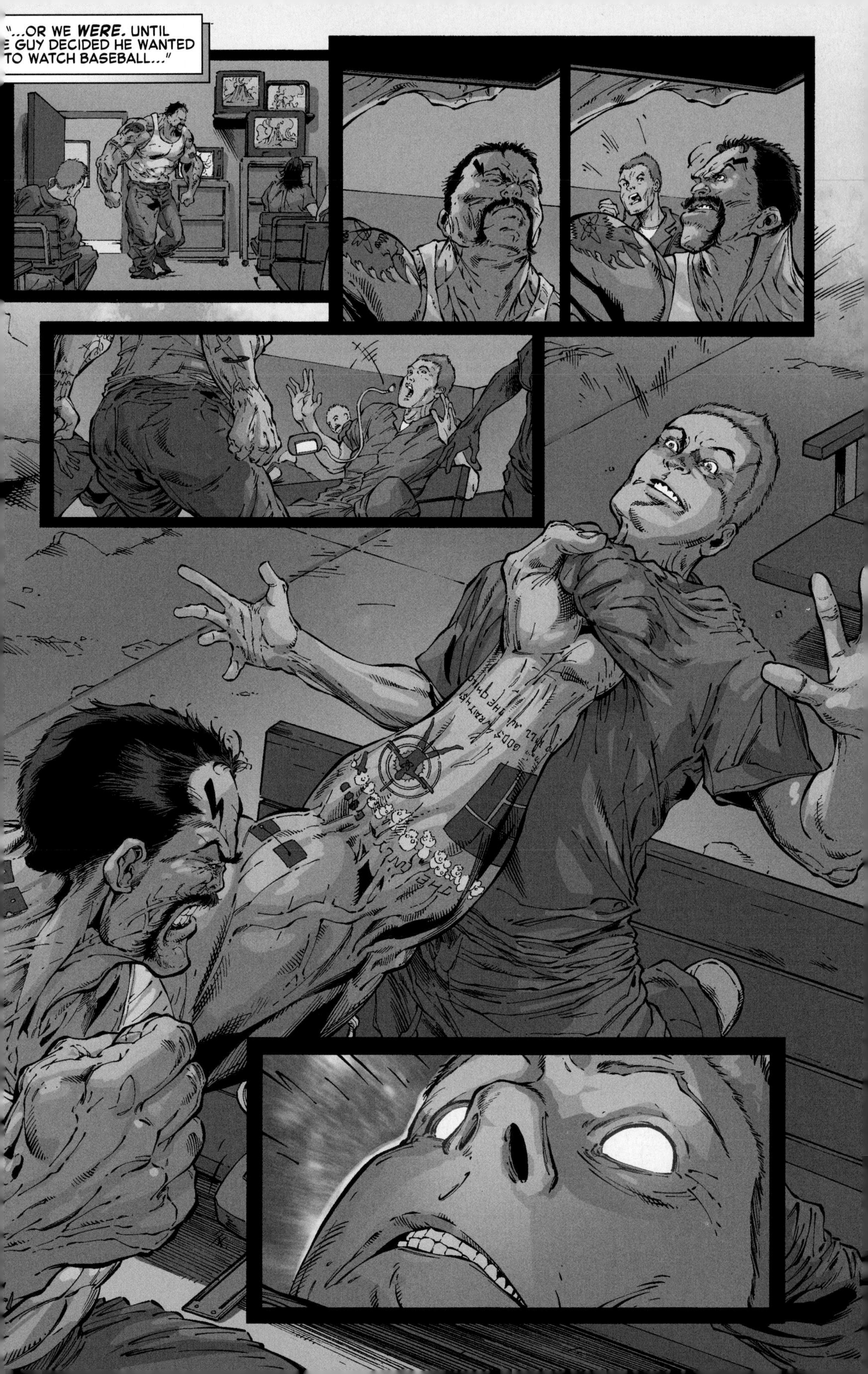
"...OR WE **WERE.** UNTIL
GUY DECIDED HE WANTED
TO WATCH BASEBALL..."

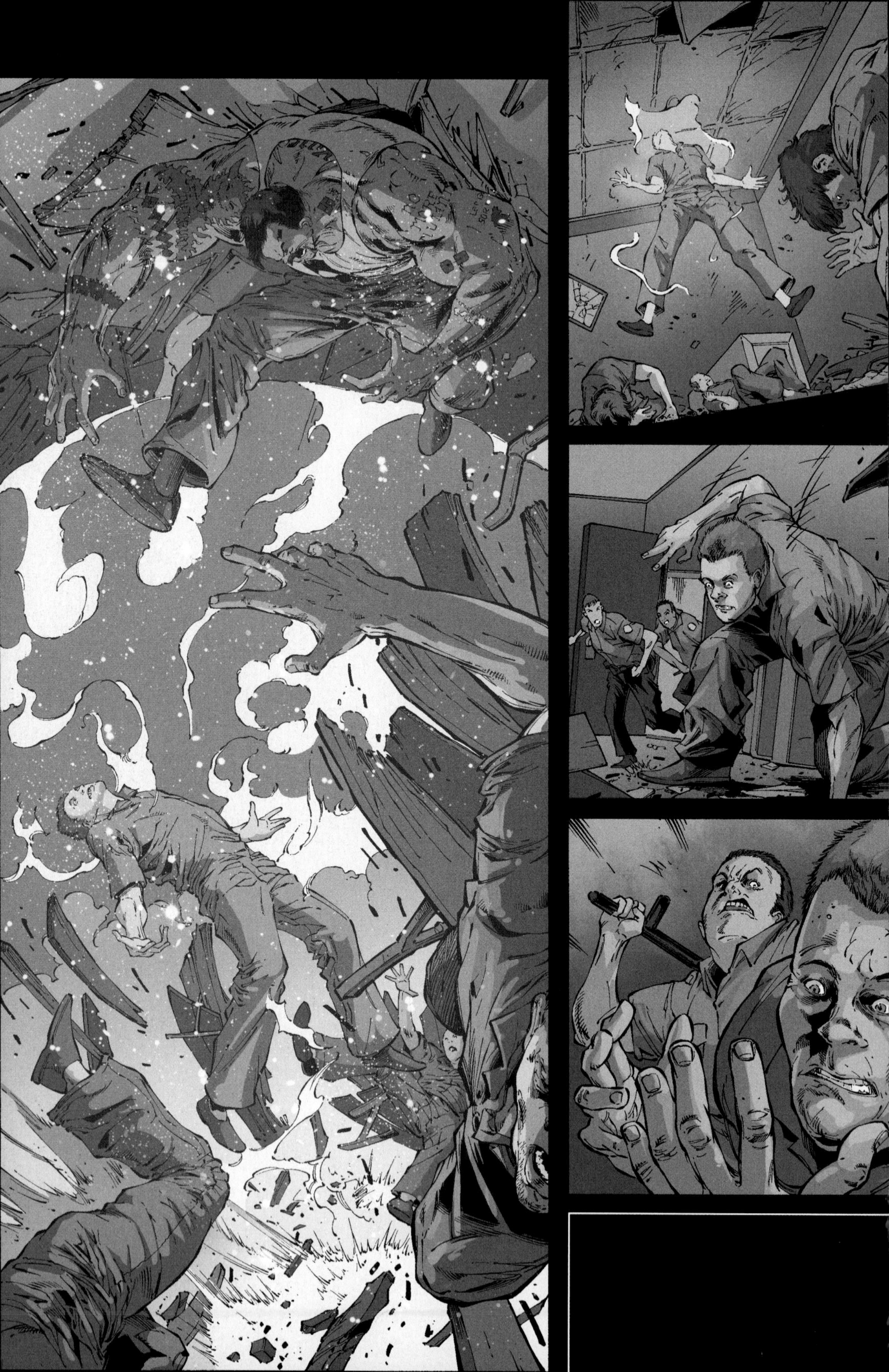

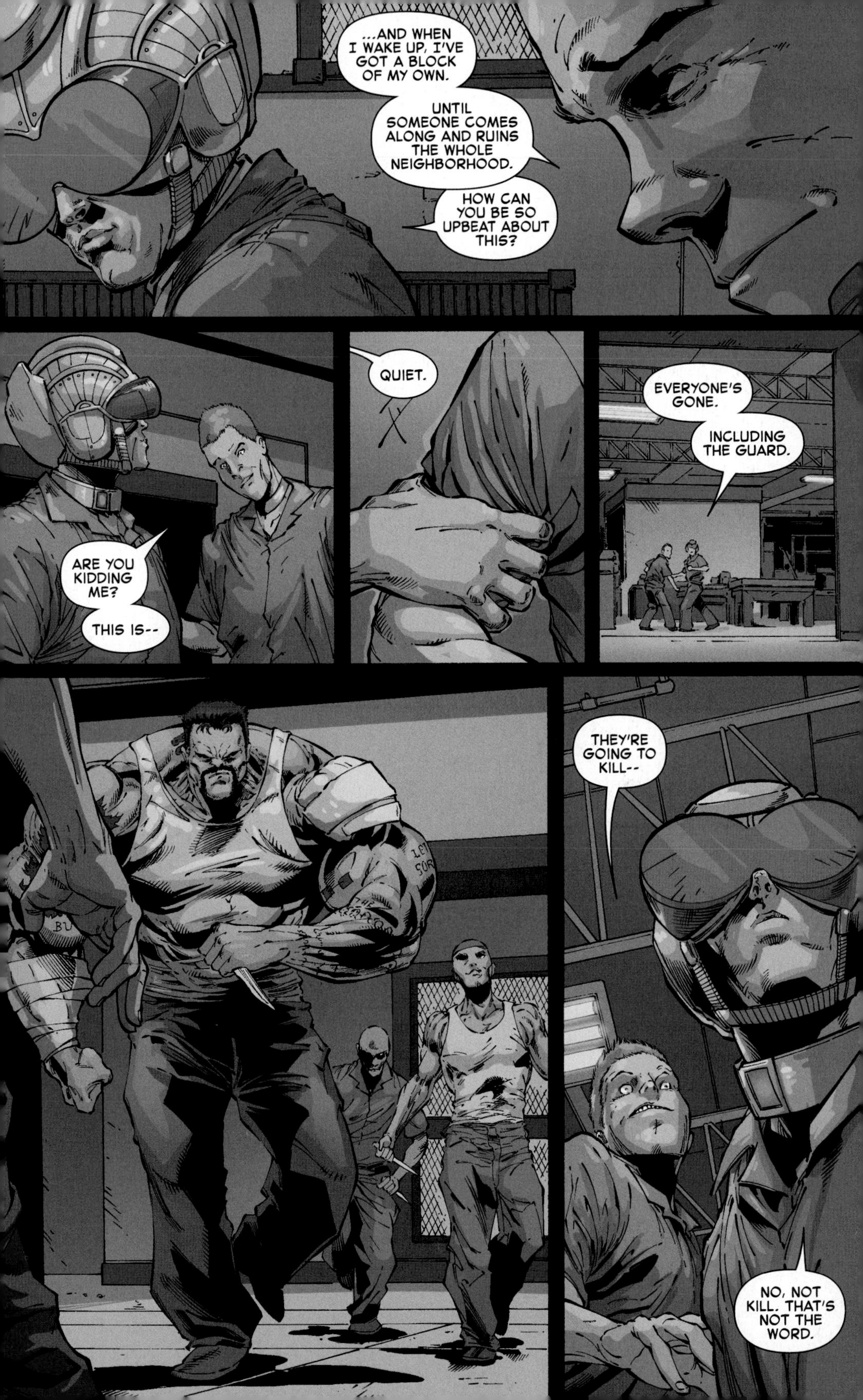
...AND WHEN I WAKE UP, I'VE GOT A BLOCK OF MY OWN.
UNTIL SOMEONE COMES ALONG AND RUINS THE WHOLE NEIGHBORHOOD.
HOW CAN YOU BE SO UPBEAT ABOUT THIS?
ARE YOU KIDDING ME?
THIS IS--
QUIET.
EVERYONE'S GONE.
INCLUDING THE GUARD.
THEY'RE GOING TO KILL--
NO, NOT KILL. THAT'S NOT THE WORD.

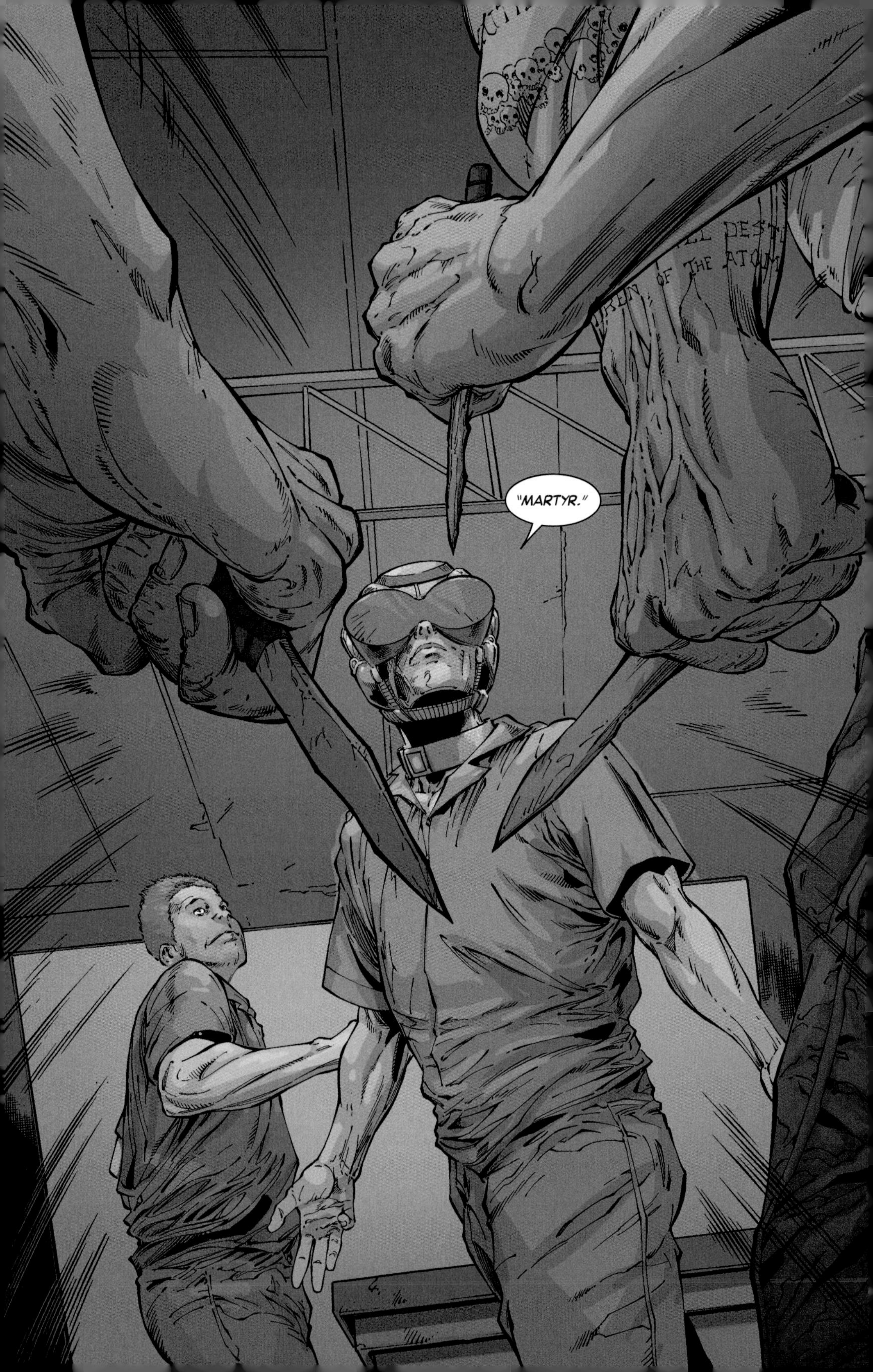
"MARTYR."

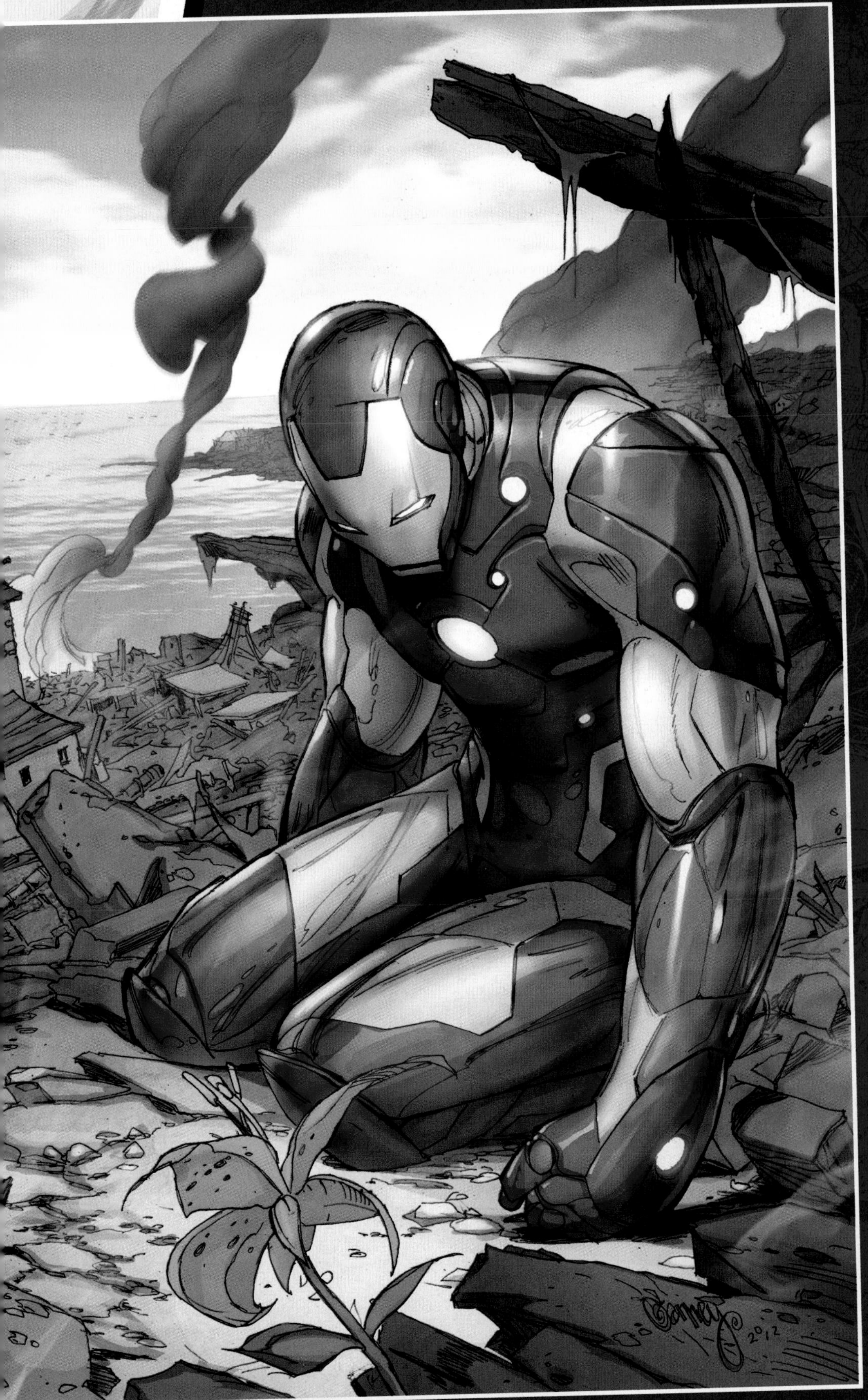

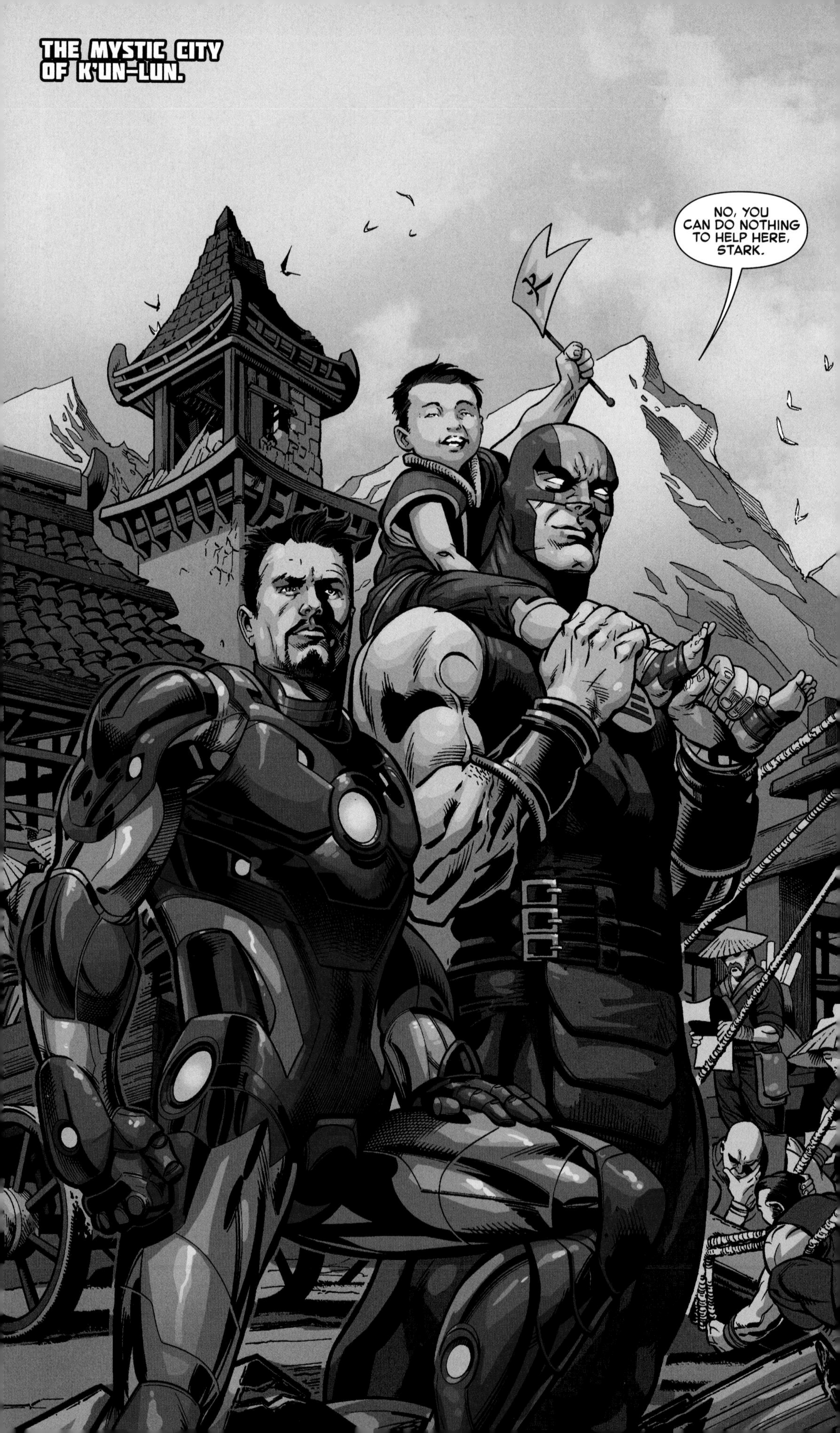
THE MYSTIC CITY OF K'UN-LUN.
NO, YOU CAN DO NOTHING TO HELP HERE, STARK.

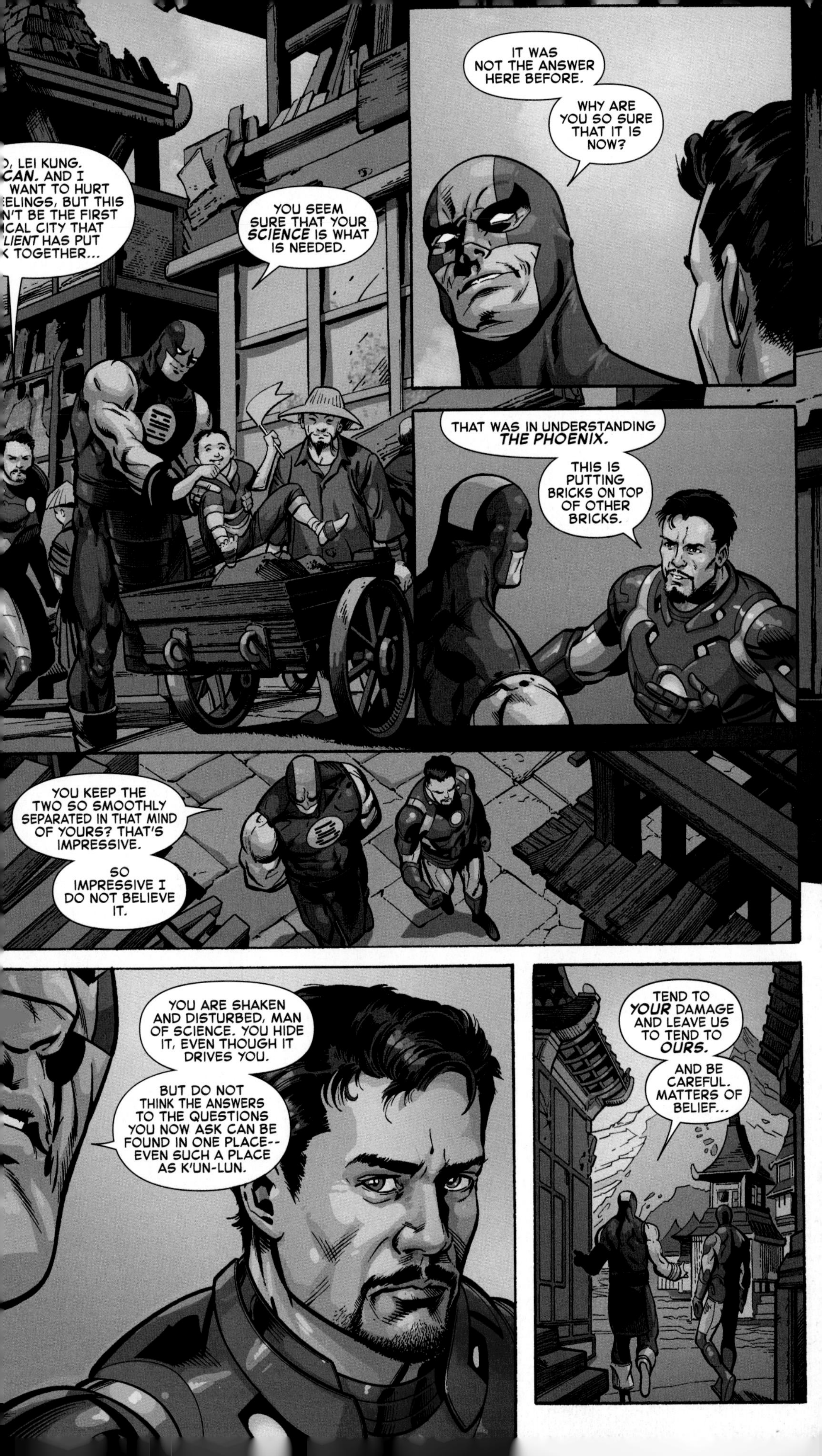

), LEI KUNG. CAN. AND I WANT TO HURT ELINGS, BUT THIS N'T BE THE FIRST ICAL CITY THAT LIENT HAS PUT K TOGETHER...
YOU SEEM SURE THAT YOUR SCIENCE IS WHAT IS NEEDED.
IT WAS NOT THE ANSWER HERE BEFORE.
WHY ARE YOU SO SURE THAT IT IS NOW?
THAT WAS IN UNDERSTANDING THE PHOENIX.
THIS IS PUTTING BRICKS ON TOP OF OTHER BRICKS.
YOU KEEP THE TWO SO SMOOTHLY SEPARATED IN THAT MIND OF YOURS? THAT'S IMPRESSIVE.
SO IMPRESSIVE I DO NOT BELIEVE IT.
YOU ARE SHAKEN AND DISTURBED, MAN OF SCIENCE. YOU HIDE IT, EVEN THOUGH IT DRIVES YOU.
BUT DO NOT THINK THE ANSWERS TO THE QUESTIONS YOU NOW ASK CAN BE FOUND IN ONE PLACE-- EVEN SUCH A PLACE AS K'UN-LUN.
TEND TO YOUR DAMAGE AND LEAVE US TO TEND TO OURS.
AND BE CAREFUL. MATTERS OF BELIEF...

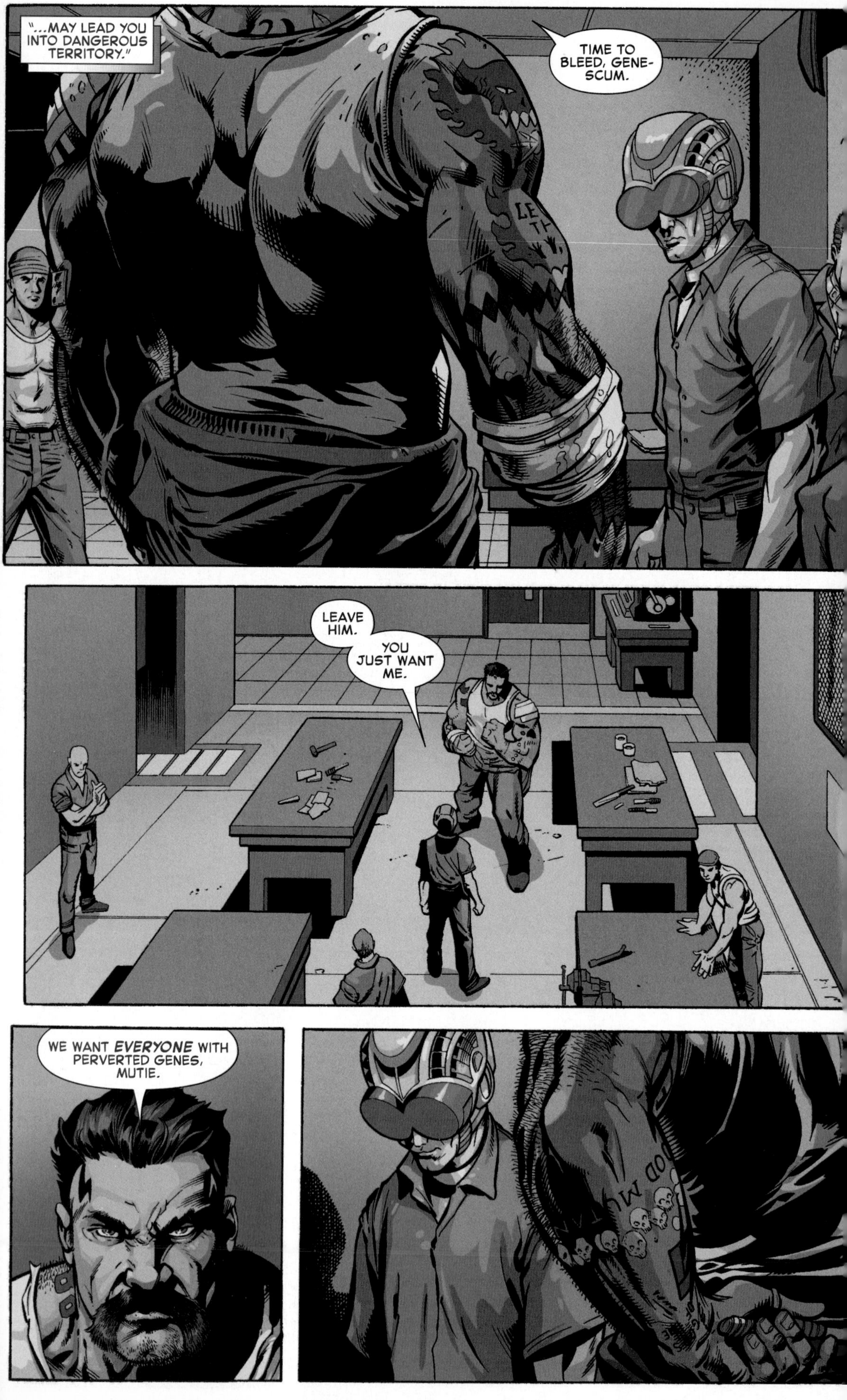
"...MAY LEAD YOU INTO DANGEROUS TERRITORY."
TIME TO BLEED, GENE-SCUM.
LEAVE HIM.
YOU JUST WANT ME.
WE WANT *EVERYONE* WITH PERVERTED GENES, MUTIE.

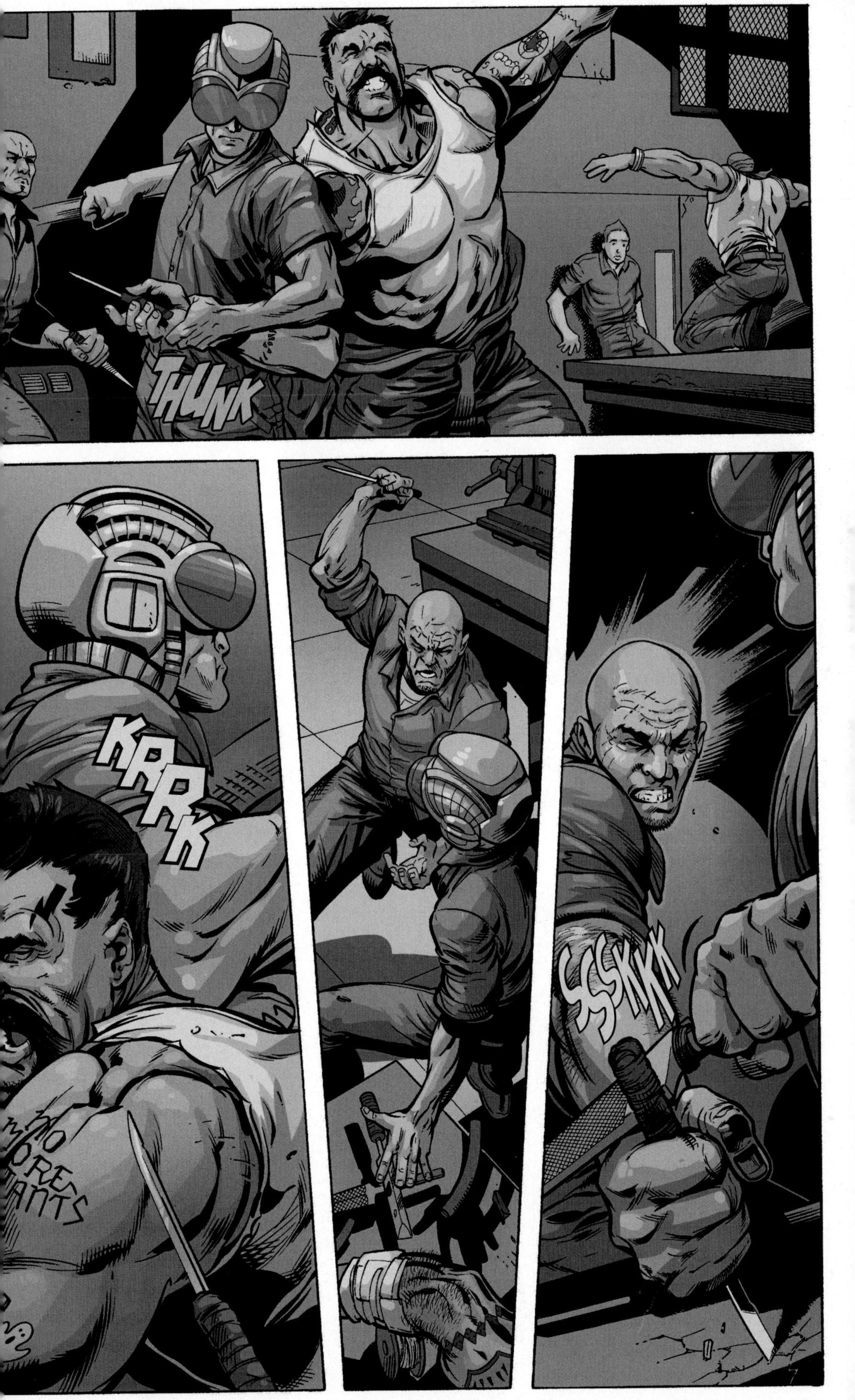
THUNK
KRRK
NO MORE
SSSKKK

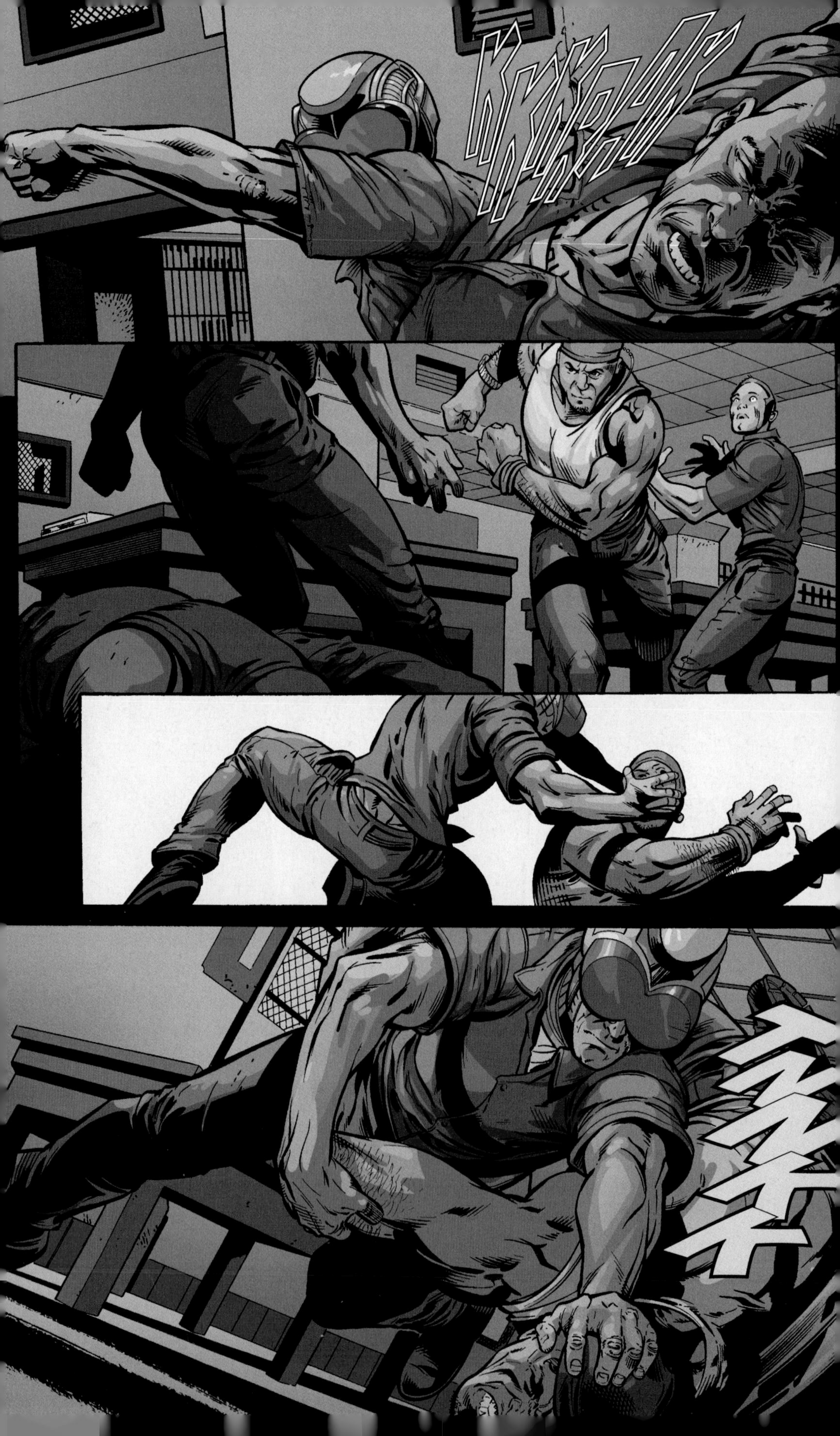

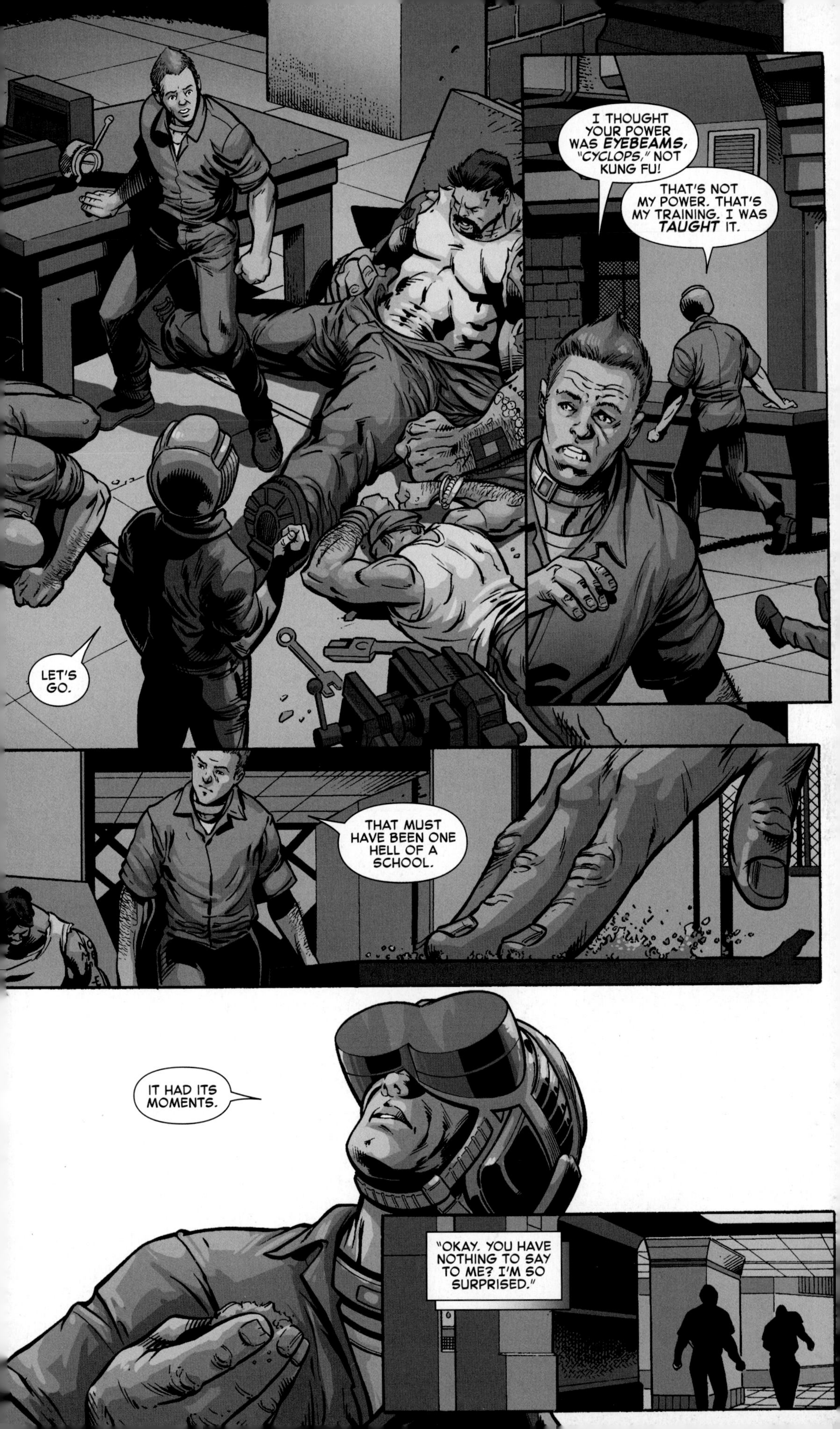
I THOUGHT YOUR POWER WAS EYEBEAMS, "CYCLOPS," NOT KUNG FU!
THAT'S NOT MY POWER. THAT'S MY TRAINING. I WAS TAUGHT IT.
LET'S GO.
THAT MUST HAVE BEEN ONE HELL OF A SCHOOL.
IT HAD ITS MOMENTS.
"OKAY. YOU HAVE NOTHING TO SAY TO ME? I'M SO SURPRISED."

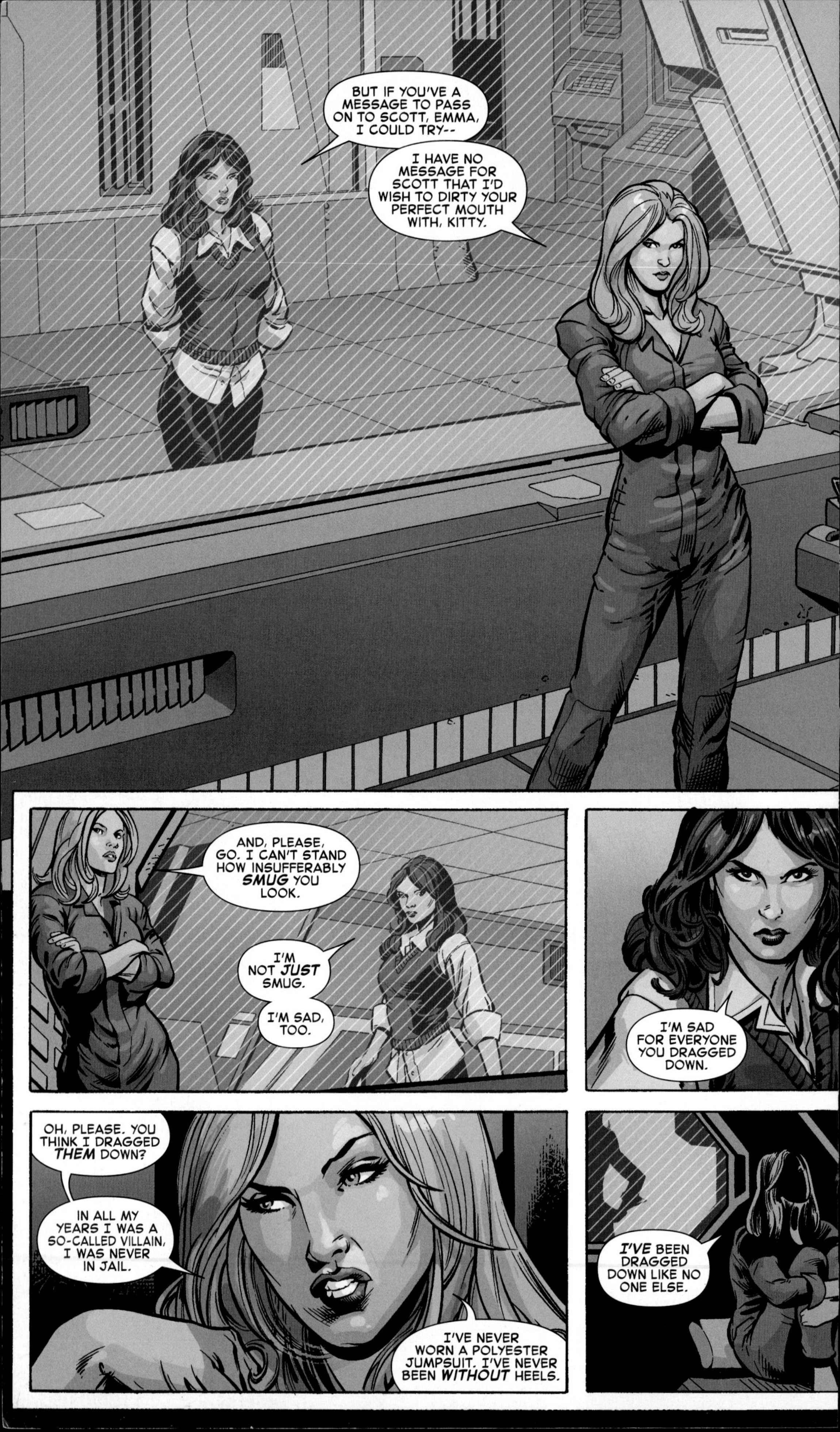
BUT IF YOU'VE A MESSAGE TO PASS ON TO SCOTT, EMMA, I COULD TRY--
I HAVE NO MESSAGE FOR SCOTT THAT I'D WISH TO DIRTY YOUR PERFECT MOUTH WITH, KITTY.
AND, PLEASE, GO. I CAN'T STAND HOW INSUFFERABLY SMUG YOU LOOK.
I'M NOT JUST SMUG.
I'M SAD, TOO.
I'M SAD FOR EVERYONE YOU DRAGGED DOWN.
OH, PLEASE. YOU THINK I DRAGGED THEM DOWN?
IN ALL MY YEARS I WAS A SO-CALLED VILLAIN, I WAS NEVER IN JAIL.
I'VE NEVER WORN A POLYESTER JUMPSUIT. I'VE NEVER BEEN WITHOUT HEELS.
I'VE BEEN DRAGGED DOWN LIKE NO ONE ELSE.

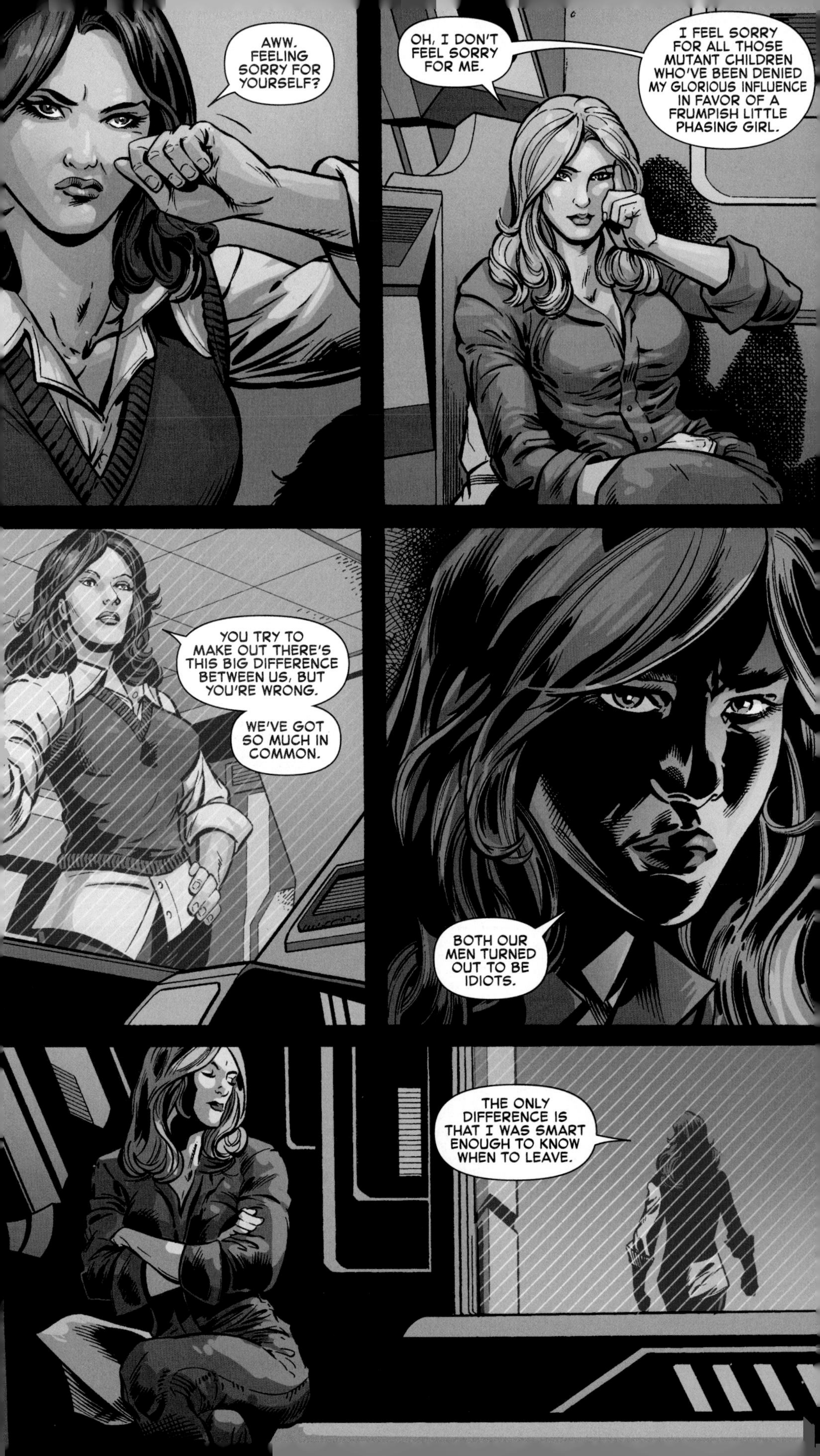
AWW. FEELING SORRY FOR YOURSELF?
OH, I DON'T FEEL SORRY FOR ME.
I FEEL SORRY FOR ALL THOSE MUTANT CHILDREN WHO'VE BEEN DENIED MY GLORIOUS INFLUENCE IN FAVOR OF A FRUMPISH LITTLE PHASING GIRL.
YOU TRY TO MAKE OUT THERE'S THIS BIG DIFFERENCE BETWEEN US, BUT YOU'RE WRONG.
WE'VE GOT SO MUCH IN COMMON.
BOTH OUR MEN TURNED OUT TO BE IDIOTS.
THE ONLY DIFFERENCE IS THAT I WAS SMART ENOUGH TO KNOW WHEN TO LEAVE.

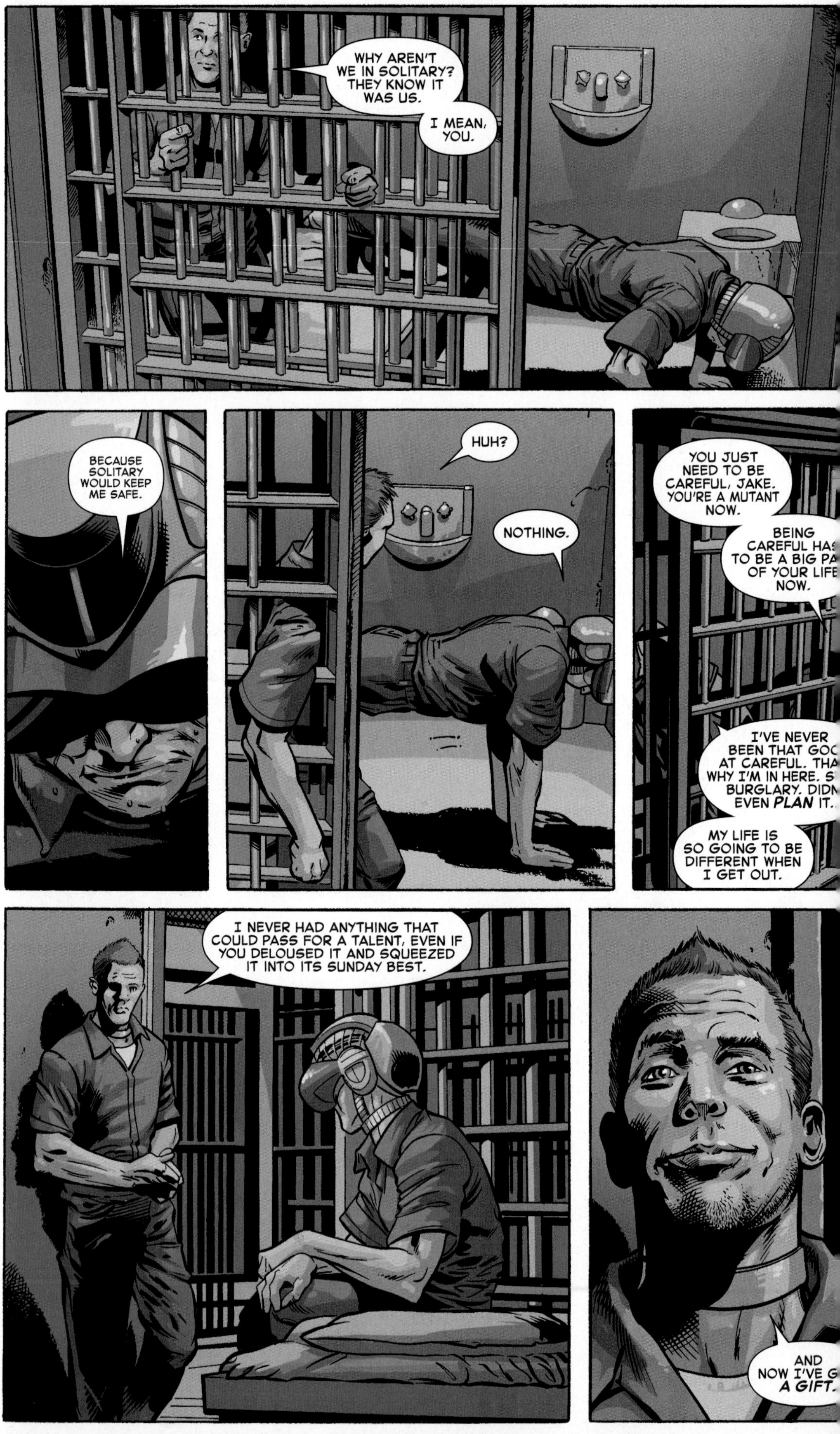
WHY AREN'T WE IN SOLITARY? THEY KNOW IT WAS US.
I MEAN, YOU.
BECAUSE SOLITARY WOULD KEEP ME SAFE.
HUH?
NOTHING.
YOU JUST NEED TO BE CAREFUL, JAKE. YOU'RE A MUTANT NOW.
BEING CAREFUL HAS TO BE A BIG PA OF YOUR LIFE NOW.
I'VE NEVER BEEN THAT GOO AT CAREFUL. THA WHY I'M IN HERE. BURGLARY. DIDN EVEN PLAN IT.
MY LIFE IS SO GOING TO BE DIFFERENT WHEN I GET OUT.
I NEVER HAD ANYTHING THAT COULD PASS FOR A TALENT, EVEN IF YOU DELOUSED IT AND SQUEEZED IT INTO ITS SUNDAY BEST.
AND NOW I'VE G A GIFT.

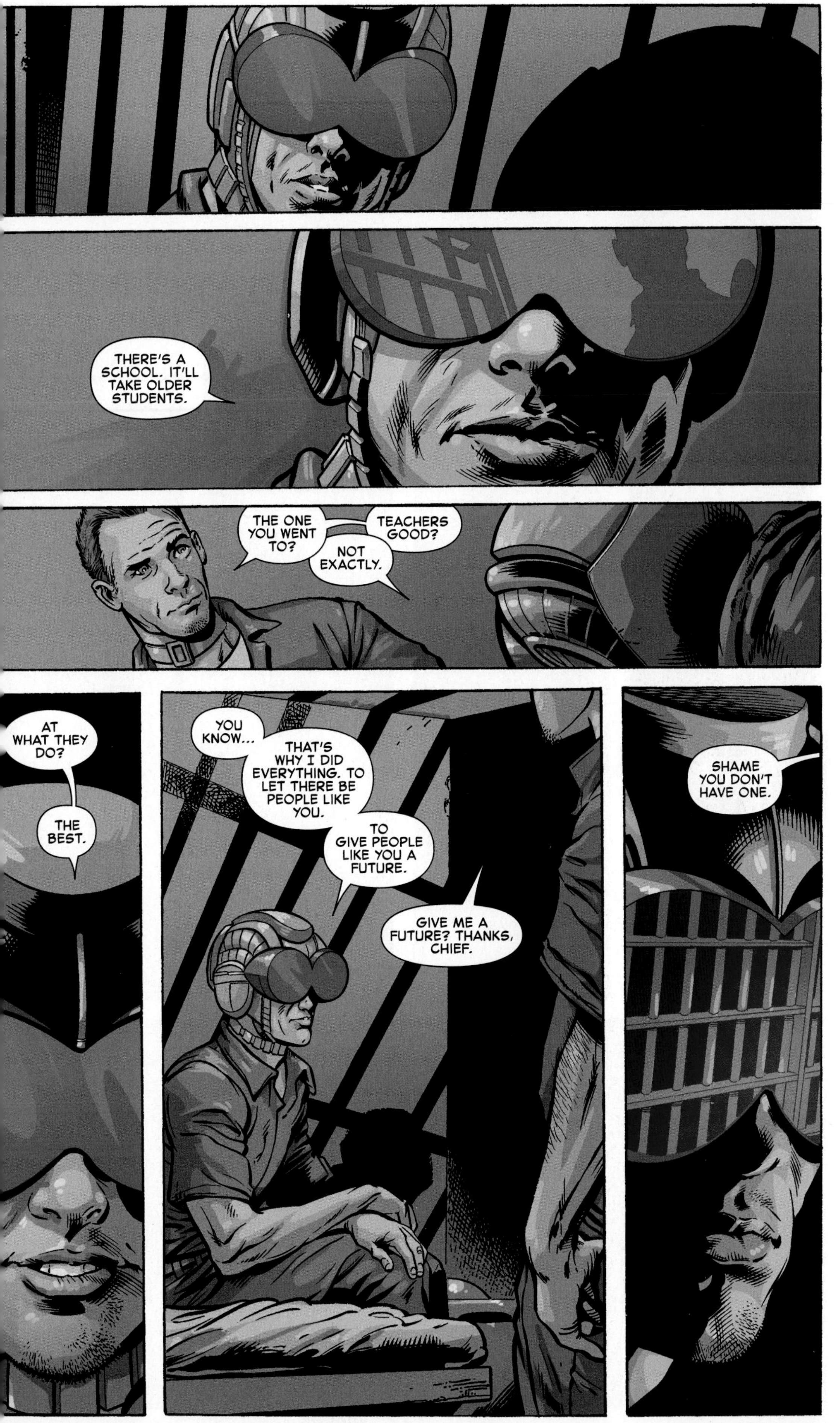
THERE'S A SCHOOL. IT'LL TAKE OLDER STUDENTS.
THE ONE YOU WENT TO?
TEACHERS GOOD?
NOT EXACTLY.
AT WHAT THEY DO?
THE BEST.
YOU KNOW...
THAT'S WHY I DID EVERYTHING. TO LET THERE BE PEOPLE LIKE YOU.
TO GIVE PEOPLE LIKE YOU A FUTURE.
GIVE ME A FUTURE? THANKS, CHIEF.
SHAME YOU DON'T HAVE ONE.

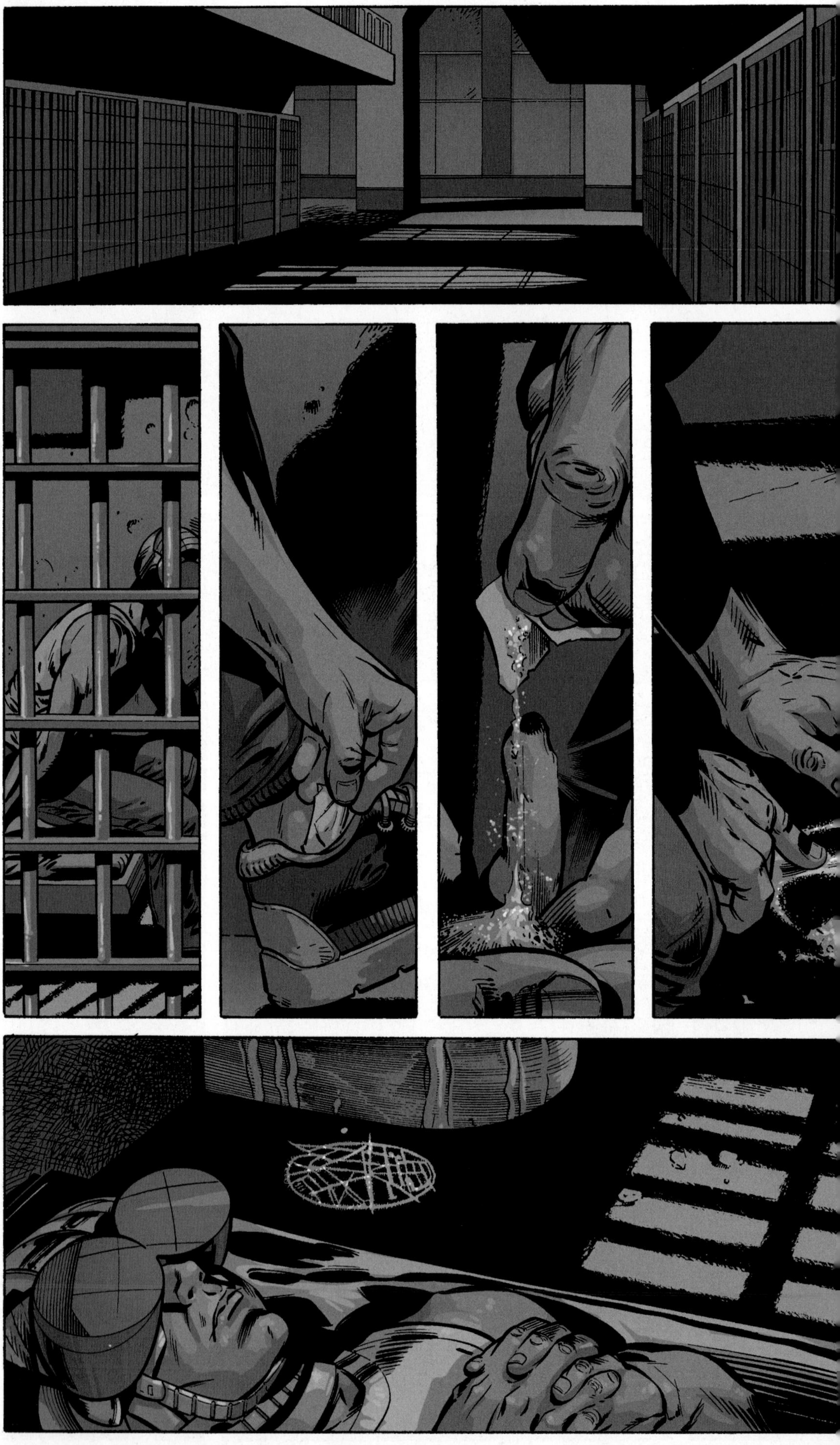

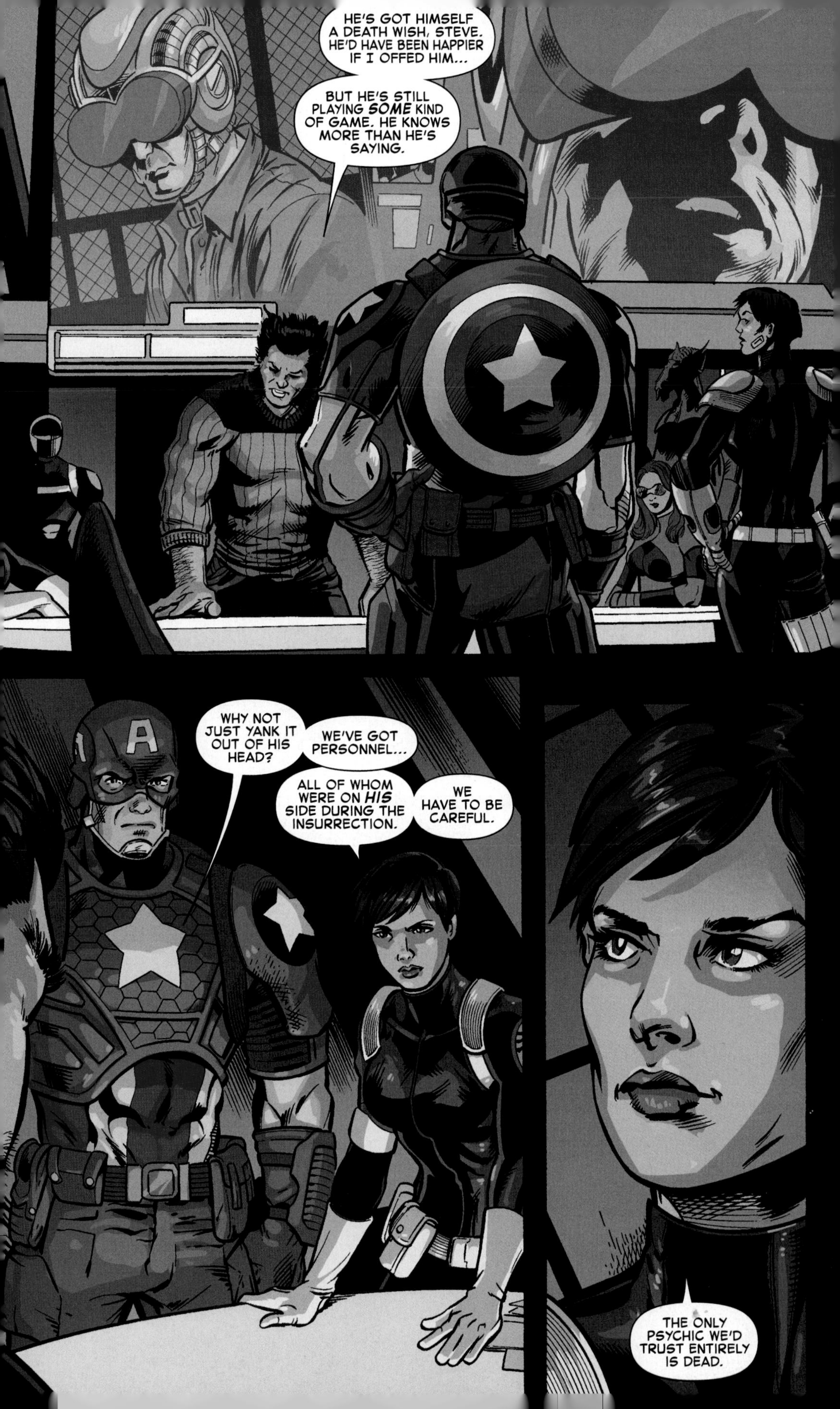
HE'S GOT HIMSELF A DEATH WISH, STEVE. HE'D HAVE BEEN HAPPIER IF I OFFED HIM...
BUT HE'S STILL PLAYING SOME KIND OF GAME. HE KNOWS MORE THAN HE'S SAYING.
WHY NOT JUST YANK IT OUT OF HIS HEAD?
WE'VE GOT PERSONNEL...
ALL OF WHOM WERE ON HIS SIDE DURING THE INSURRECTION.
WE HAVE TO BE CAREFUL.
THE ONLY PSYCHIC WE'D TRUST ENTIRELY IS DEAD.

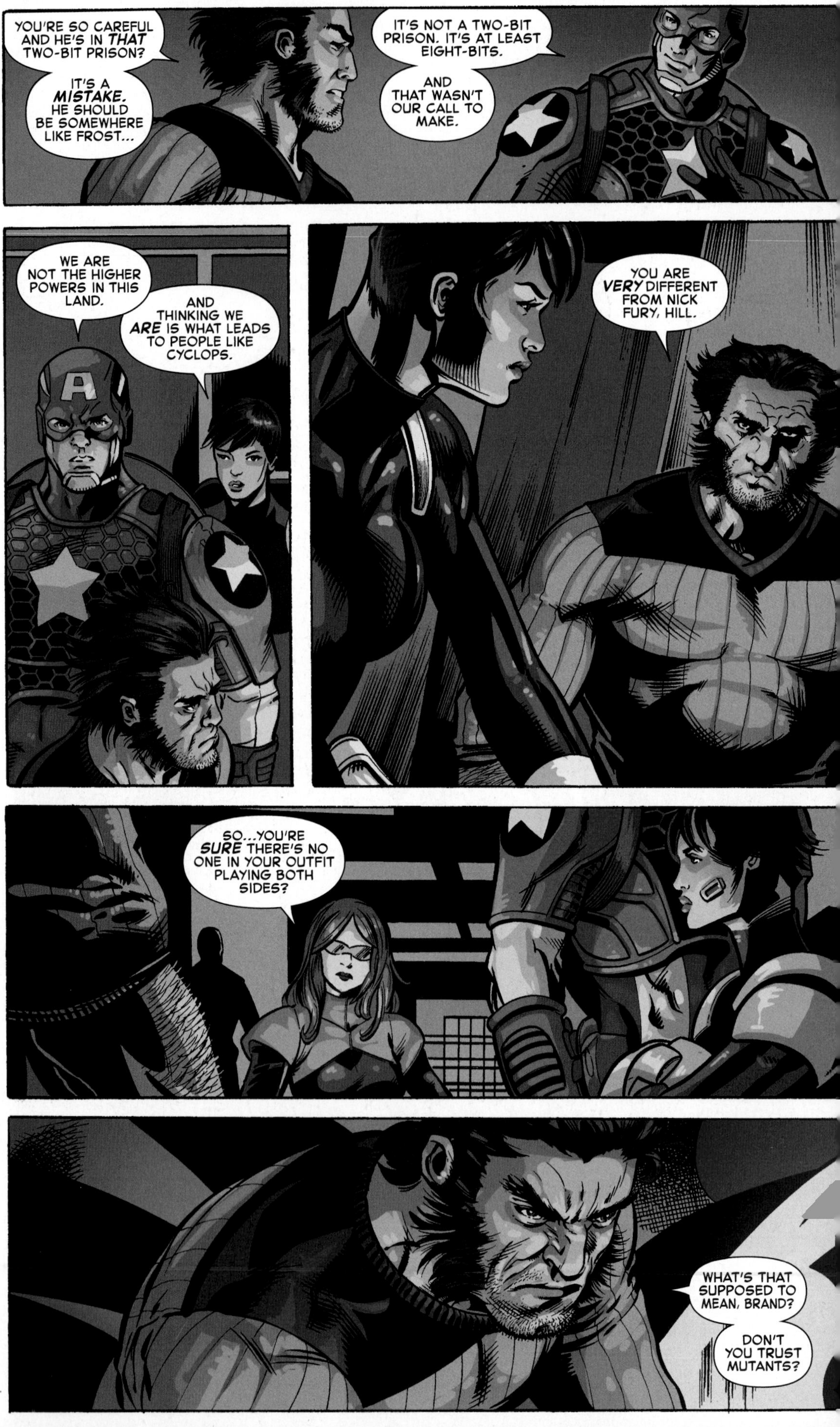
YOU'RE SO CAREFUL AND HE'S IN THAT TWO-BIT PRISON?
IT'S A MISTAKE. HE SHOULD BE SOMEWHERE LIKE FROST...
IT'S NOT A TWO-BIT PRISON. IT'S AT LEAST EIGHT-BITS.
AND THAT WASN'T OUR CALL TO MAKE.
WE ARE NOT THE HIGHER POWERS IN THIS LAND.
AND THINKING WE ARE IS WHAT LEADS TO PEOPLE LIKE CYCLOPS.
YOU ARE VERY DIFFERENT FROM NICK FURY, HILL.
SO...YOU'RE SURE THERE'S NO ONE IN YOUR OUTFIT PLAYING BOTH SIDES?
WHAT'S THAT SUPPOSED TO MEAN, BRAND?
DON'T YOU TRUST MUTANTS?

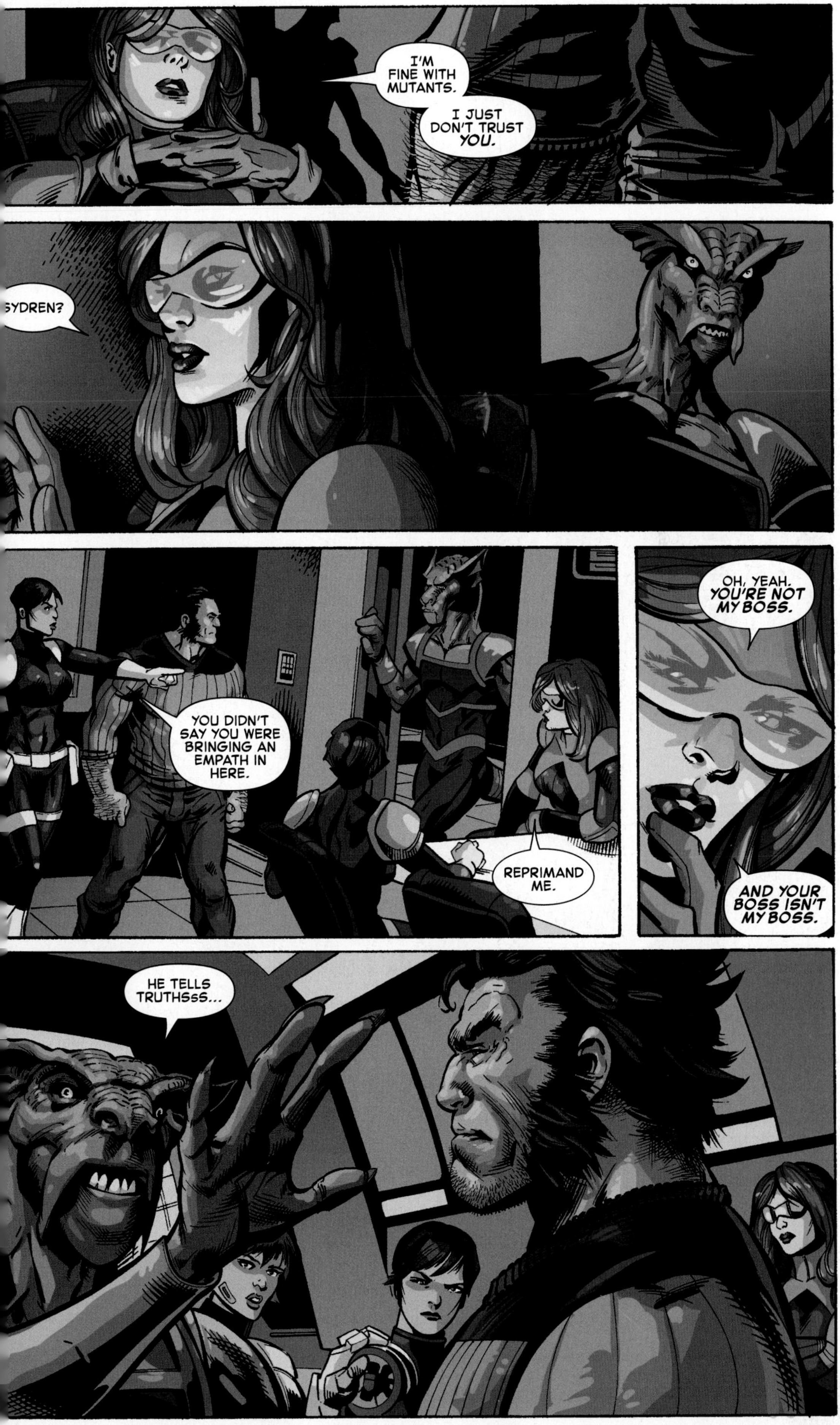
I'M FINE WITH MUTANTS.
I JUST DON'T TRUST YOU.
SYDREN?
YOU DIDN'T SAY YOU WERE BRINGING AN EMPATH IN HERE.
REPRIMAND ME.
OH, YEAH. YOU'RE NOT MY BOSS.
AND YOUR BOSS ISN'T MY BOSS.
HE TELLS TRUTHSSS...

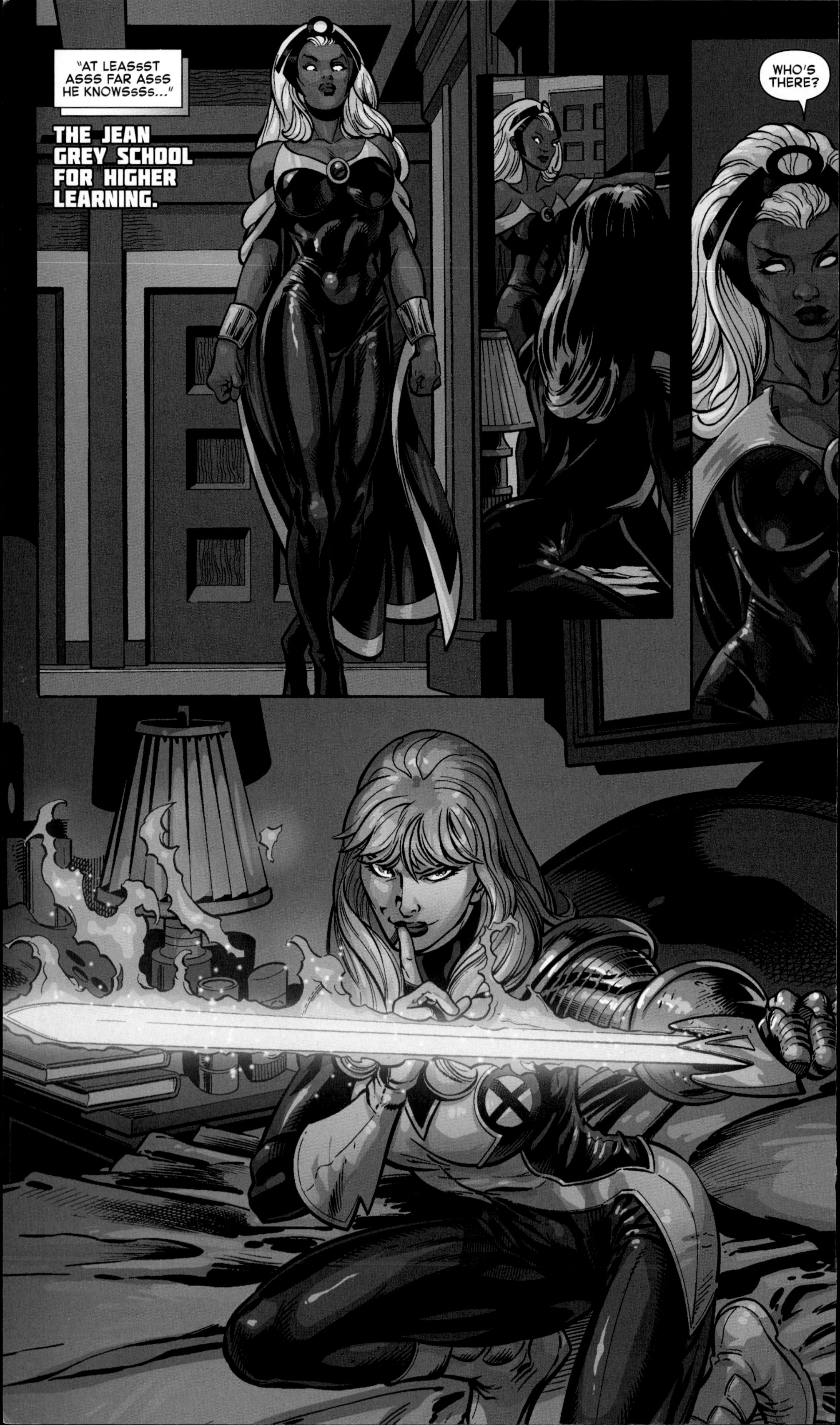
"AT LEASSST ASSS FAR ASSS HE KNOWSSSS..."
THE JEAN GREY SCHOOL FOR HIGHER LEARNING.
WHO'S THERE?

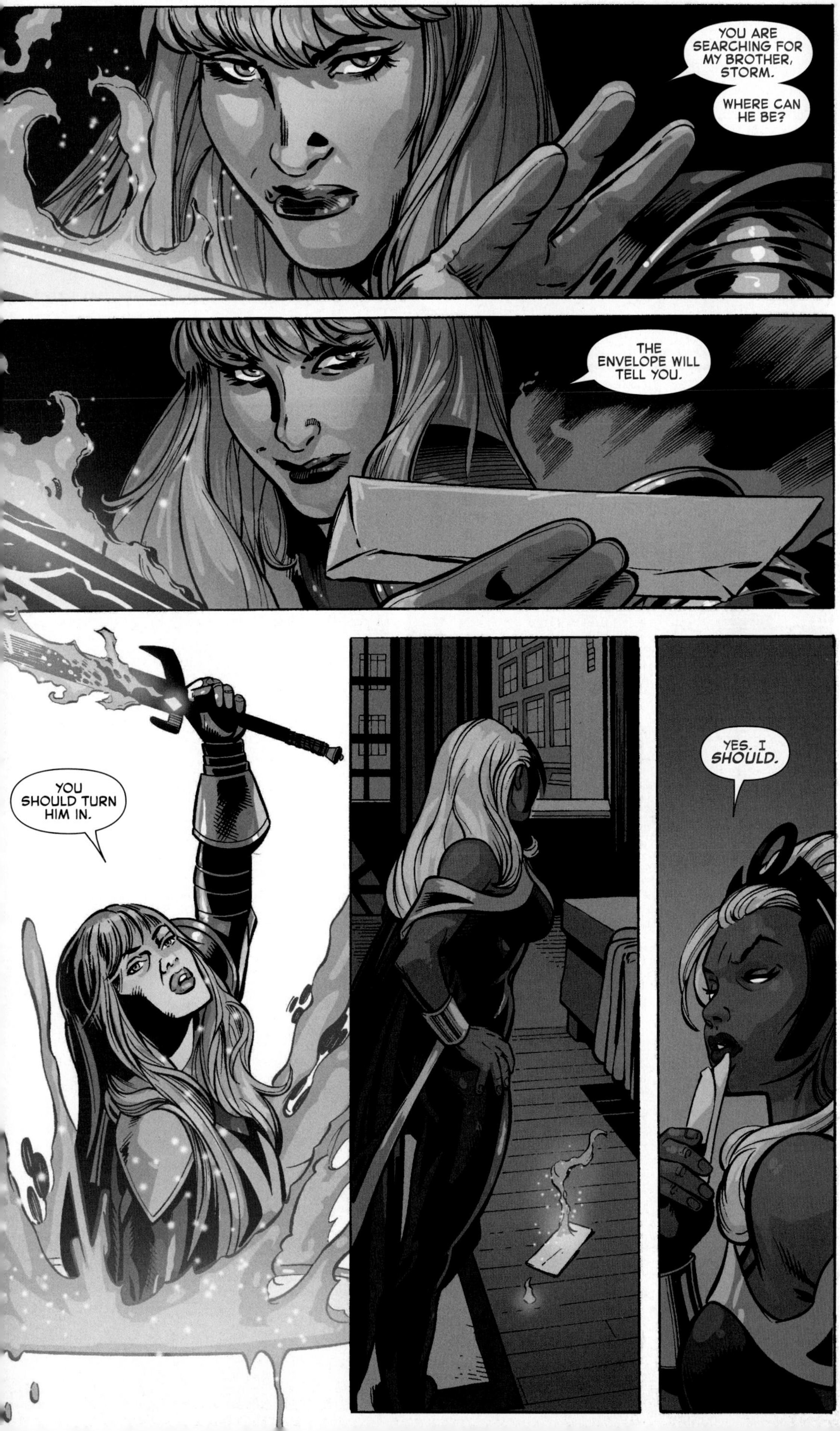
YOU ARE SEARCHING FOR MY BROTHER, STORM.
WHERE CAN HE BE?
THE ENVELOPE WILL TELL YOU.
YOU SHOULD TURN HIM IN.
YES. I *SHOULD.*

DEAR LAURIE...

I COULD NEVER HAVE HANDLED A SCHOOL LIKE THIS BEFORE I WAS ON A TEAM WITH YOU GUYS. SO I OWE YOU. AGAIN.

YOU MADE ME SO MUCH BETTER. YOU *ALL* DID. I KNOW I TREATED YOU BADLY, BUT I OWE YOU ALL SO MUCH.

I THINK OF YOU ALL THE TIME.

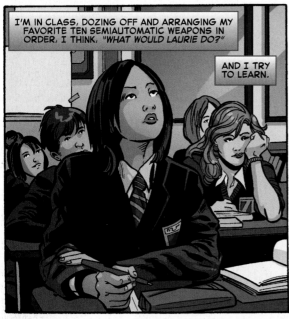

I'M IN CLASS, DOZING OFF AND ARRANGING MY FAVORITE TEN SEMIAUTOMATIC WEAPONS IN ORDER, I THINK, *"WHAT WOULD LAURIE DO?"*

AND I TRY TO LEARN.

WHEN CONVERSATIONS TURN AWKWARD, I THINK OF HOW GABRIEL WOULD ACT, AND TRY AND BE AS FRIENDLY AS HIM.

WHEN I HAVE TO LISTEN, I THINK OF I LISTEN TO WHAT T SAY AND WHAT THE DON'T AND MAKE M OWN MIND UP.

HELL...WHEN I RUN, I THINK OF TEON.

AND JUST TRY TO BE NOTHING MORE THAN THE MOVEMENT OF MY BODY.

I EVEN THINK OF KENJI.

BECAUSE NO MATTE HOW MUCH I'M TRYIN TO FIT IN HERE, THE ARE TIMES YOU HAV TO SAY "NO."

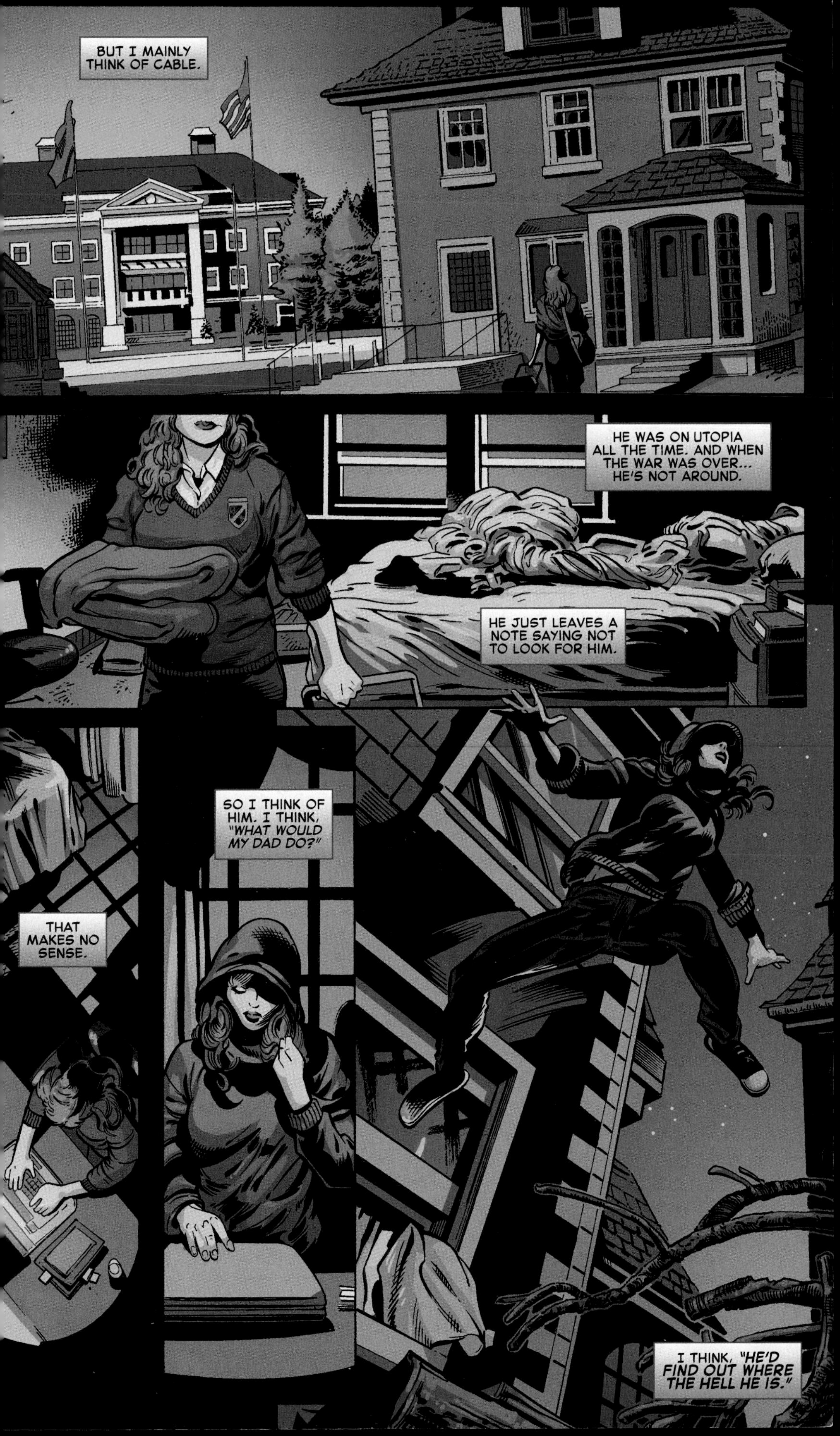
BUT I MAINLY THINK OF CABLE.
HE WAS ON UTOPIA ALL THE TIME. AND WHEN THE WAR WAS OVER... HE'S NOT AROUND.
HE JUST LEAVES A NOTE SAYING NOT TO LOOK FOR HIM.
THAT MAKES NO SENSE.
SO I THINK OF HIM. I THINK, *"WHAT WOULD MY DAD DO?"*
I THINK, *"HE'D FIND OUT WHERE THE HELL HE IS."*

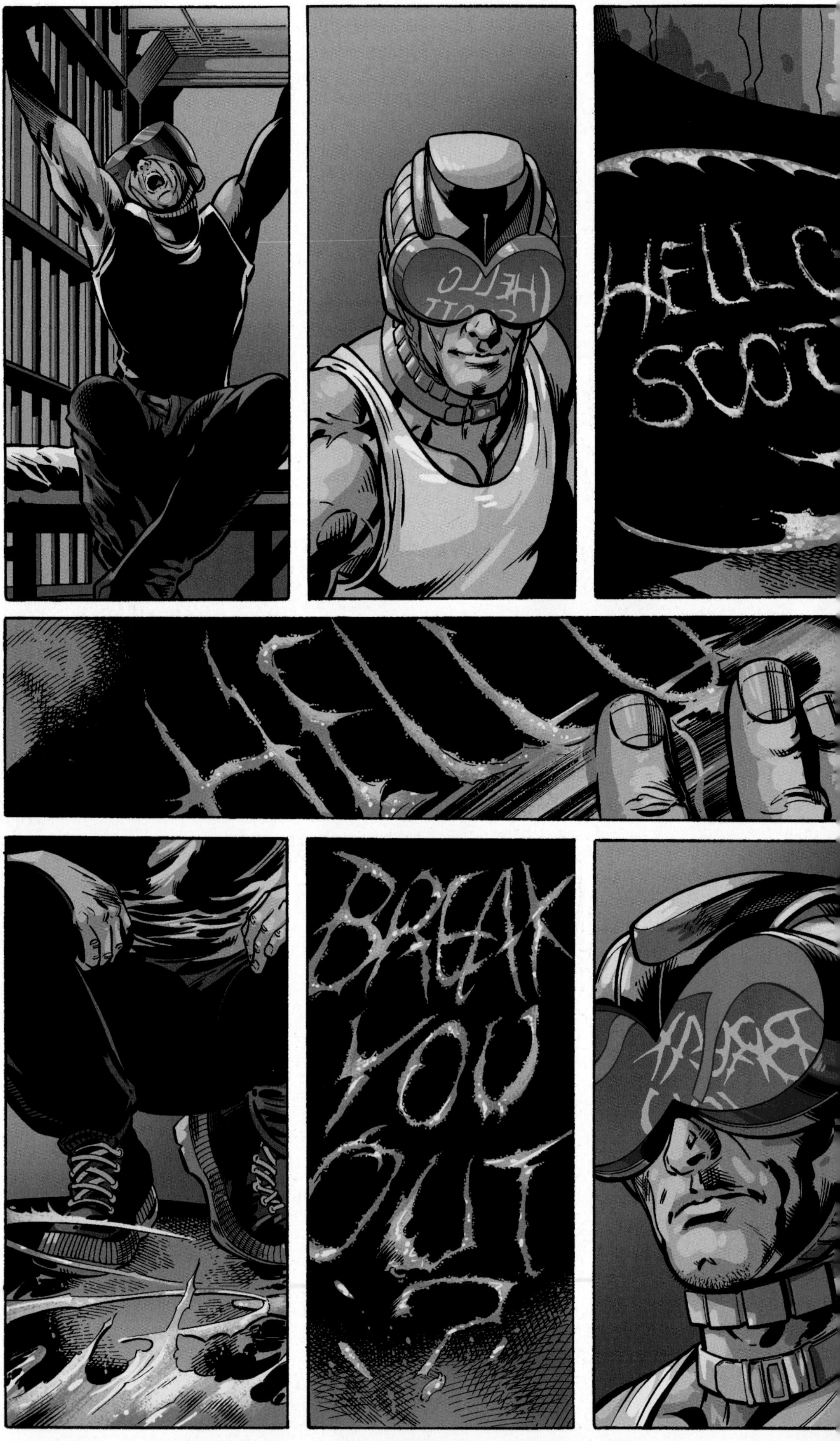
BREAK YOU OUT ?

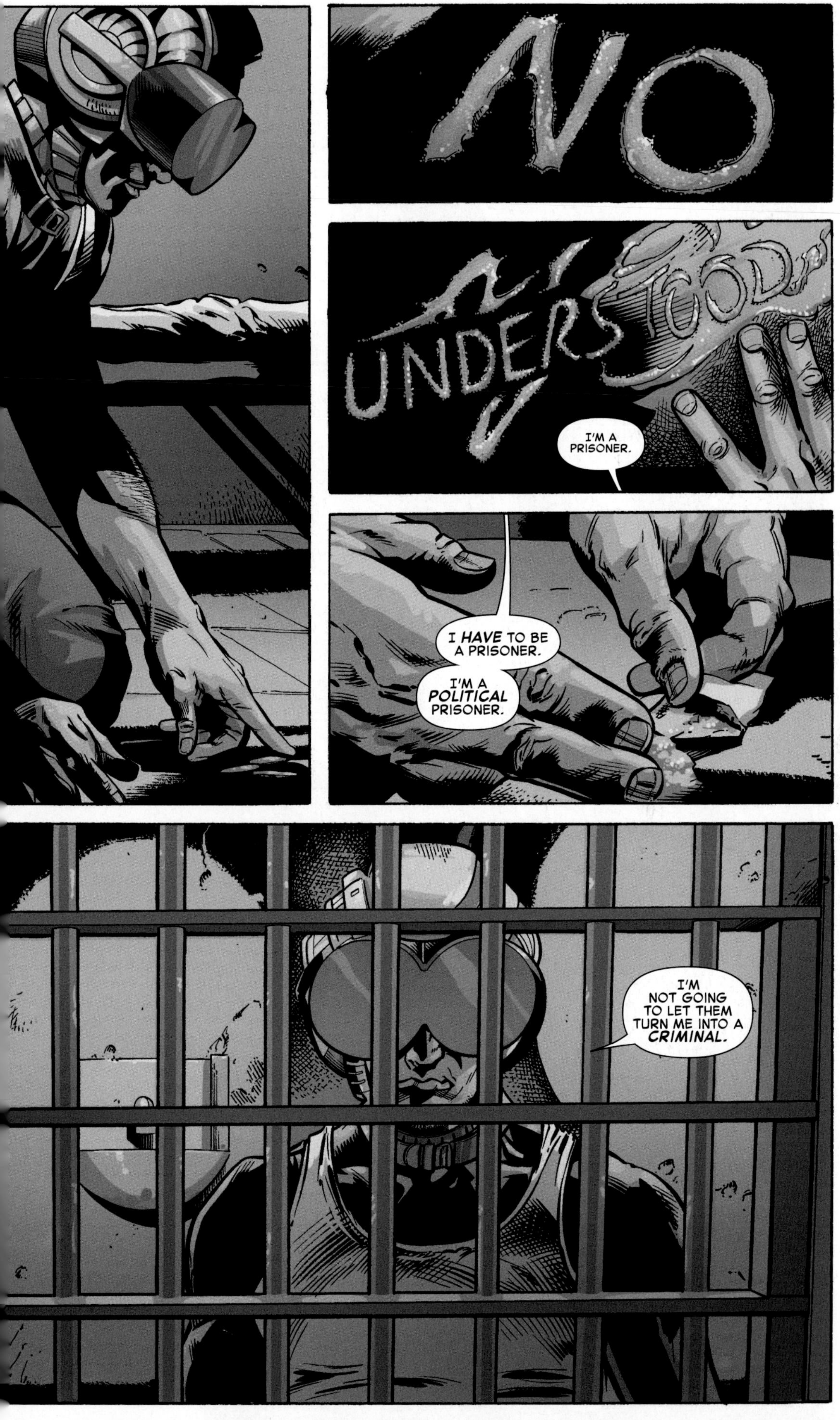
NO
UNDERSTOOD
I'M A PRISONER.
I *HAVE* TO BE A PRISONER.
I'M A *POLITICAL* PRISONER.
I'M NOT GOING TO LET THEM TURN ME INTO A *CRIMINAL.*

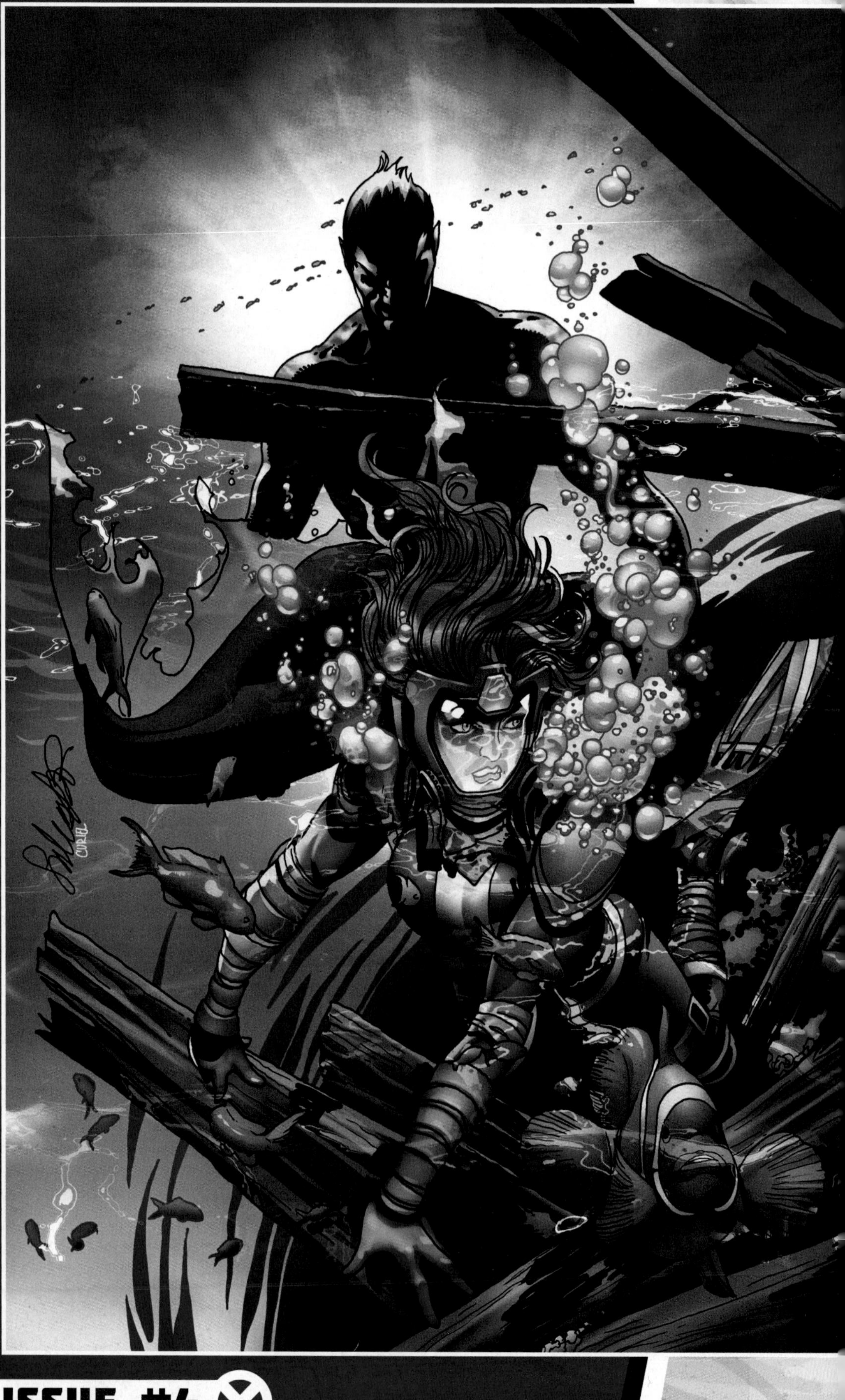

ISSUE #4

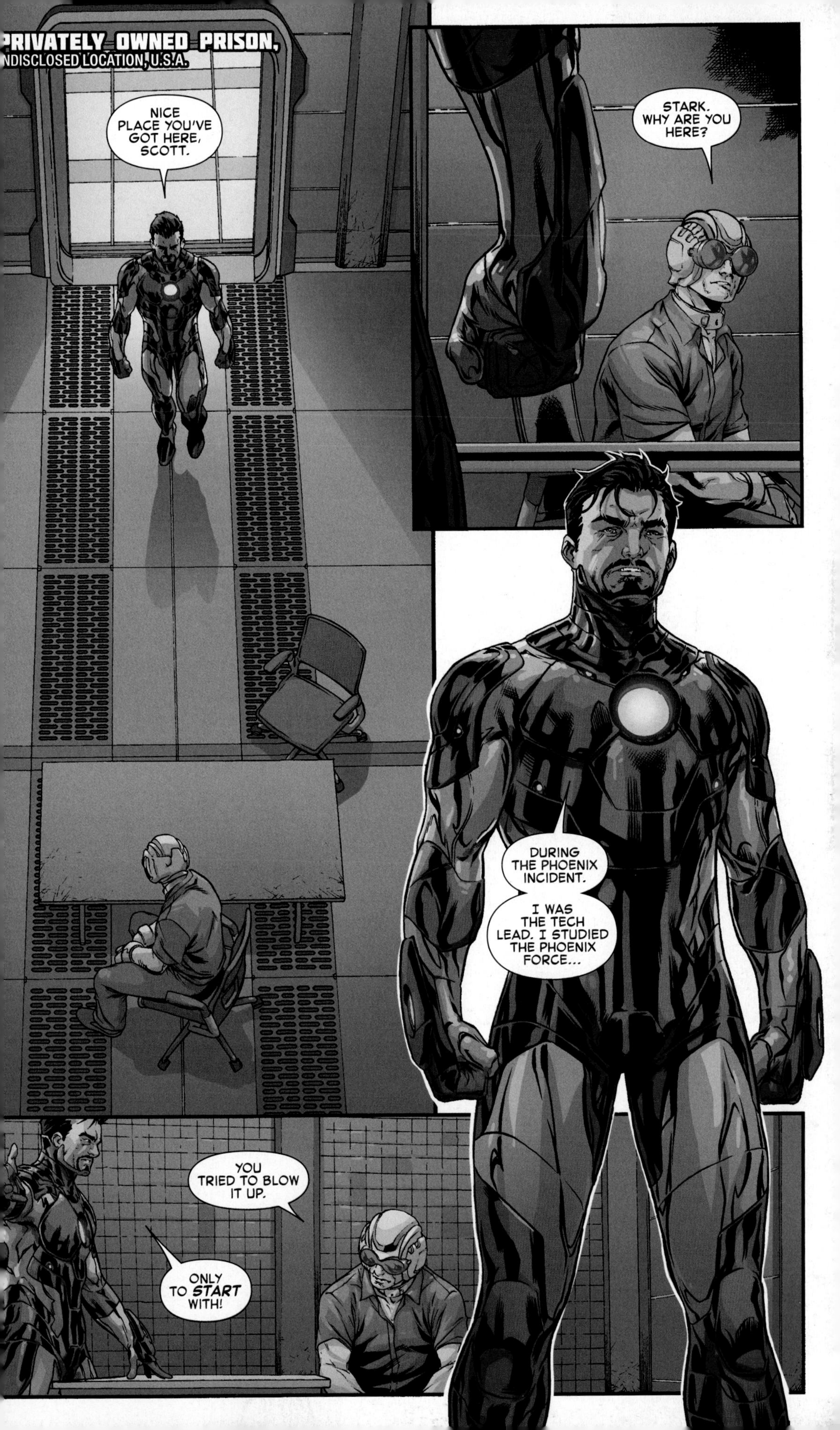
PRIVATELY OWNED PRISON,
UNDISCLOSED LOCATION, U.S.A.
NICE PLACE YOU'VE GOT HERE, SCOTT.
STARK. WHY ARE YOU HERE?
DURING THE PHOENIX INCIDENT.
I WAS THE TECH LEAD. I STUDIED THE PHOENIX FORCE...
YOU TRIED TO BLOW IT UP.
ONLY TO START WITH!

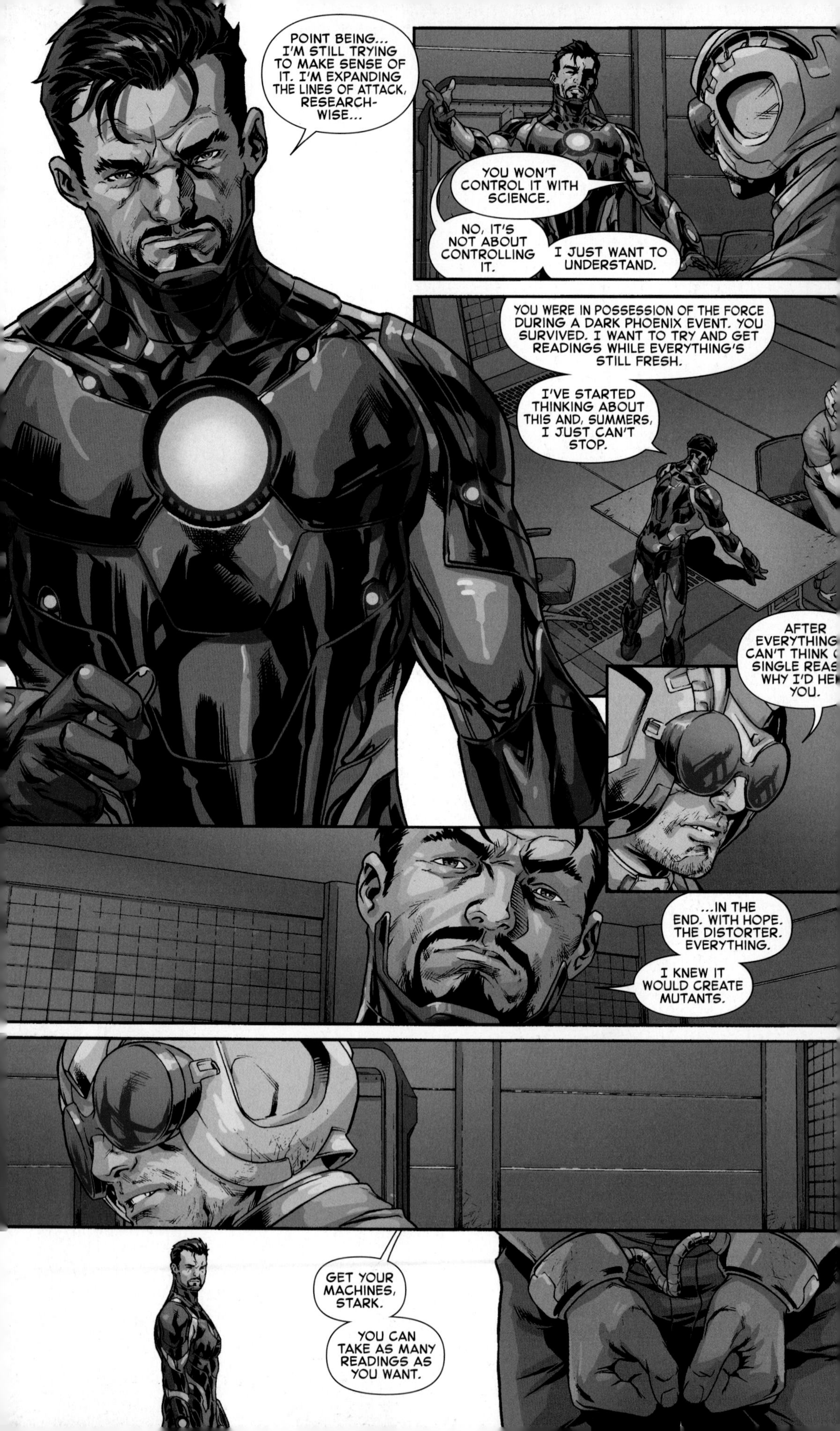

POINT BEING... I'M STILL TRYING TO MAKE SENSE OF IT. I'M EXPANDING THE LINES OF ATTACK, RESEARCH-WISE...
YOU WON'T CONTROL IT WITH SCIENCE.
NO, IT'S NOT ABOUT CONTROLLING IT.
I JUST WANT TO UNDERSTAND.
YOU WERE IN POSSESSION OF THE FORCE DURING A DARK PHOENIX EVENT. YOU SURVIVED. I WANT TO TRY AND GET READINGS WHILE EVERYTHING'S STILL FRESH.
I'VE STARTED THINKING ABOUT THIS AND, SUMMERS, I JUST CAN'T STOP.
...IN THE END. WITH HOPE. THE DISTORTER. EVERYTHING.
I KNEW IT WOULD CREATE MUTANTS.
GET YOUR MACHINES, STARK.
YOU CAN TAKE AS MANY READINGS AS YOU WANT.

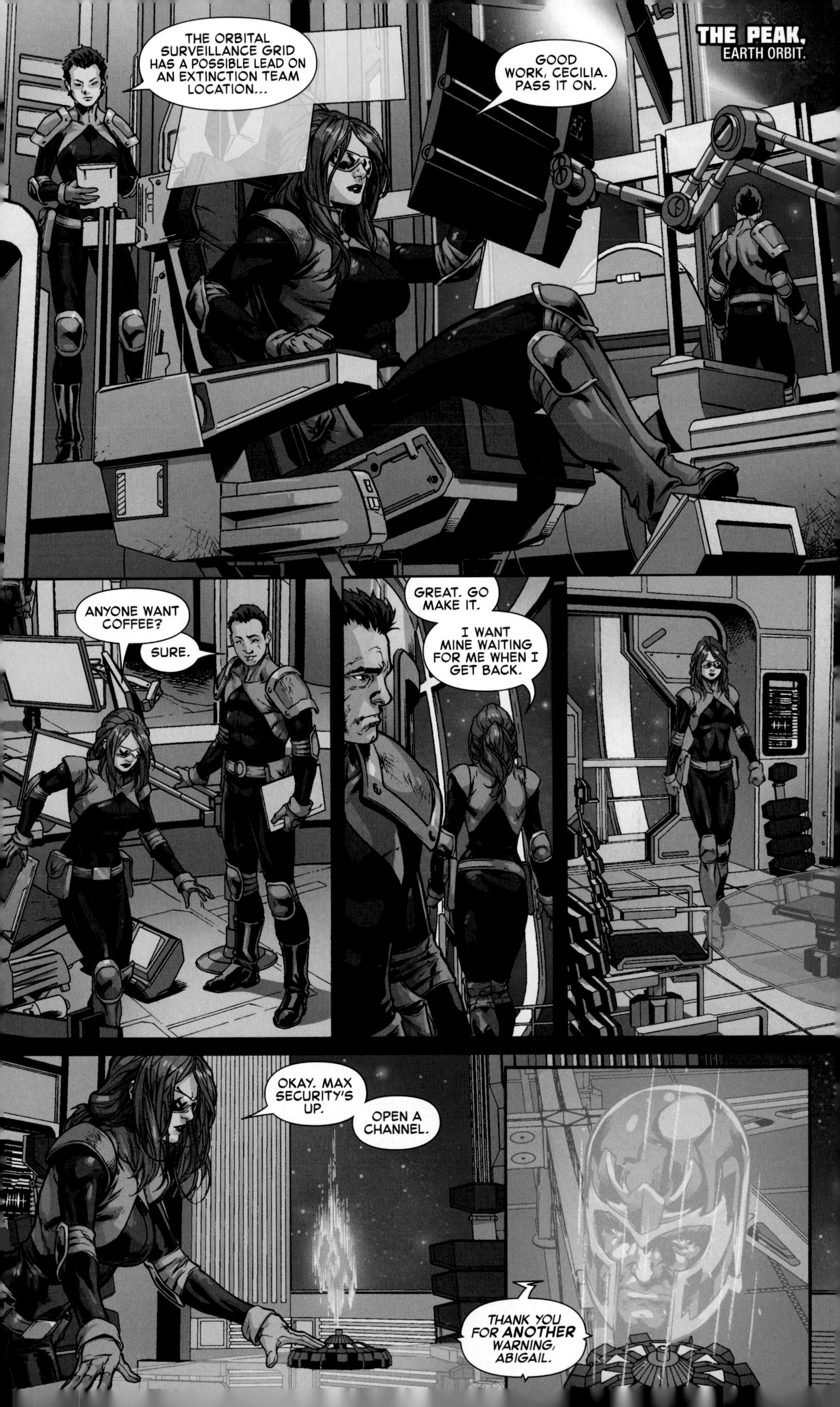
THE PEAK, EARTH ORBIT.
THE ORBITAL SURVEILLANCE GRID HAS A POSSIBLE LEAD ON AN EXTINCTION TEAM LOCATION...
GOOD WORK, CECILIA. PASS IT ON.
ANYONE WANT COFFEE?
SURE.
GREAT. GO MAKE IT.
I WANT MINE WAITING FOR ME WHEN I GET BACK.
OKAY. MAX SECURITY'S UP.
OPEN A CHANNEL.
THANK YOU FOR ANOTHER WARNING, ABIGAIL.

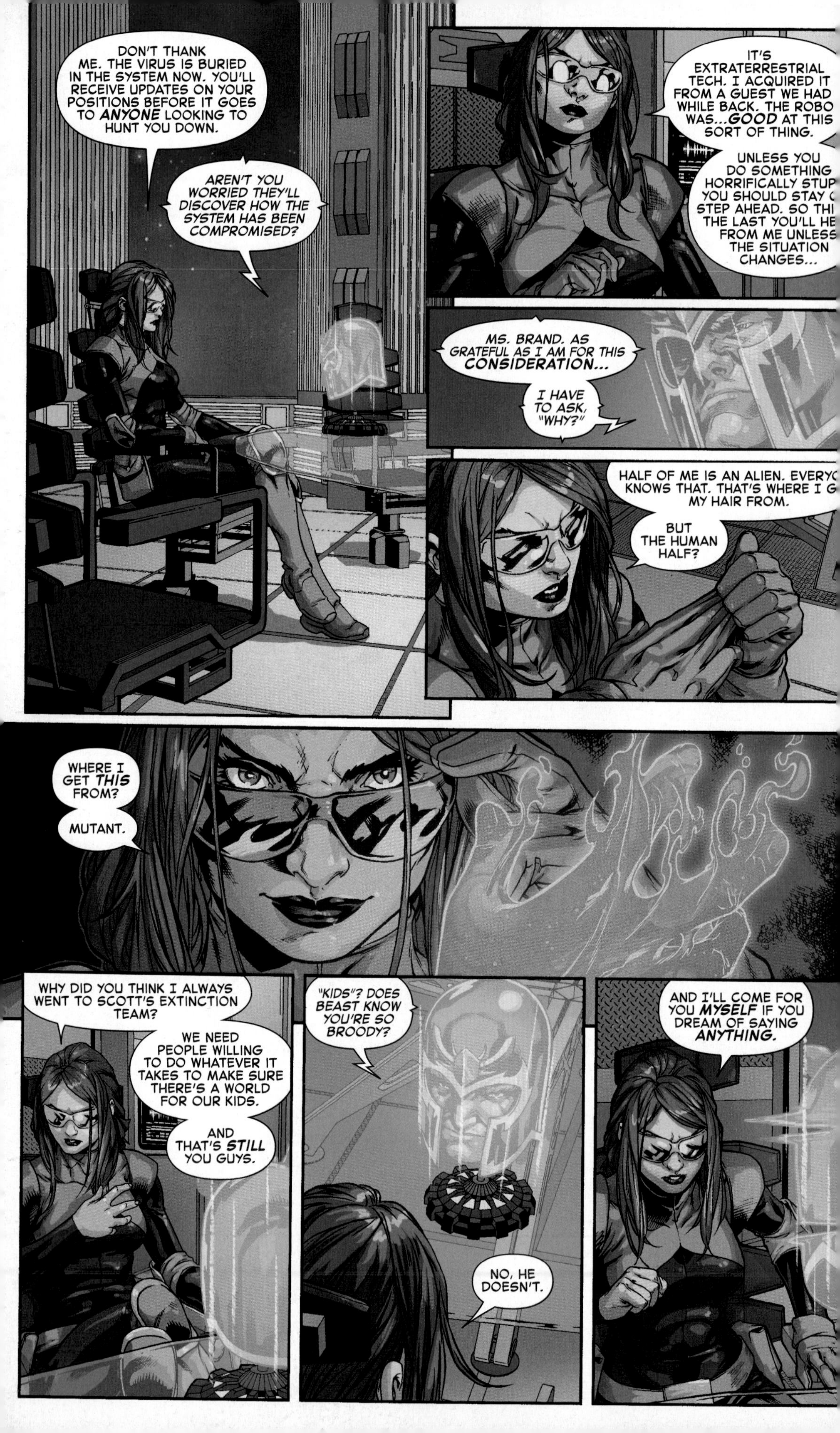
DON'T THANK ME. THE VIRUS IS BURIED IN THE SYSTEM NOW. YOU'LL RECEIVE UPDATES ON YOUR POSITIONS BEFORE IT GOES TO ANYONE LOOKING TO HUNT YOU DOWN.
AREN'T YOU WORRIED THEY'LL DISCOVER HOW THE SYSTEM HAS BEEN COMPROMISED?
IT'S EXTRATERRESTRIAL TECH. I ACQUIRED IT FROM A GUEST WE HAD WHILE BACK. THE ROBO WAS...GOOD AT THIS SORT OF THING.
UNLESS YOU DO SOMETHING HORRIFICALLY STUP YOU SHOULD STAY STEP AHEAD. SO THI THE LAST YOU'LL HE FROM ME UNLESS THE SITUATION CHANGES...
MS. BRAND. AS GRATEFUL AS I AM FOR THIS CONSIDERATION...
I HAVE TO ASK, "WHY?"
HALF OF ME IS AN ALIEN. EVERY KNOWS THAT. THAT'S WHERE I G MY HAIR FROM.
BUT THE HUMAN HALF?
WHERE I GET THIS FROM?
MUTANT.
WHY DID YOU THINK I ALWAYS WENT TO SCOTT'S EXTINCTION TEAM?
WE NEED PEOPLE WILLING TO DO WHATEVER IT TAKES TO MAKE SURE THERE'S A WORLD FOR OUR KIDS.
AND THAT'S STILL YOU GUYS.
"KIDS"? DOES BEAST KNOW YOU'RE SO BROODY?
NO, HE DOESN'T.
AND I'LL COME FOR YOU MYSELF IF YOU DREAM OF SAYING ANYTHING.

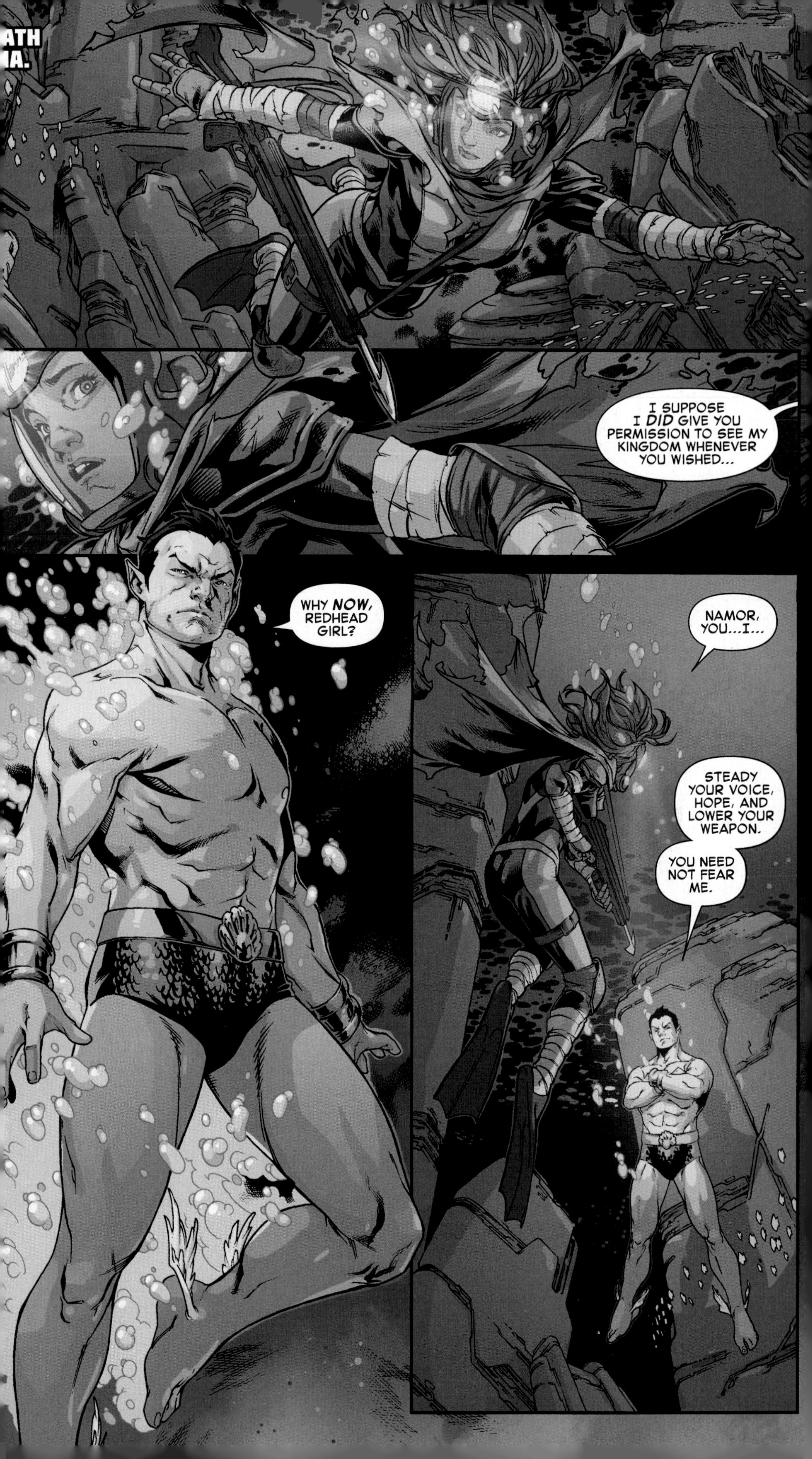
I SUPPOSE I DID GIVE YOU PERMISSION TO SEE MY KINGDOM WHENEVER YOU WISHED...
WHY NOW, REDHEAD GIRL?
NAMOR, YOU...I...
STEADY YOUR VOICE, HOPE, AND LOWER YOUR WEAPON.
YOU NEED NOT FEAR ME.

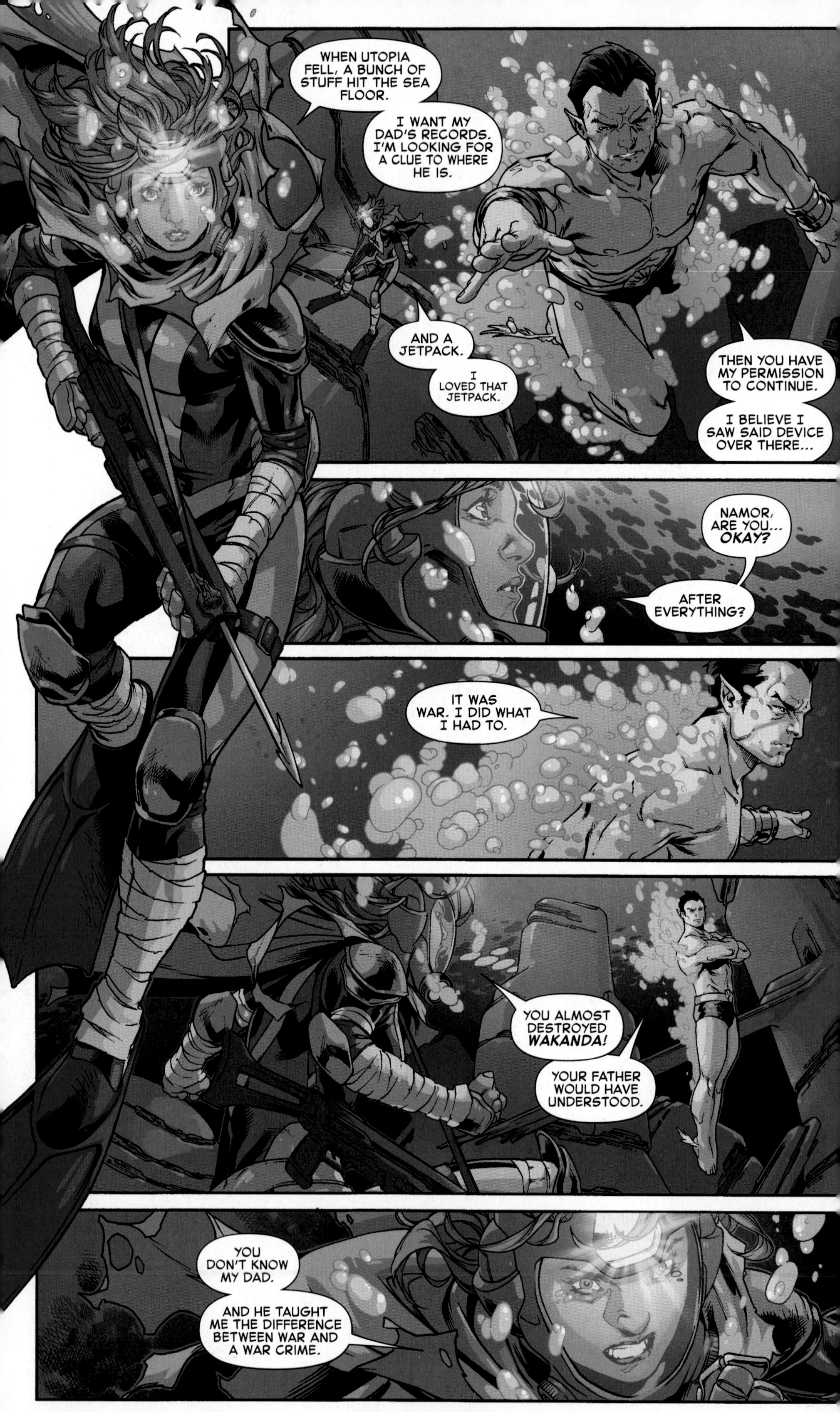
WHEN UTOPIA FELL, A BUNCH OF STUFF HIT THE SEA FLOOR.
I WANT MY DAD'S RECORDS. I'M LOOKING FOR A CLUE TO WHERE HE IS.
AND A JETPACK.
I LOVED THAT JETPACK.
THEN YOU HAVE MY PERMISSION TO CONTINUE.
I BELIEVE I SAW SAID DEVICE OVER THERE...
NAMOR, ARE YOU... OKAY?
AFTER EVERYTHING?
IT WAS WAR. I DID WHAT I HAD TO.
YOU ALMOST DESTROYED WAKANDA!
YOUR FATHER WOULD HAVE UNDERSTOOD.
YOU DON'T KNOW MY DAD.
AND HE TAUGHT ME THE DIFFERENCE BETWEEN WAR AND A WAR CRIME.

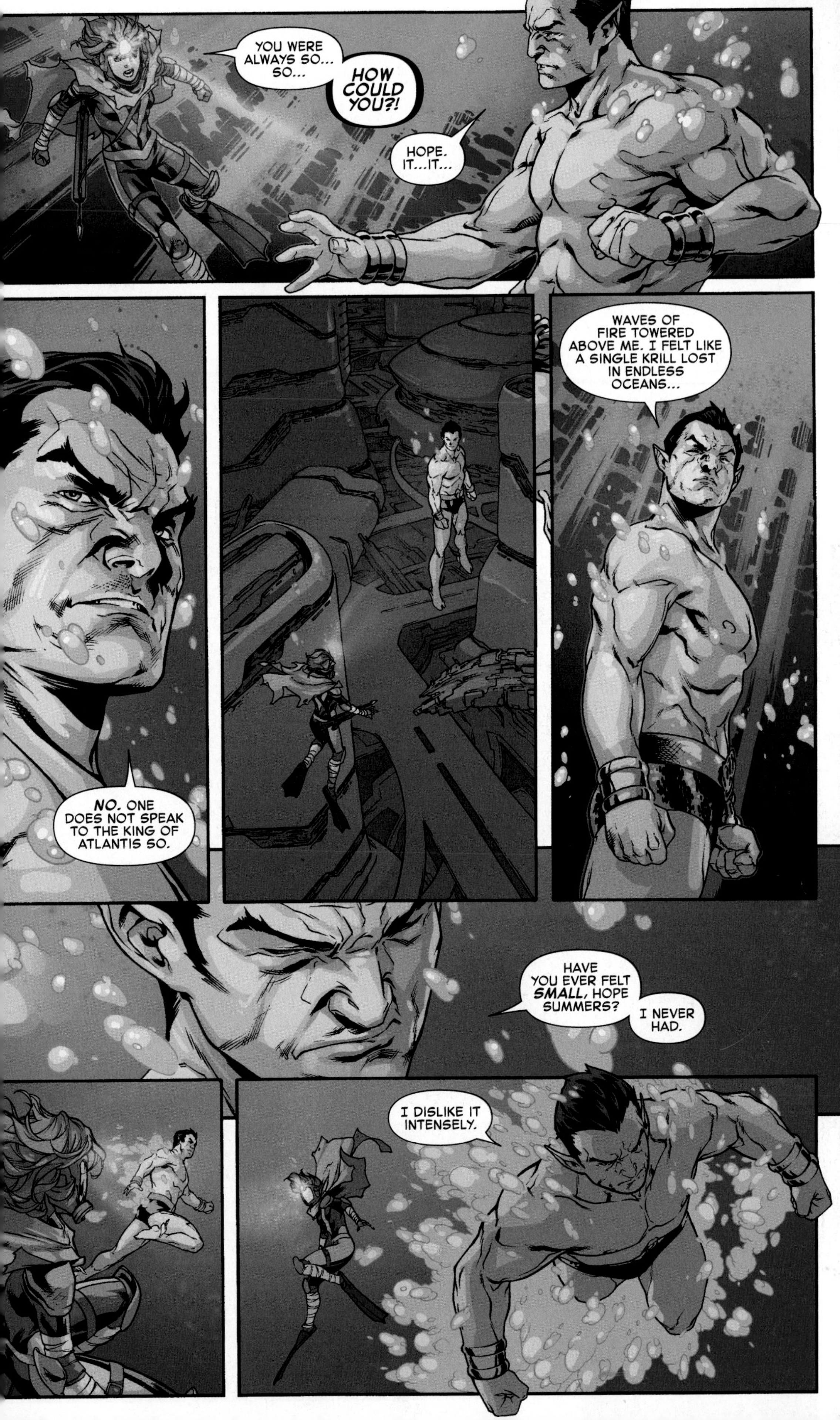
YOU WERE ALWAYS SO... SO...
HOW COULD YOU?!
HOPE. IT...IT...
NO. ONE DOES NOT SPEAK TO THE KING OF ATLANTIS SO.
WAVES OF FIRE TOWERED ABOVE ME. I FELT LIKE A SINGLE KRILL LOST IN ENDLESS OCEANS...
HAVE YOU EVER FELT SMALL, HOPE SUMMERS?
I NEVER HAD.
I DISLIKE IT INTENSELY.

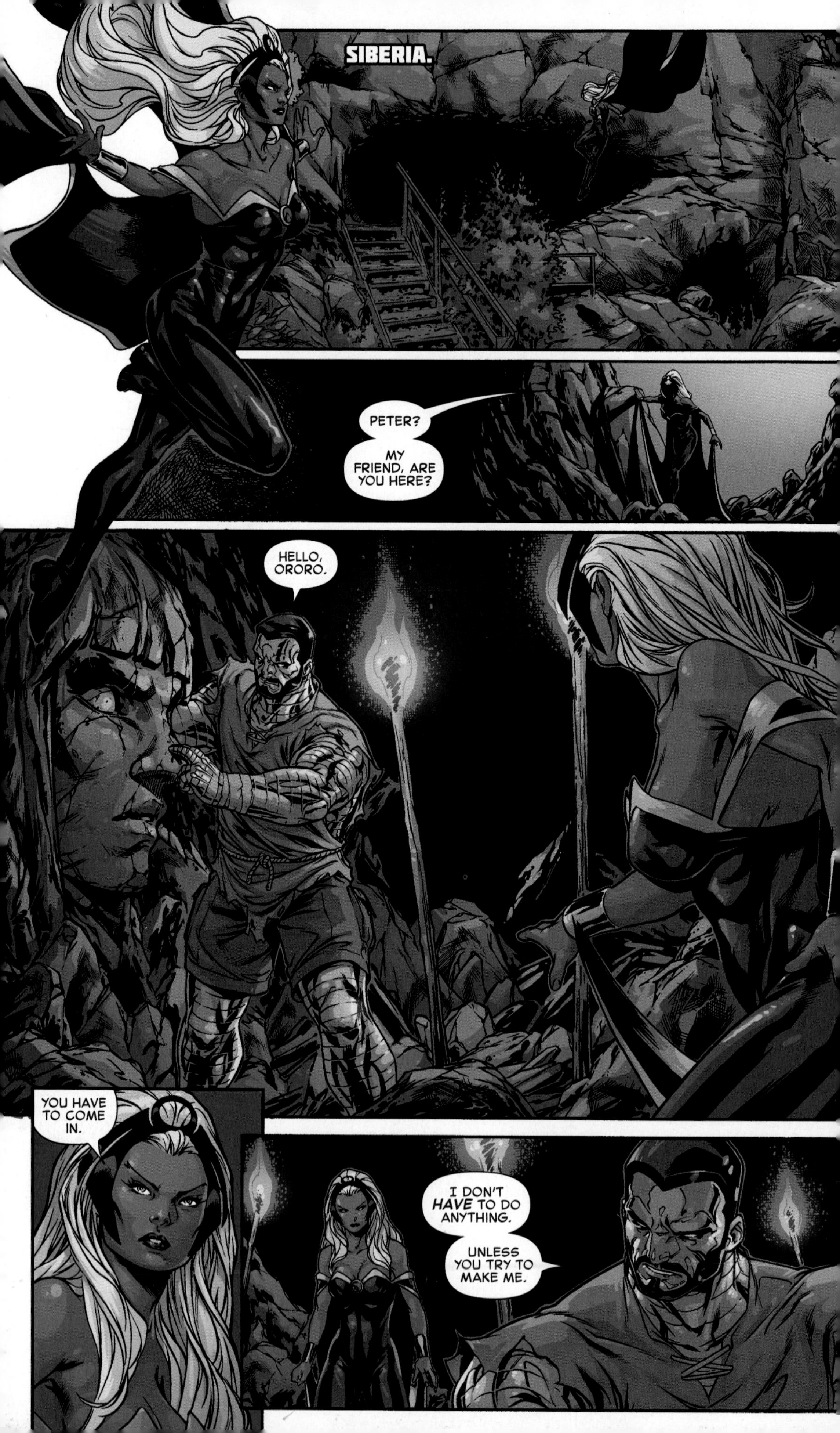
SIBERIA.
PETER?
MY FRIEND, ARE YOU HERE?
HELLO, ORORO.
YOU HAVE TO COME IN.
I DON'T *HAVE* TO DO ANYTHING.
UNLESS YOU TRY TO MAKE ME.

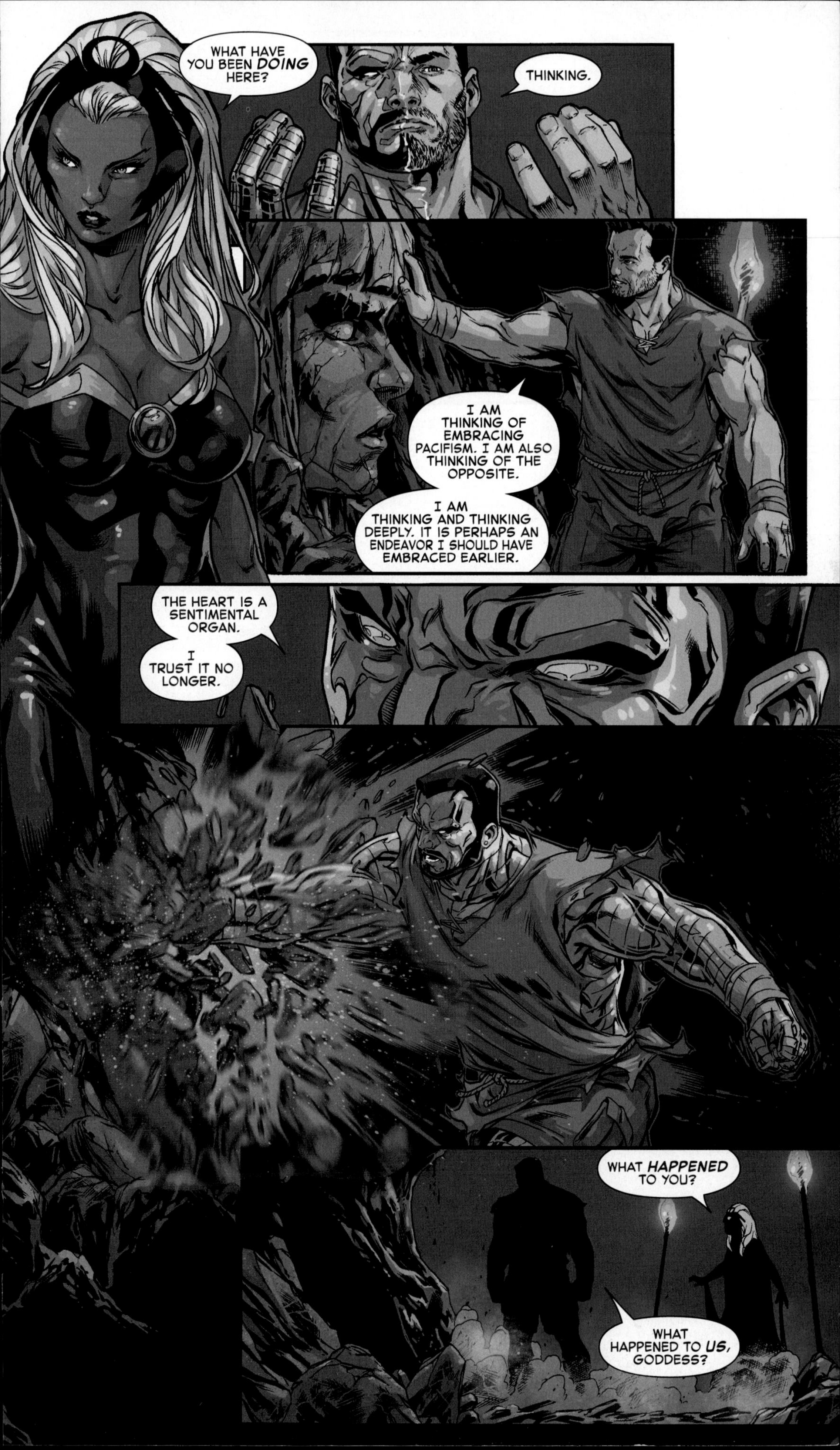
WHAT HAVE YOU BEEN *DOING* HERE?
THINKING.
I AM THINKING OF EMBRACING PACIFISM. I AM ALSO THINKING OF THE OPPOSITE.
I AM THINKING AND THINKING DEEPLY. IT IS PERHAPS AN ENDEAVOR I SHOULD HAVE EMBRACED EARLIER.
THE HEART IS A SENTIMENTAL ORGAN.
I TRUST IT NO LONGER.
WHAT *HAPPENED* TO YOU?
WHAT HAPPENED TO *US,* GODDESS?

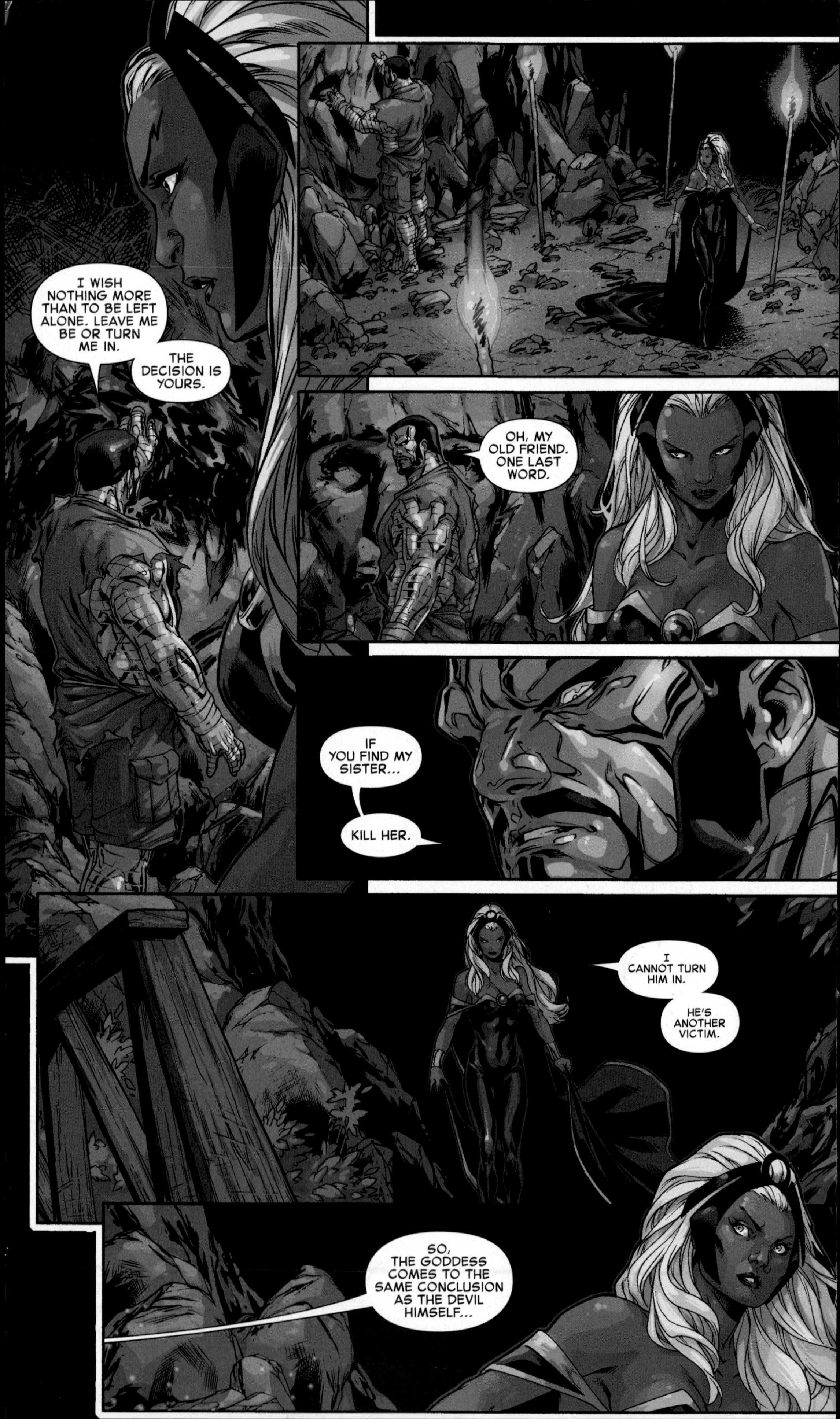
I WISH NOTHING MORE THAN TO BE LEFT ALONE. LEAVE ME BE OR TURN ME IN.
THE DECISION IS YOURS.
OH, MY OLD FRIEND. ONE LAST WORD.
IF YOU FIND MY SISTER...
KILL HER.
I CANNOT TURN HIM IN.
HE'S ANOTHER VICTIM.
SO, THE GODDESS COMES TO THE SAME CONCLUSION AS THE DEVIL HIMSELF...

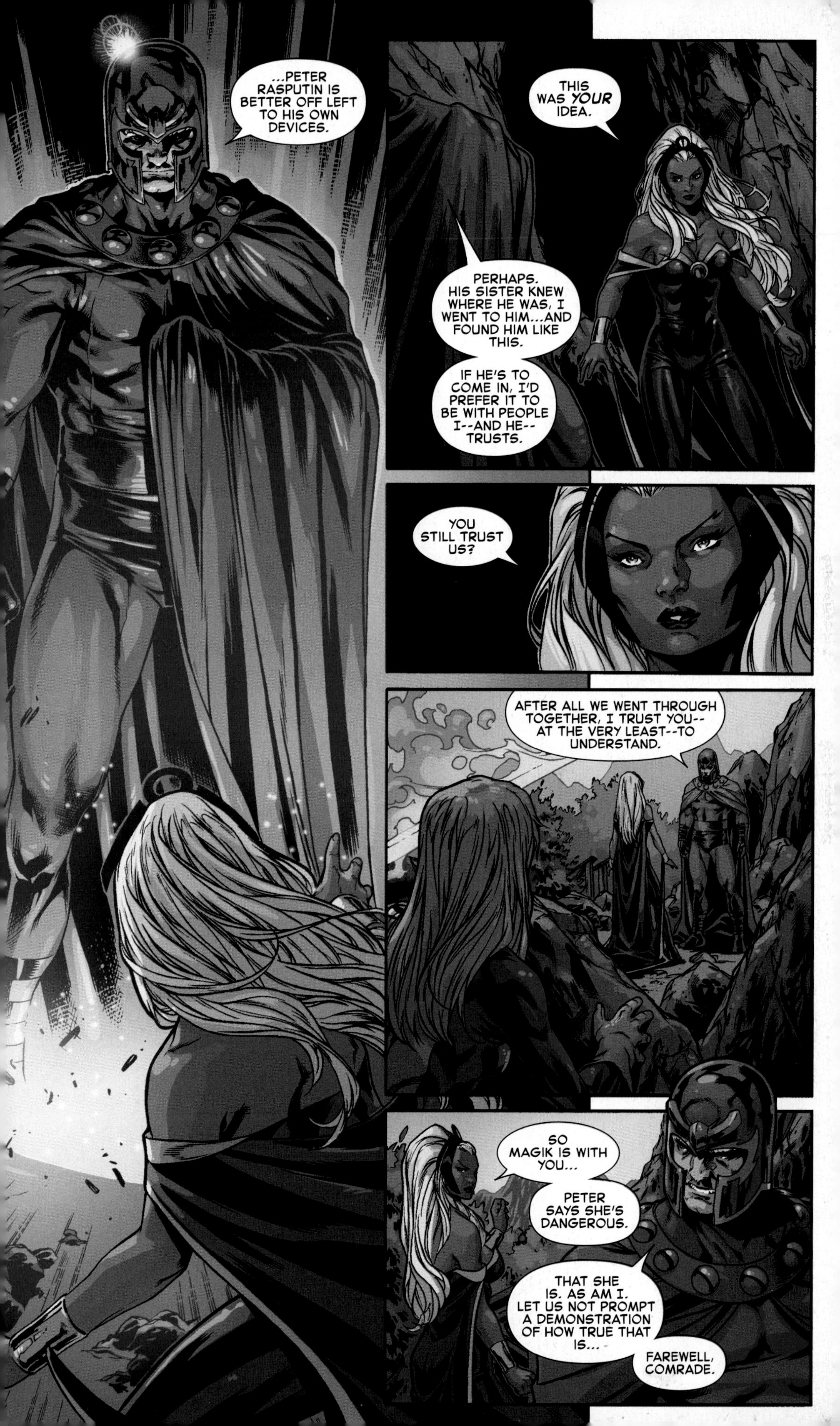
...PETER RASPUTIN IS BETTER OFF LEFT TO HIS OWN DEVICES.
THIS WAS *YOUR* IDEA.
PERHAPS. HIS SISTER KNEW WHERE HE WAS, I WENT TO HIM...AND FOUND HIM LIKE THIS.
IF HE'S TO COME IN, I'D PREFER IT TO BE WITH PEOPLE I--AND HE--TRUSTS.
YOU STILL TRUST US?
AFTER ALL WE WENT THROUGH TOGETHER, I TRUST YOU--AT THE VERY LEAST--TO UNDERSTAND.
SO MAGIK IS WITH YOU...
PETER SAYS SHE'S DANGEROUS.
THAT SHE IS. AS AM I. LET US NOT PROMPT A DEMONSTRATION OF HOW TRUE THAT IS...
FAREWELL, COMRADE.

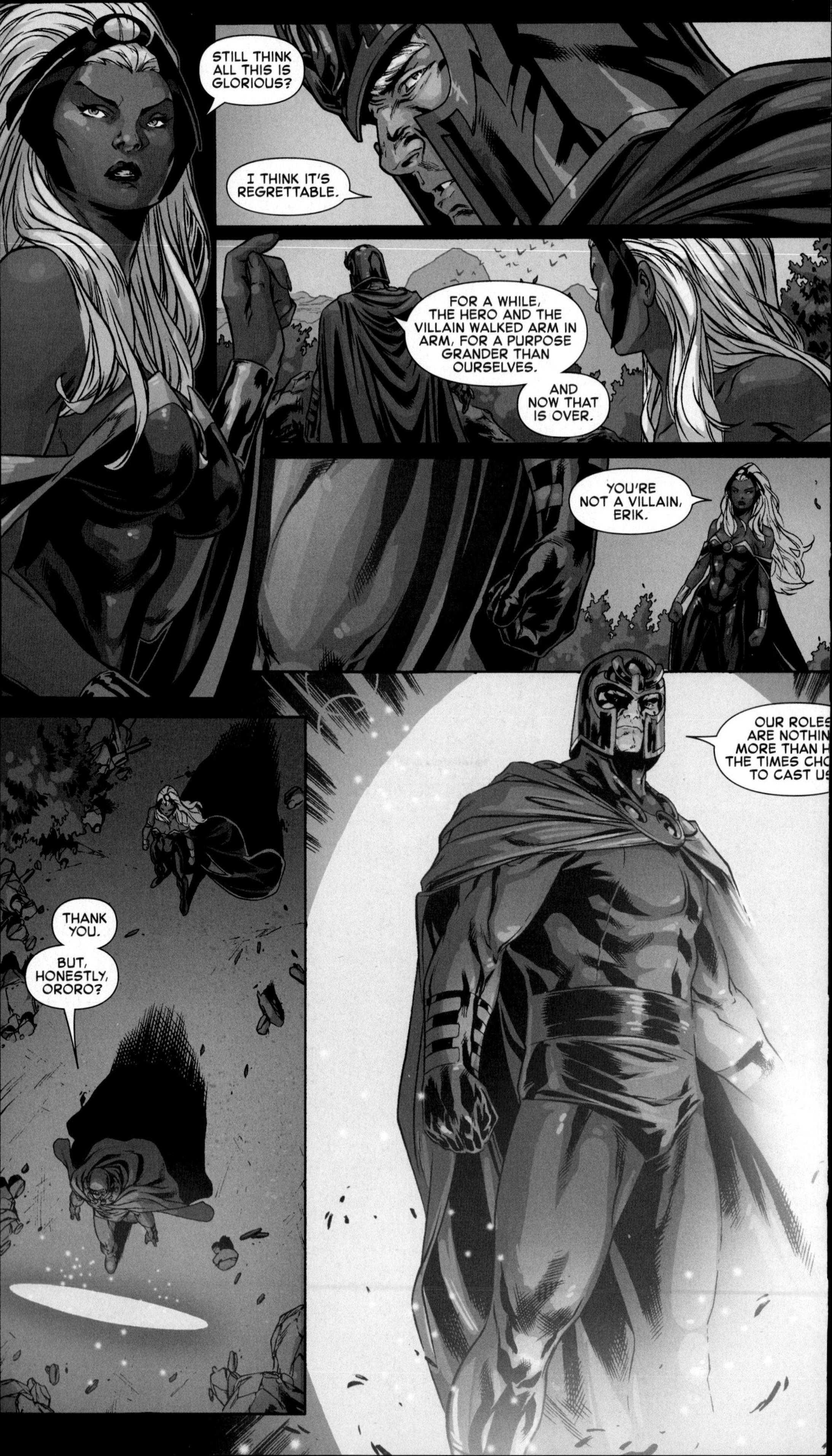
STILL THINK ALL THIS IS GLORIOUS?
I THINK IT'S REGRETTABLE.
FOR A WHILE, THE HERO AND THE VILLAIN WALKED ARM IN ARM, FOR A PURPOSE GRANDER THAN OURSELVES.
AND NOW THAT IS OVER.
YOU'RE NOT A VILLAIN, ERIK.
THANK YOU.
BUT, HONESTLY, ORORO?
OUR ROLES ARE NOTHIN MORE THAN H THE TIMES CHO TO CAST US

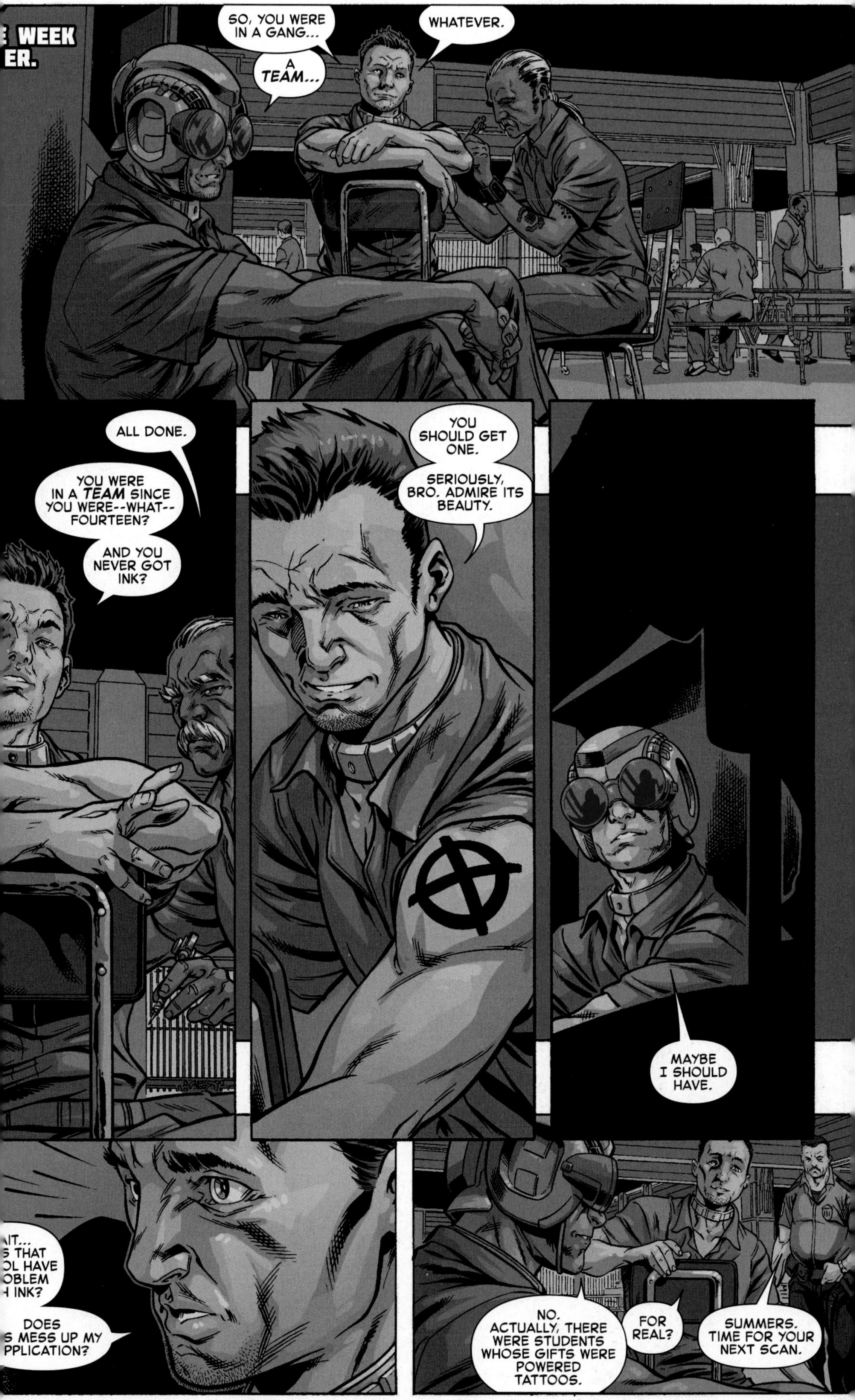

WEEK
ER.
SO, YOU WERE IN A GANG...
A TEAM...
WHATEVER.
ALL DONE.
YOU WERE IN A TEAM SINCE YOU WERE--WHAT--FOURTEEN?
AND YOU NEVER GOT INK?
YOU SHOULD GET ONE.
SERIOUSLY, BRO. ADMIRE ITS BEAUTY.
MAYBE I SHOULD HAVE.
DOES
NO. ACTUALLY, THERE WERE STUDENTS WHOSE GIFTS WERE POWERED TATTOOS.
FOR REAL?
SUMMERS. TIME FOR YOUR NEXT SCAN.

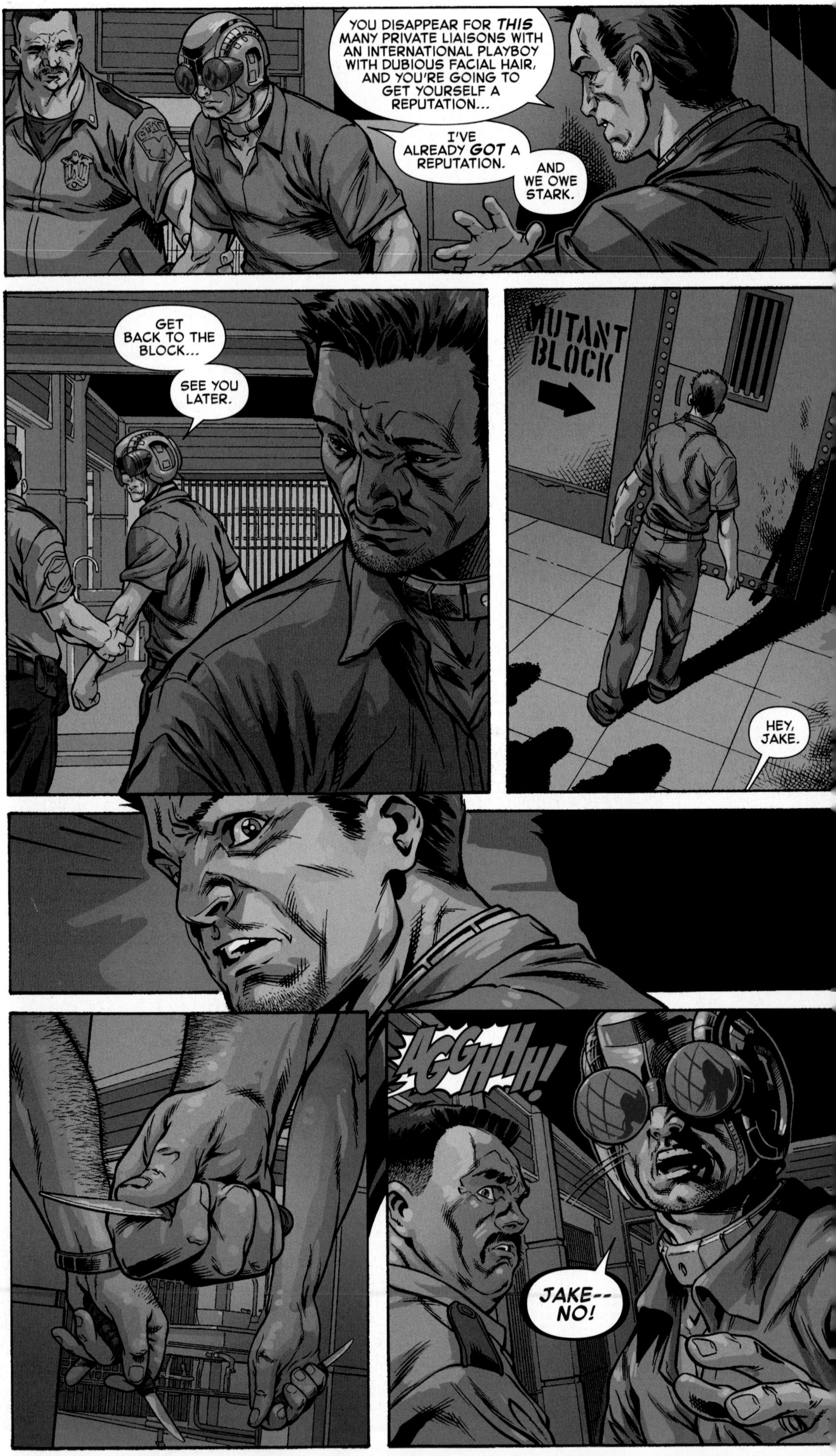

YOU DISAPPEAR FOR THIS MANY PRIVATE LIAISONS WITH AN INTERNATIONAL PLAYBOY WITH DUBIOUS FACIAL HAIR, AND YOU'RE GOING TO GET YOURSELF A REPUTATION...
I'VE ALREADY GOT A REPUTATION.
AND WE OWE STARK.
GET BACK TO THE BLOCK...
SEE YOU LATER.
MUTANT BLOCK
HEY, JAKE.
AGGHHH!
JAKE-- NO!

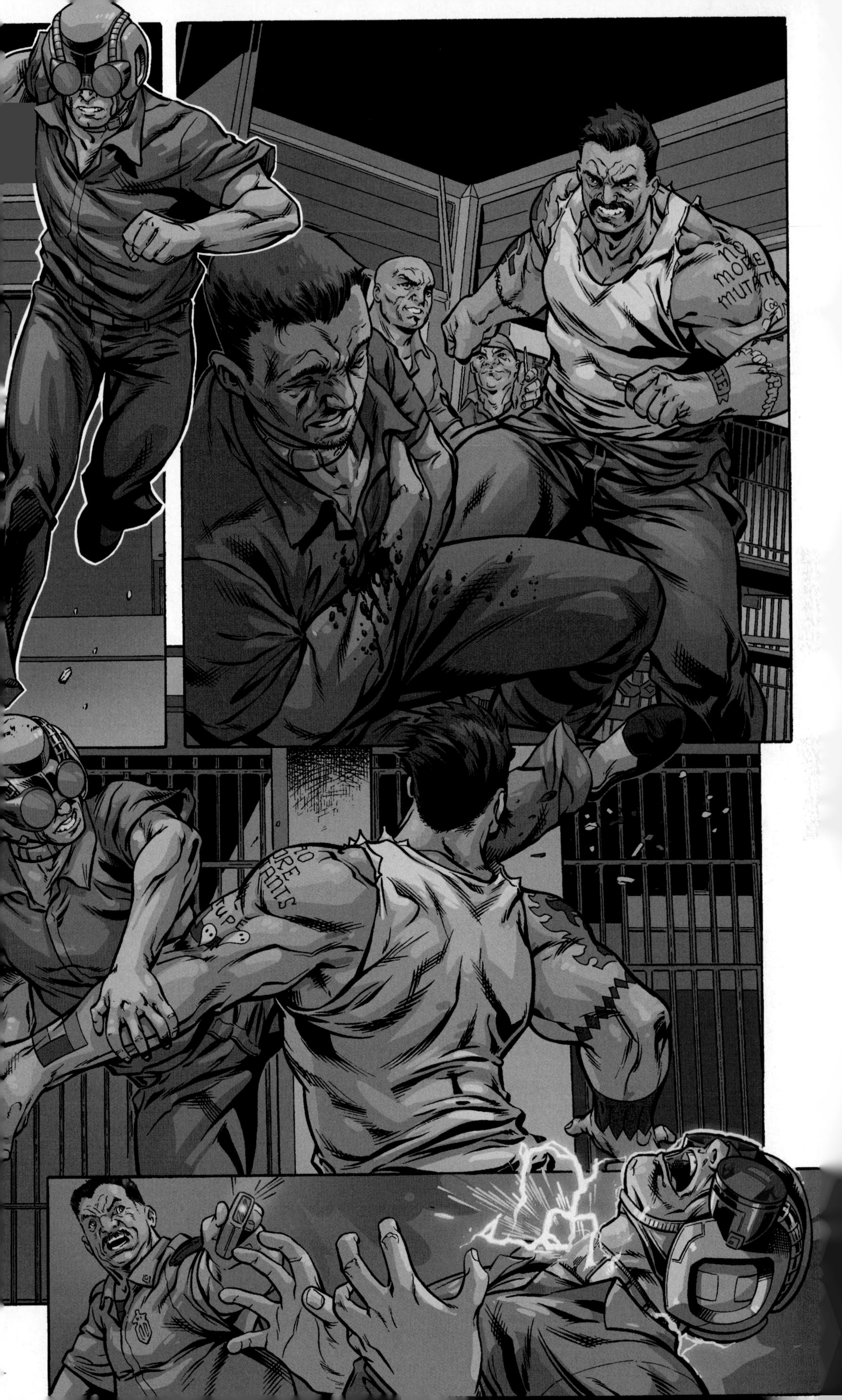

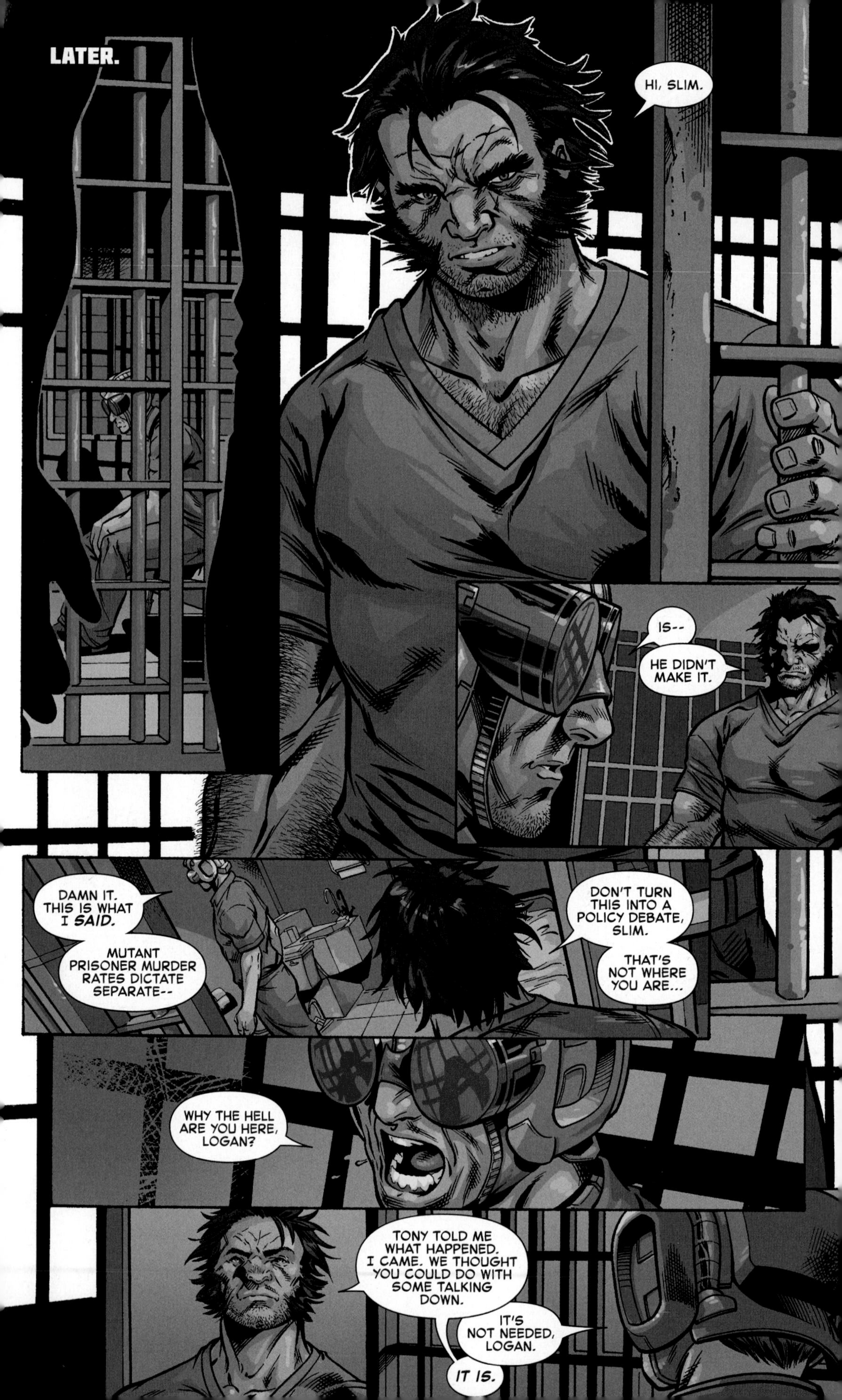
LATER.
HI, SLIM.
IS--
HE DIDN'T MAKE IT.
DAMN IT. THIS IS WHAT I *SAID.*
MUTANT PRISONER MURDER RATES DICTATE SEPARATE--
DON'T TURN THIS INTO A POLICY DEBATE, SLIM.
THAT'S NOT WHERE YOU ARE...
WHY THE HELL ARE YOU HERE, LOGAN?
TONY TOLD ME WHAT HAPPENED. I CAME. WE THOUGHT YOU COULD DO WITH SOME TALKING DOWN.
IT'S NOT NEEDED, LOGAN.
IT IS.

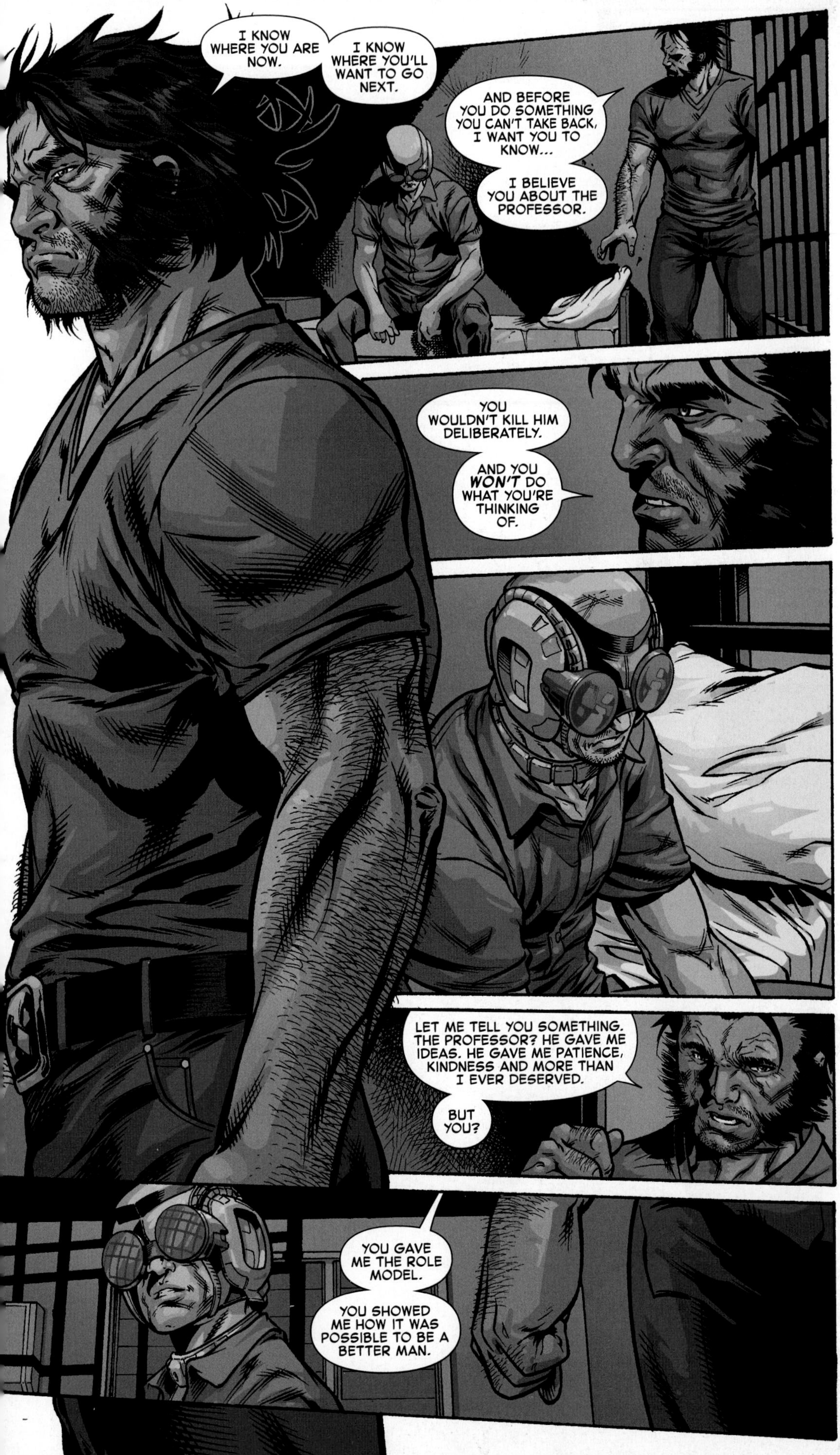
I KNOW WHERE YOU ARE NOW.
I KNOW WHERE YOU'LL WANT TO GO NEXT.
AND BEFORE YOU DO SOMETHING YOU CAN'T TAKE BACK, I WANT YOU TO KNOW...
I BELIEVE YOU ABOUT THE PROFESSOR.
YOU WOULDN'T KILL HIM DELIBERATELY.
AND YOU *WON'T* DO WHAT YOU'RE THINKING OF.
LET ME TELL YOU SOMETHING. THE PROFESSOR? HE GAVE ME IDEAS. HE GAVE ME PATIENCE, KINDNESS AND MORE THAN I EVER DESERVED.
BUT YOU?
YOU GAVE ME THE ROLE MODEL.
YOU SHOWED ME HOW IT WAS POSSIBLE TO BE A BETTER MAN.

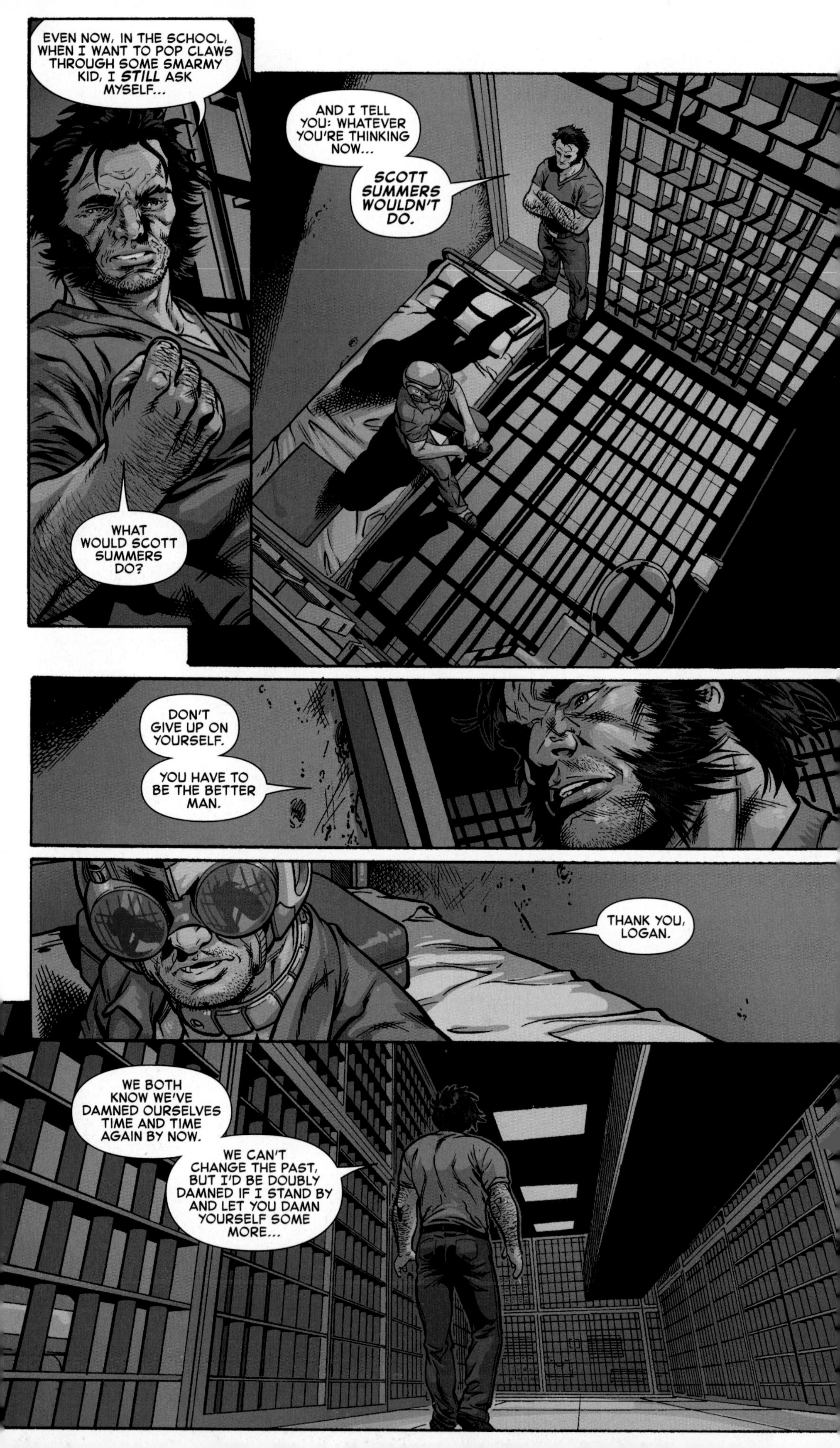
EVEN NOW, IN THE SCHOOL, WHEN I WANT TO POP CLAWS THROUGH SOME SMARMY KID, I STILL ASK MYSELF...
WHAT WOULD SCOTT SUMMERS DO?
AND I TELL YOU: WHATEVER YOU'RE THINKING NOW...
SCOTT SUMMERS WOULDN'T DO.
DON'T GIVE UP ON YOURSELF.
YOU HAVE TO BE THE BETTER MAN.
THANK YOU, LOGAN.
WE BOTH KNOW WE'VE DAMNED OURSELVES TIME AND TIME AGAIN BY NOW.
WE CAN'T CHANGE THE PAST, BUT I'D BE DOUBLY DAMNED IF I STAND BY AND LET YOU DAMN YOURSELF SOME MORE...

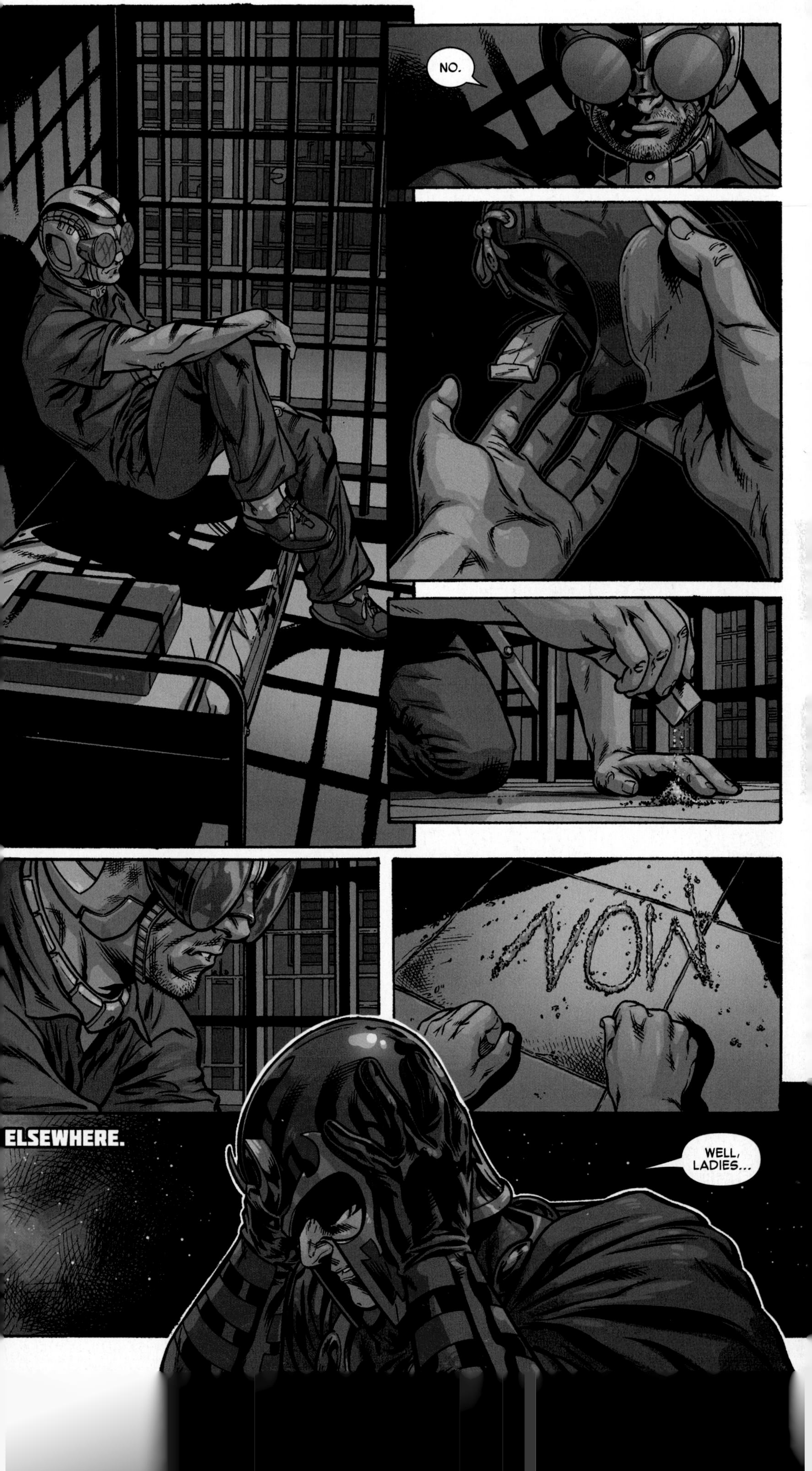
NO.
NOW
ELSEWHERE.
WELL, LADIES...

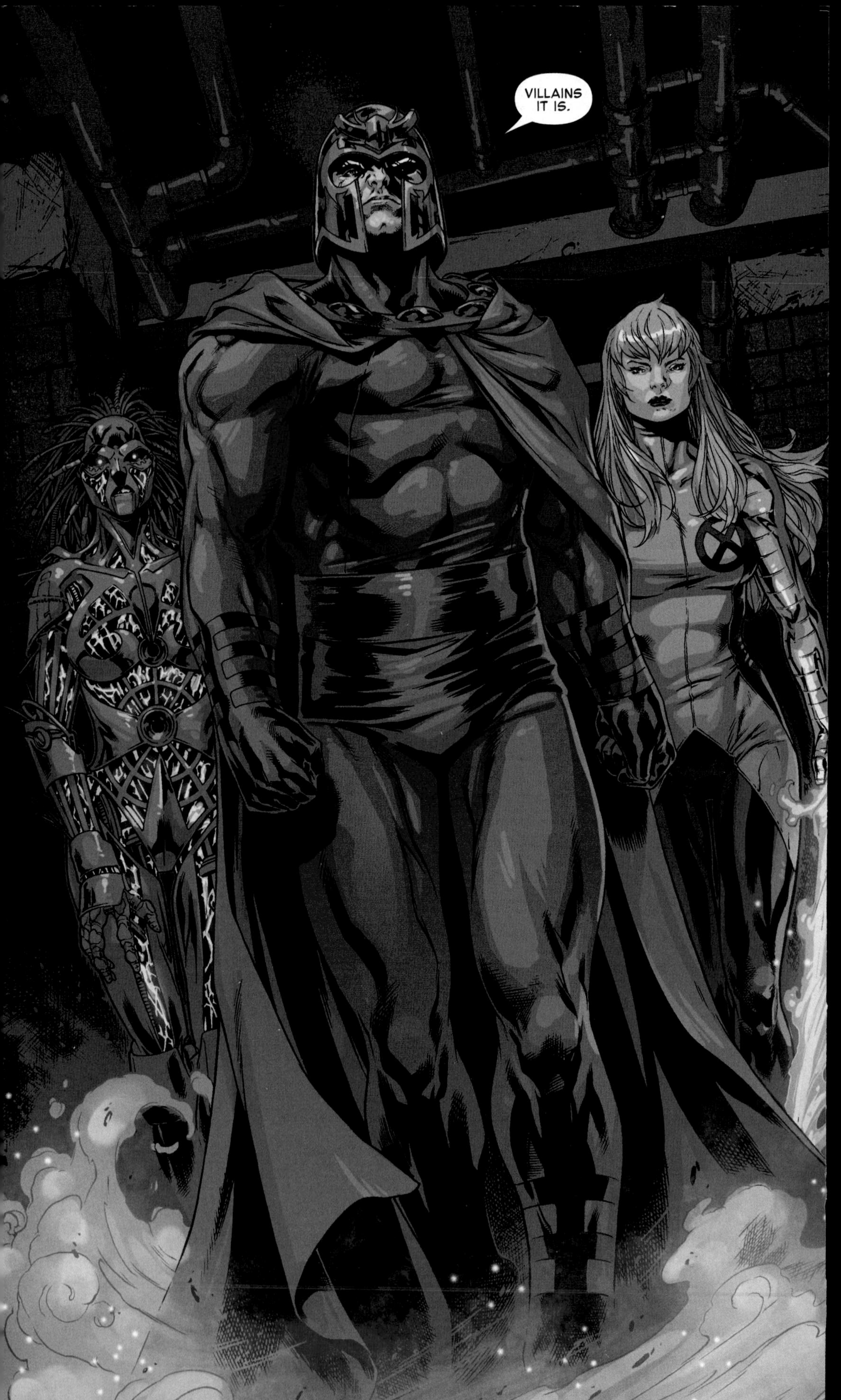
VILLAINS IT IS.

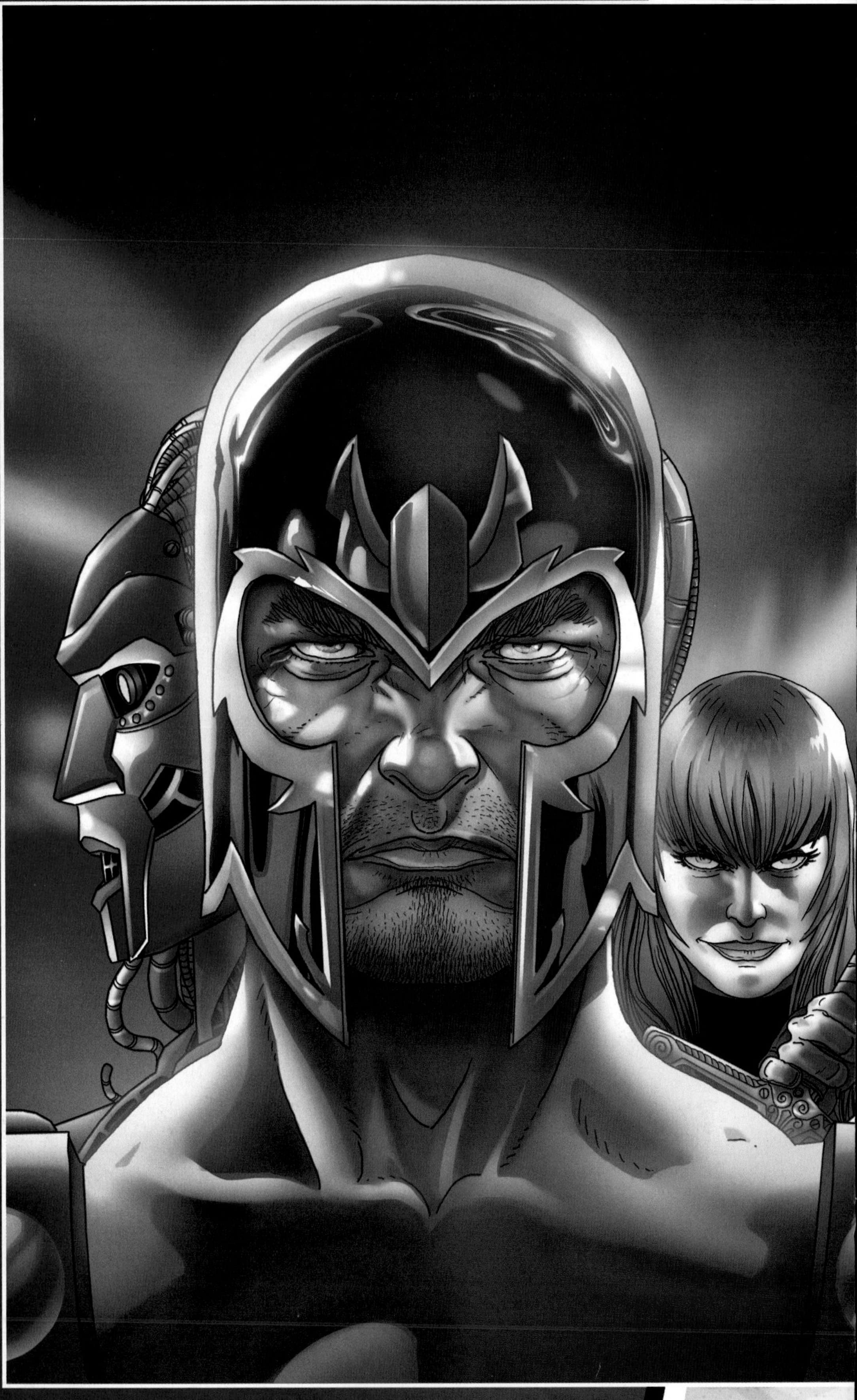

ISSUE #5

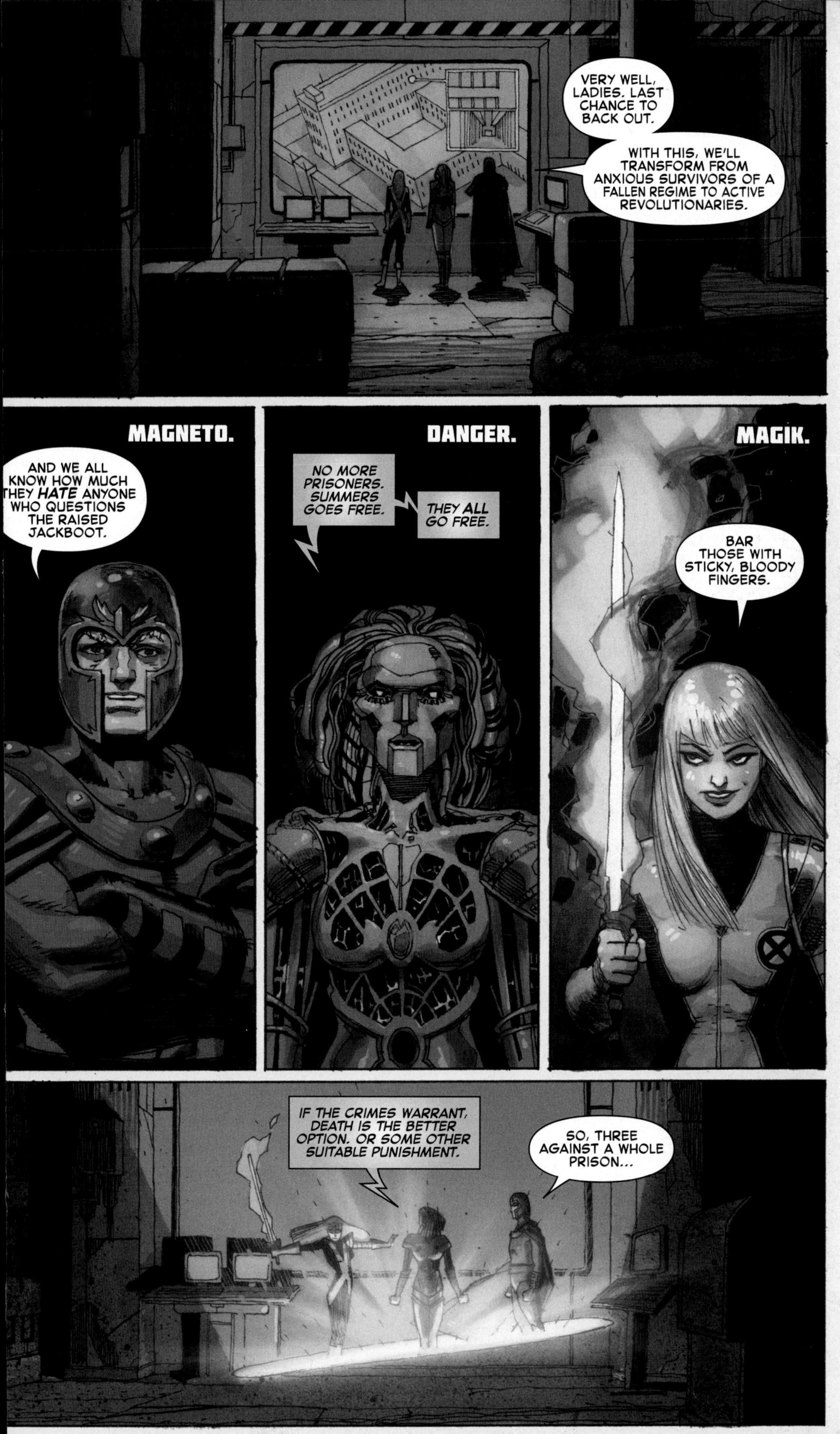
VERY WELL, LADIES. LAST CHANCE TO BACK OUT.
WITH THIS, WE'LL TRANSFORM FROM ANXIOUS SURVIVORS OF A FALLEN REGIME TO ACTIVE REVOLUTIONARIES.
MAGNETO.
AND WE ALL KNOW HOW MUCH THEY HATE ANYONE WHO QUESTIONS THE RAISED JACKBOOT.
DANGER.
NO MORE PRISONERS. SUMMERS GOES FREE.
THEY ALL GO FREE.
MAGIK.
BAR THOSE WITH STICKY, BLOODY FINGERS.
IF THE CRIMES WARRANT, DEATH IS THE BETTER OPTION. OR SOME OTHER SUITABLE PUNISHMENT.
SO, THREE AGAINST A WHOLE PRISON...

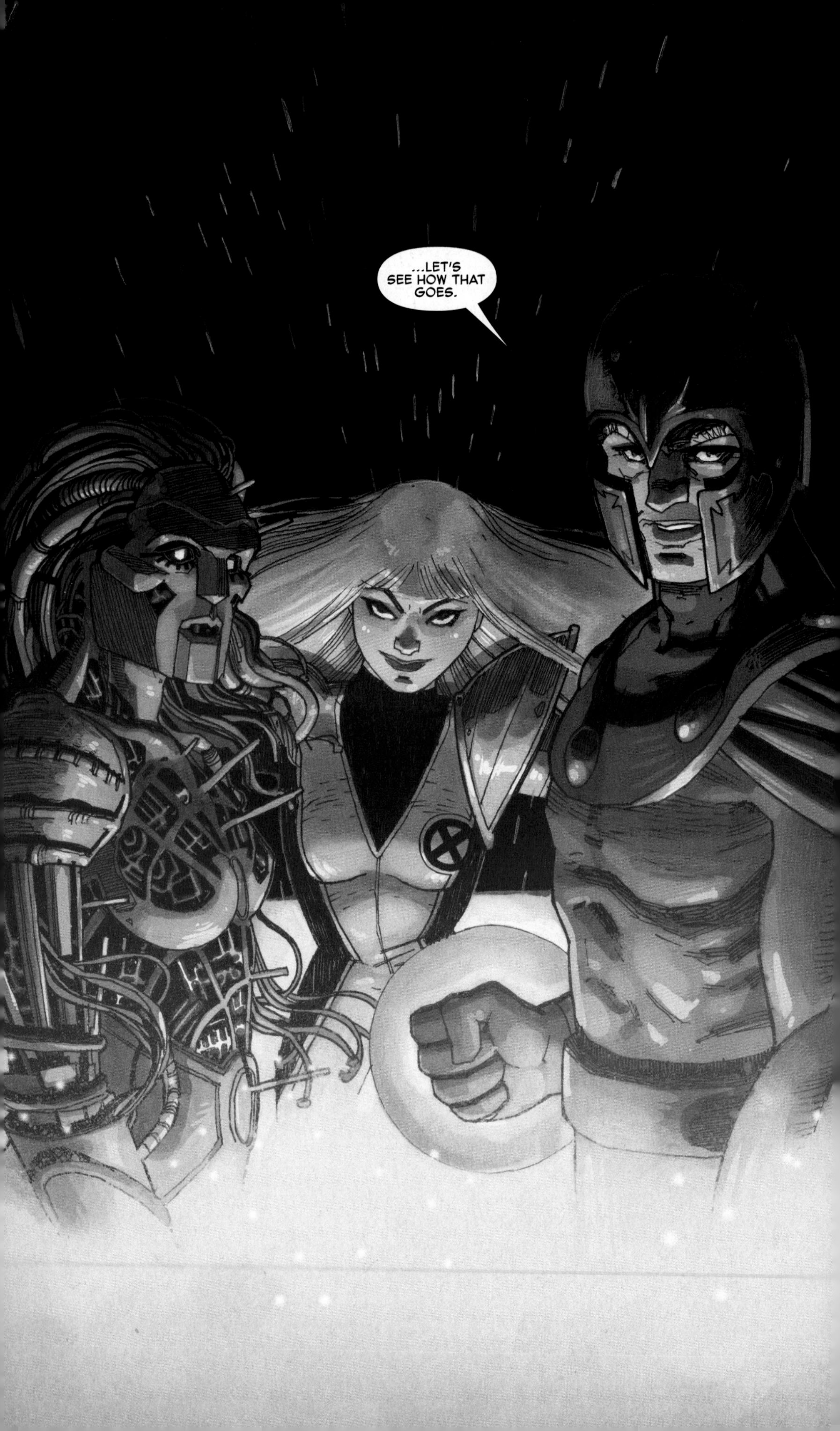
...LET'S SEE HOW THAT GOES.

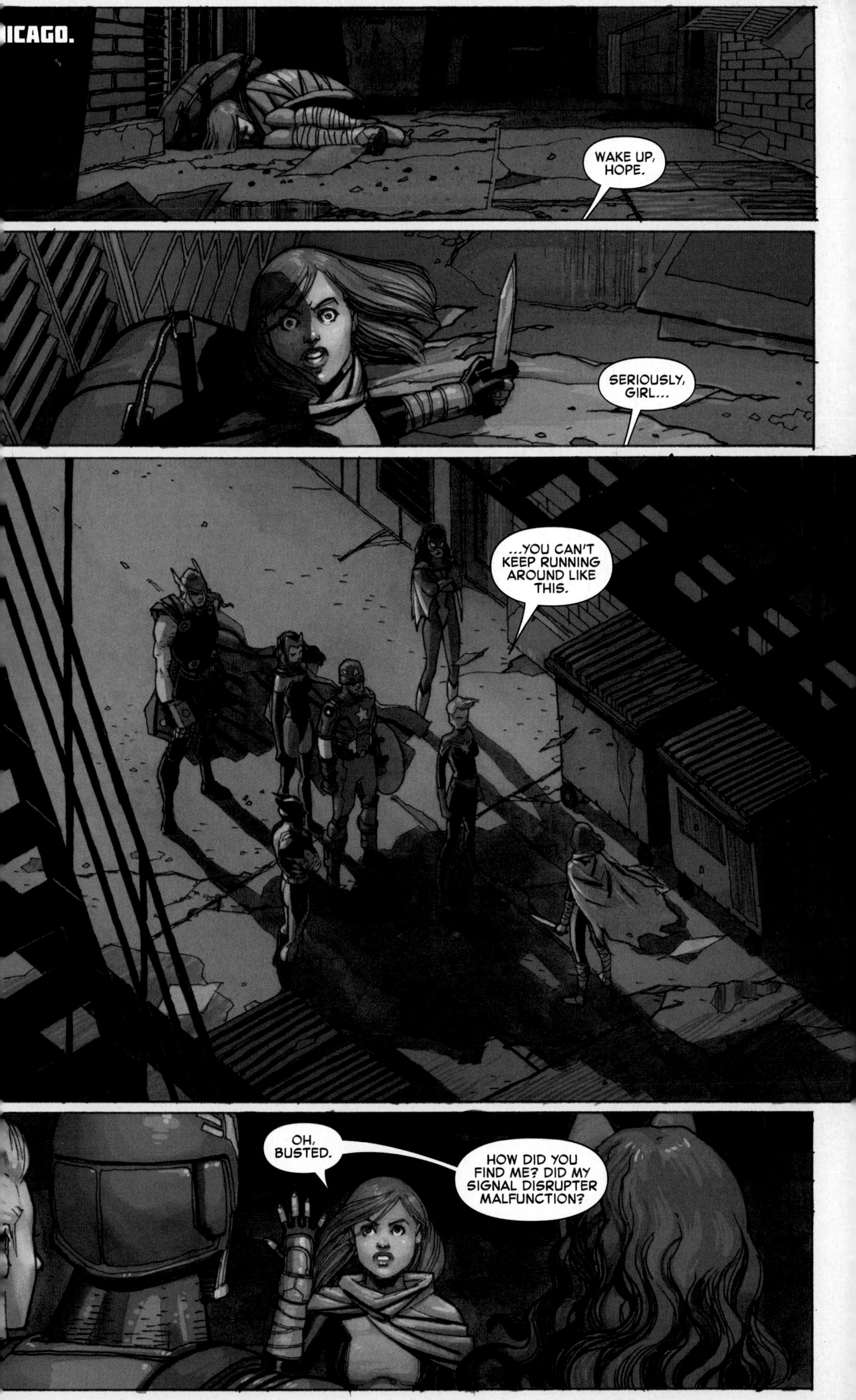
ICAGO.
WAKE UP, HOPE.
SERIOUSLY, GIRL...
...YOU CAN'T KEEP RUNNING AROUND LIKE THIS.
OH, BUSTED.
HOW DID YOU FIND ME? DID MY SIGNAL DISRUPTER MALFUNCTION?

A DIVINATION SPELL. IT NARROWED YOU DOWN TO BEING IN CHICAGO AT SOME POINT IN THE COMING TWO WEEKS.

AND MY NOSE DID THE REST...

WHERE HAVE YOU *BEEN*, HOPE?

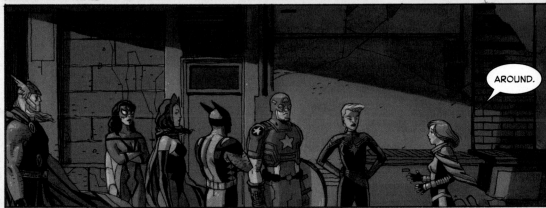

AROUND.

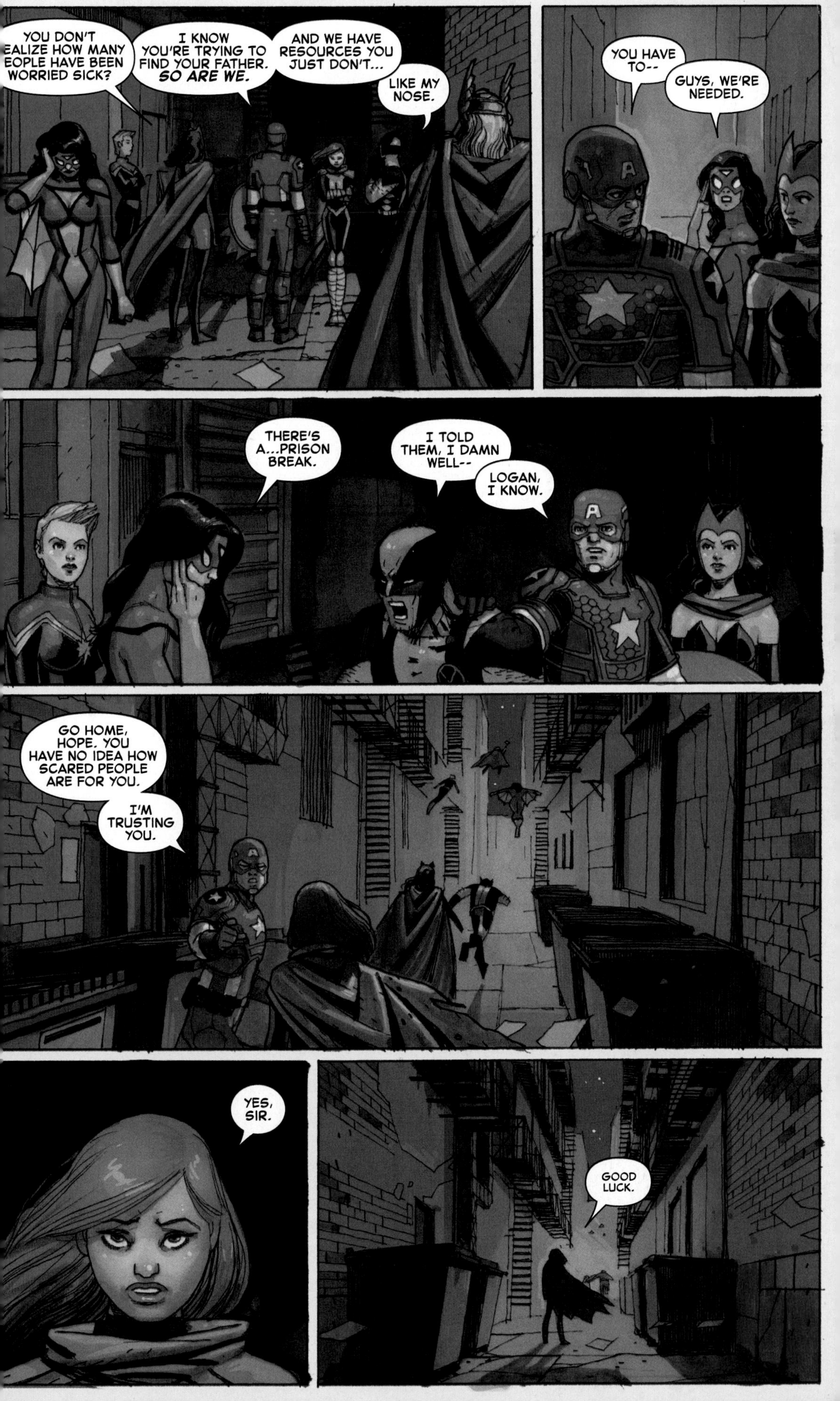
YOU DON'T EALIZE HOW MANY EOPLE HAVE BEEN WORRIED SICK?
I KNOW YOU'RE TRYING TO FIND YOUR FATHER. *SO ARE WE.*
AND WE HAVE RESOURCES YOU JUST DON'T...
LIKE MY NOSE.
YOU HAVE TO--
GUYS, WE'RE NEEDED.
THERE'S A...PRISON BREAK.
I TOLD THEM, I DAMN WELL--
LOGAN, I KNOW.
GO HOME, HOPE. YOU HAVE NO IDEA HOW SCARED PEOPLE ARE FOR YOU.
I'M TRUSTING YOU.
YES, SIR.
GOOD LUCK.

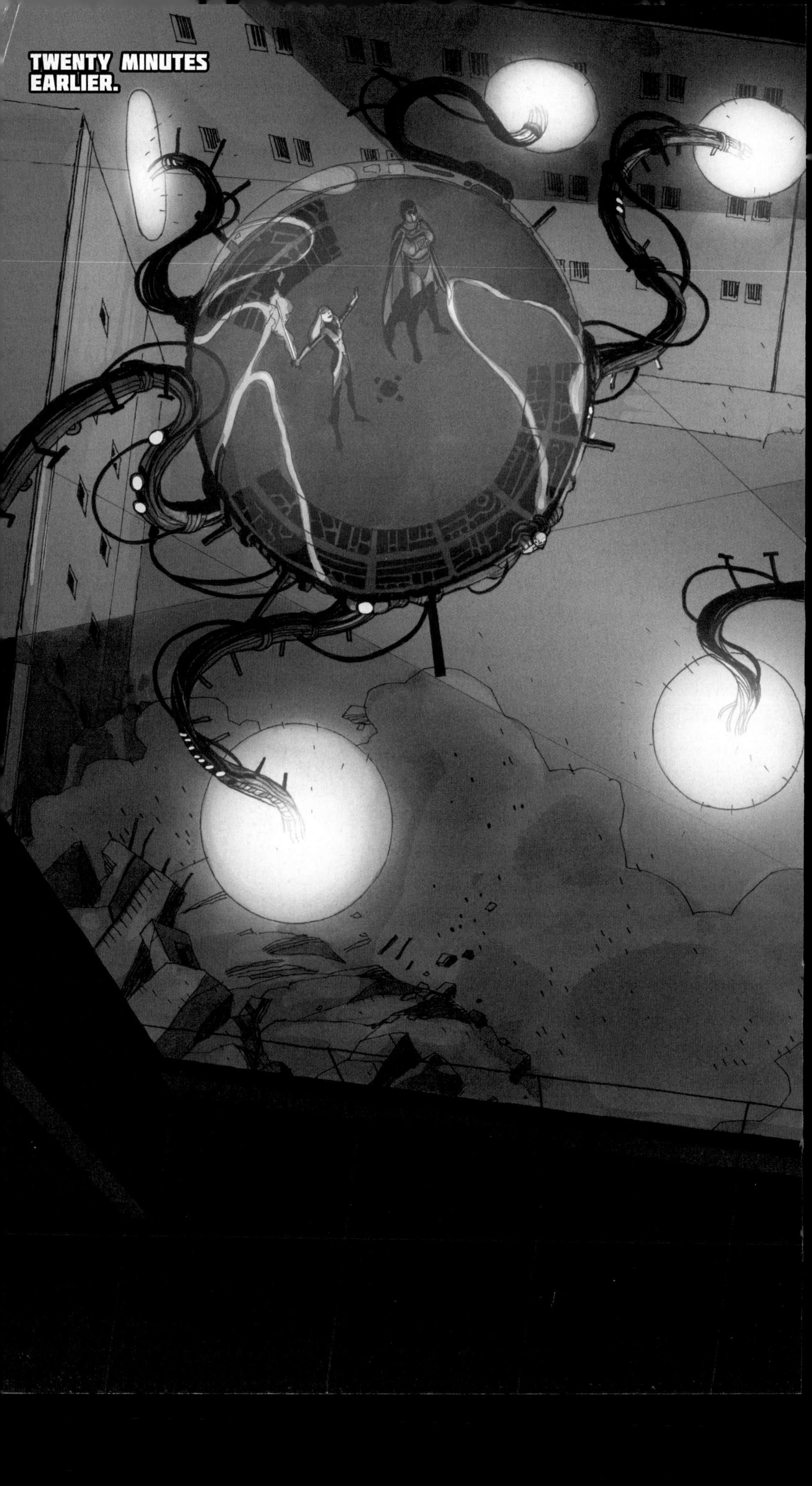
TWENTY MINUTES EARLIER.

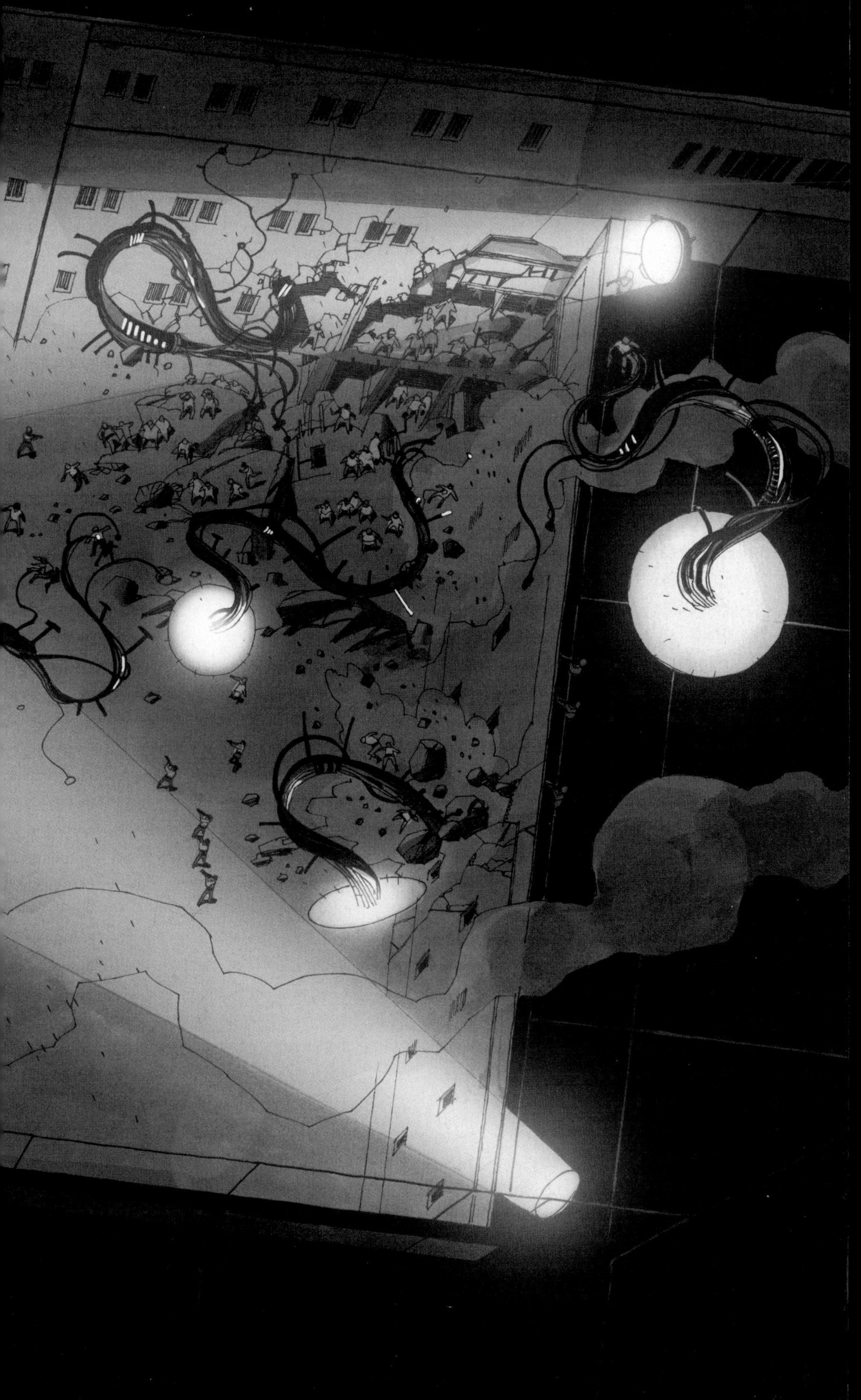

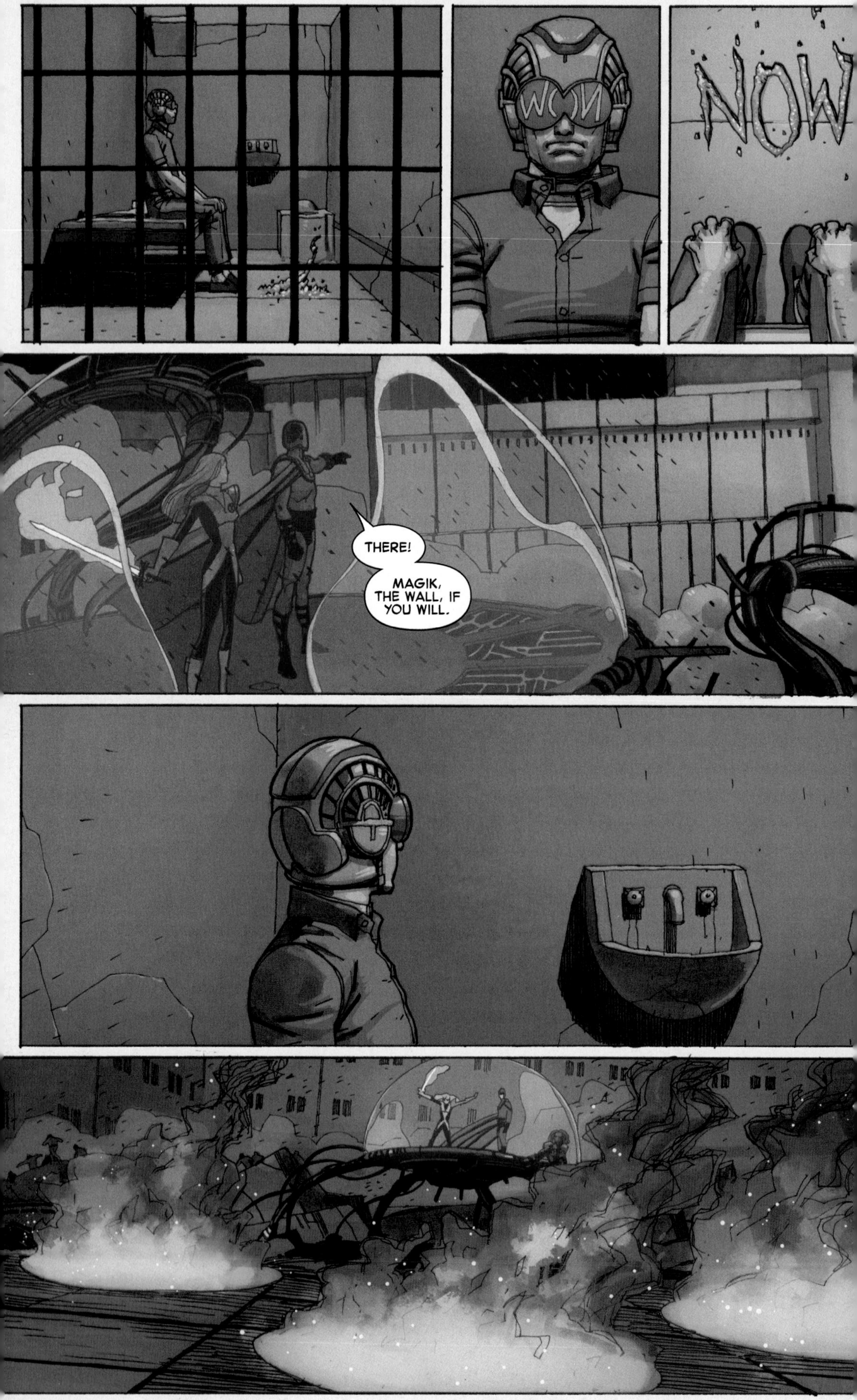

NOW
WON
THERE!
MAGIK, THE WALL, IF YOU WILL.

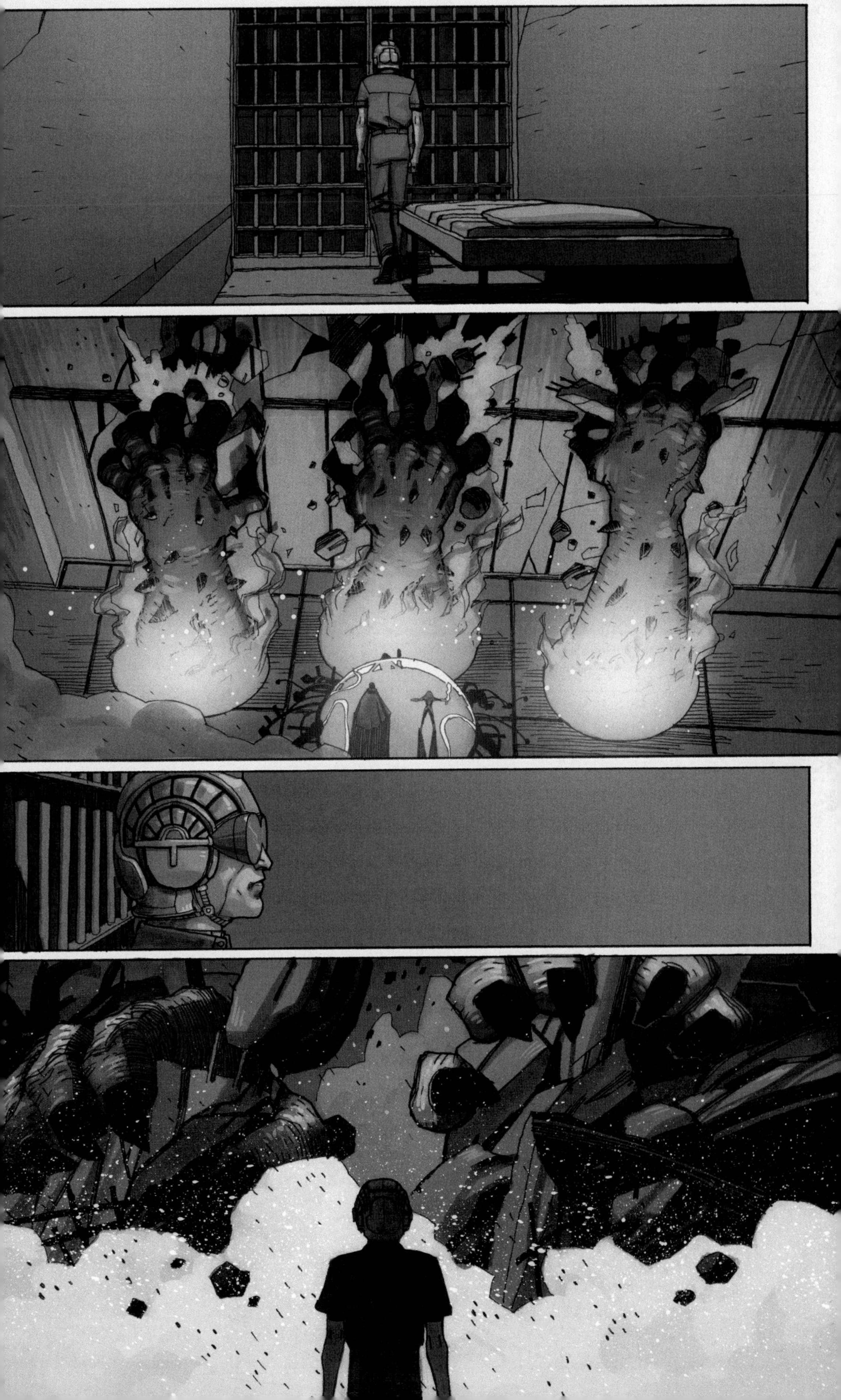

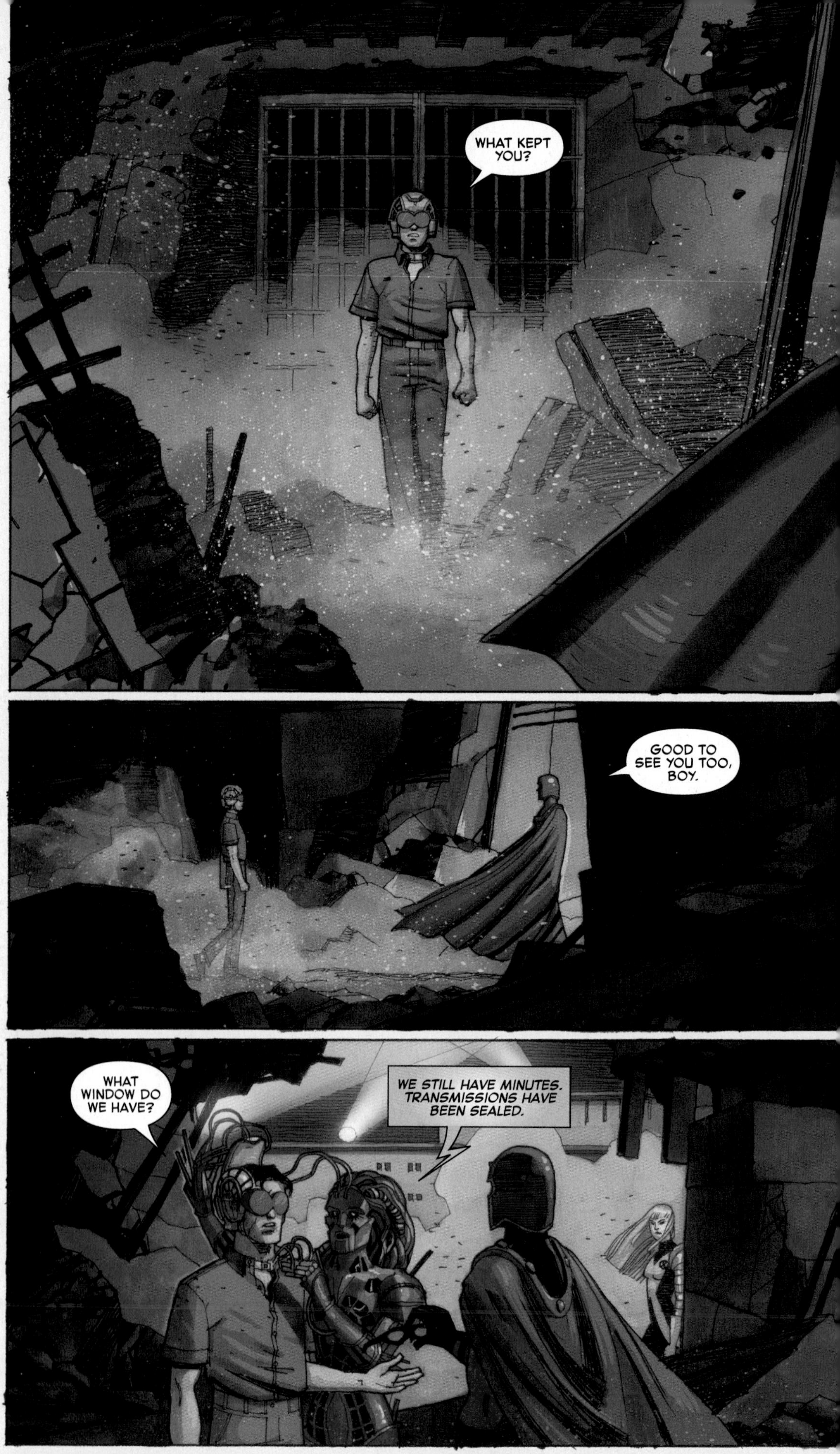
WHAT KEPT YOU?
GOOD TO SEE YOU TOO, BOY.
WHAT WINDOW DO WE HAVE?
WE STILL HAVE MINUTES. TRANSMISSIONS HAVE BEEN SEALED.

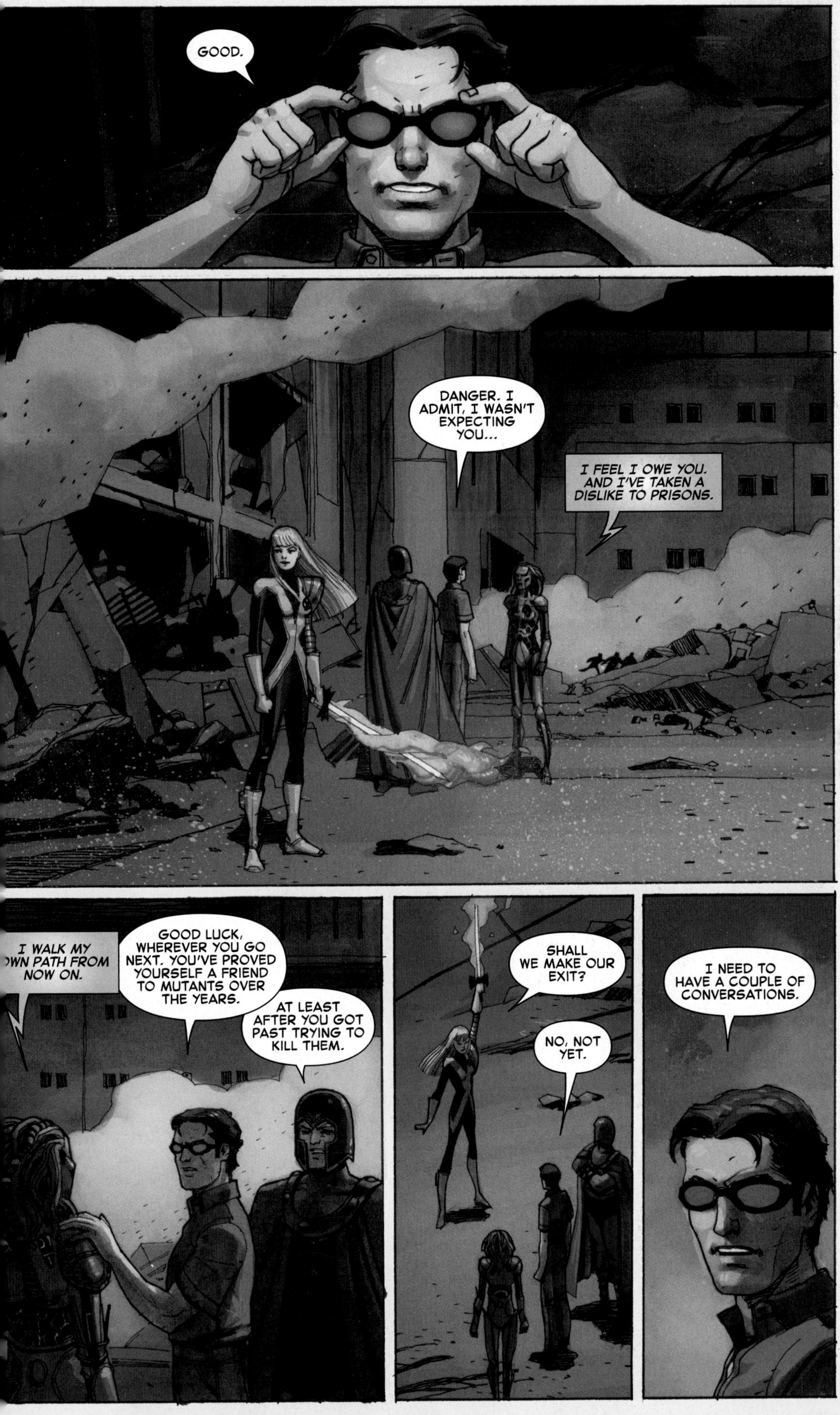
GOOD.
DANGER. I ADMIT, I WASN'T EXPECTING YOU...
I FEEL I OWE YOU. AND I'VE TAKEN A DISLIKE TO PRISONS.
I WALK MY OWN PATH FROM NOW ON.
GOOD LUCK, WHEREVER YOU GO NEXT. YOU'VE PROVED YOURSELF A FRIEND TO MUTANTS OVER THE YEARS.
AT LEAST AFTER YOU GOT PAST TRYING TO KILL THEM.
SHALL WE MAKE OUR EXIT?
NO, NOT YET.
I NEED TO HAVE A COUPLE OF CONVERSATIONS.

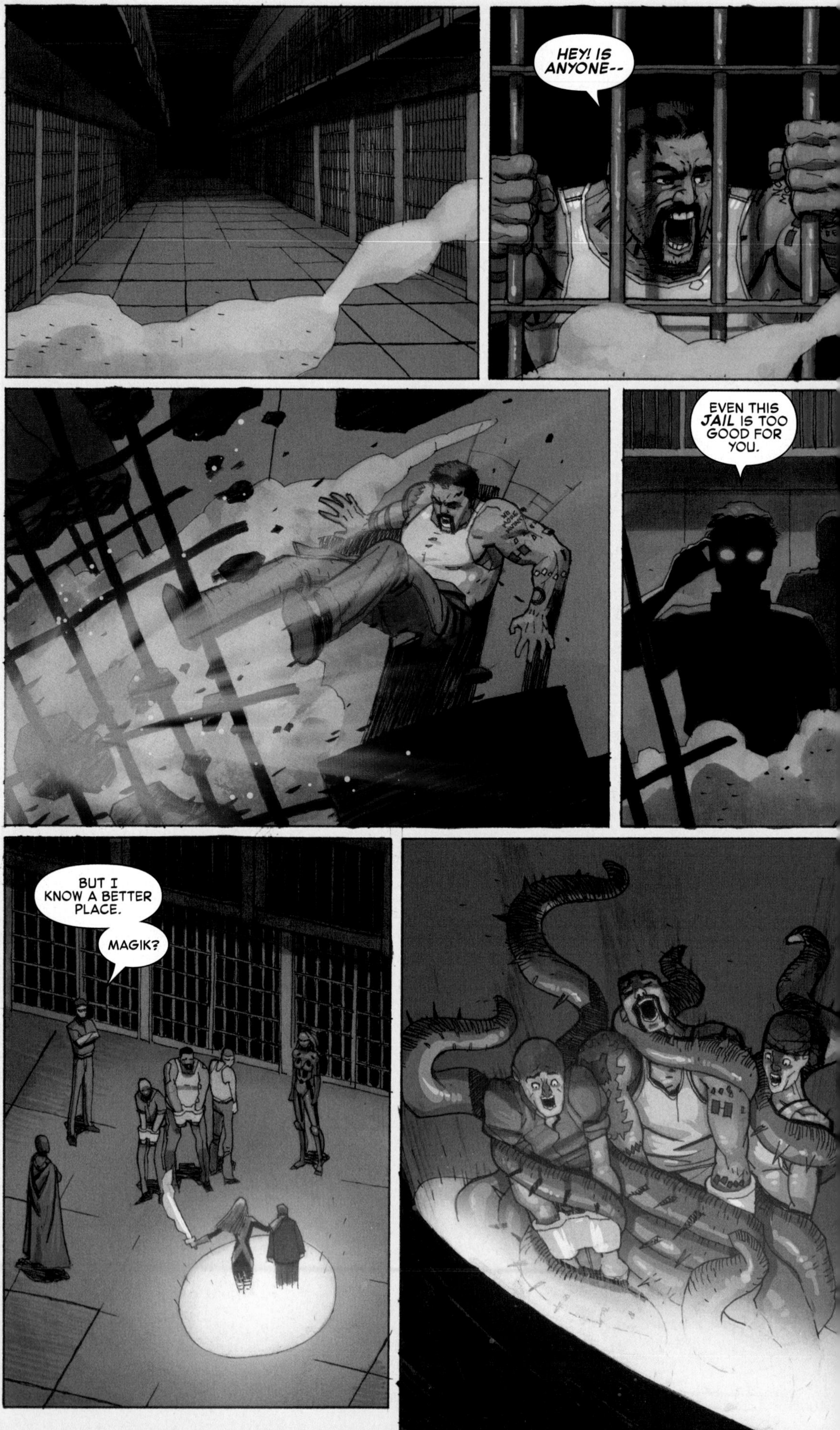
HEY! IS ANYONE--
EVEN THIS JAIL IS TOO GOOD FOR YOU.
BUT I KNOW A BETTER PLACE.
MAGIK?

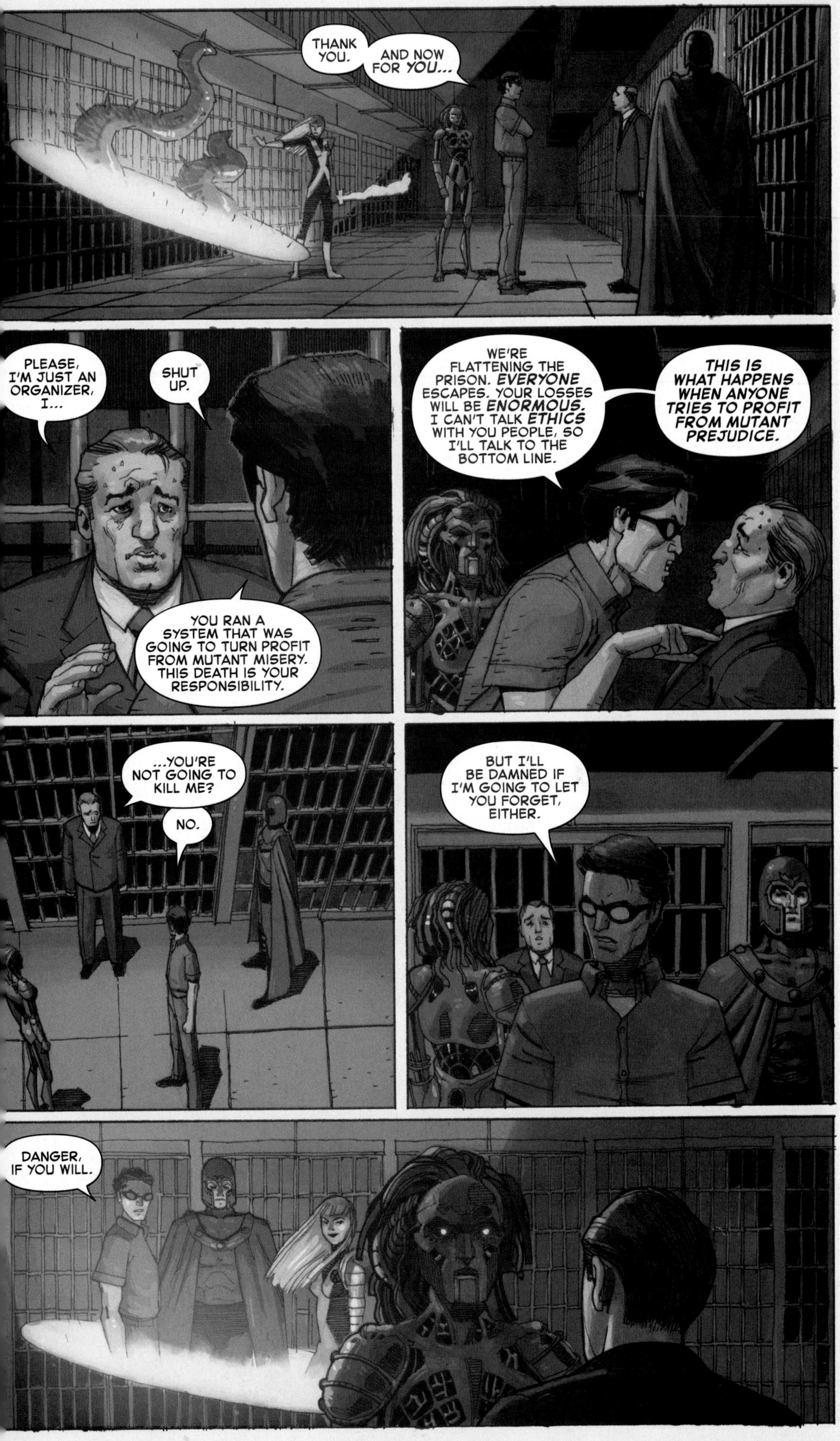

THANK YOU.
AND NOW FOR YOU...
PLEASE, I'M JUST AN ORGANIZER, I...
SHUT UP.
YOU RAN A SYSTEM THAT WAS GOING TO TURN PROFIT FROM MUTANT MISERY. THIS DEATH IS YOUR RESPONSIBILITY.
WE'RE FLATTENING THE PRISON. EVERYONE ESCAPES. YOUR LOSSES WILL BE ENORMOUS. I CAN'T TALK ETHICS WITH YOU PEOPLE, SO I'LL TALK TO THE BOTTOM LINE.
THIS IS WHAT HAPPENS WHEN ANYONE TRIES TO PROFIT FROM MUTANT PREJUDICE.
...YOU'RE NOT GOING TO KILL ME?
NO.
BUT I'LL BE DAMNED IF I'M GOING TO LET YOU FORGET, EITHER.
DANGER, IF YOU WILL.

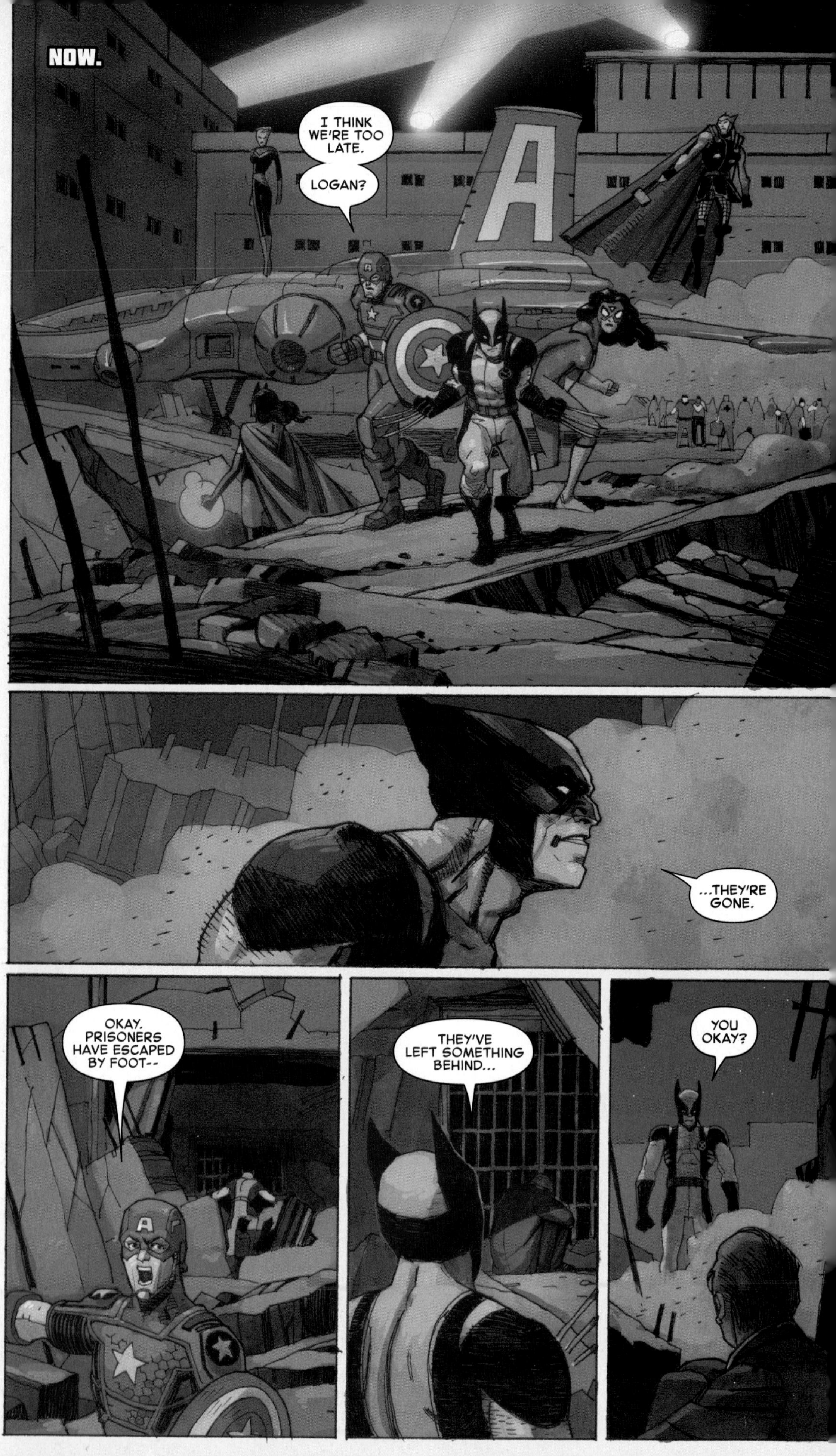
NOW.
I THINK WE'RE TOO LATE.
LOGAN?
...THEY'RE GONE.
OKAY. PRISONERS HAVE ESCAPED BY FOOT--
THEY'VE LEFT SOMETHING BEHIND...
YOU OKAY?

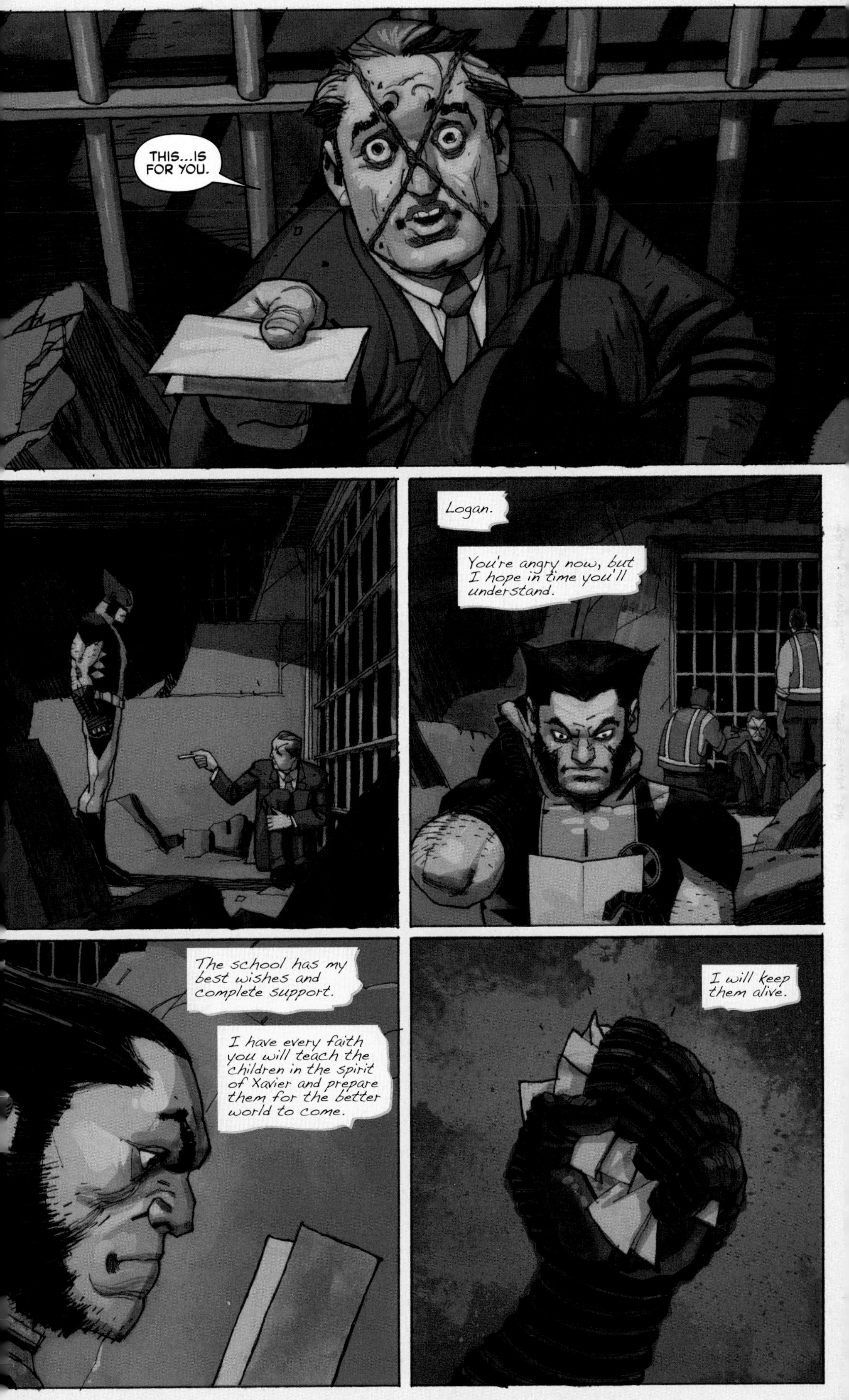
THIS...IS FOR YOU.
Logan.
You're angry now, but I hope in time you'll understand.
The school has my best wishes and complete support.
I have every faith you will teach the children in the spirit of Xavier and prepare them for the better world to come.
I will keep them alive.

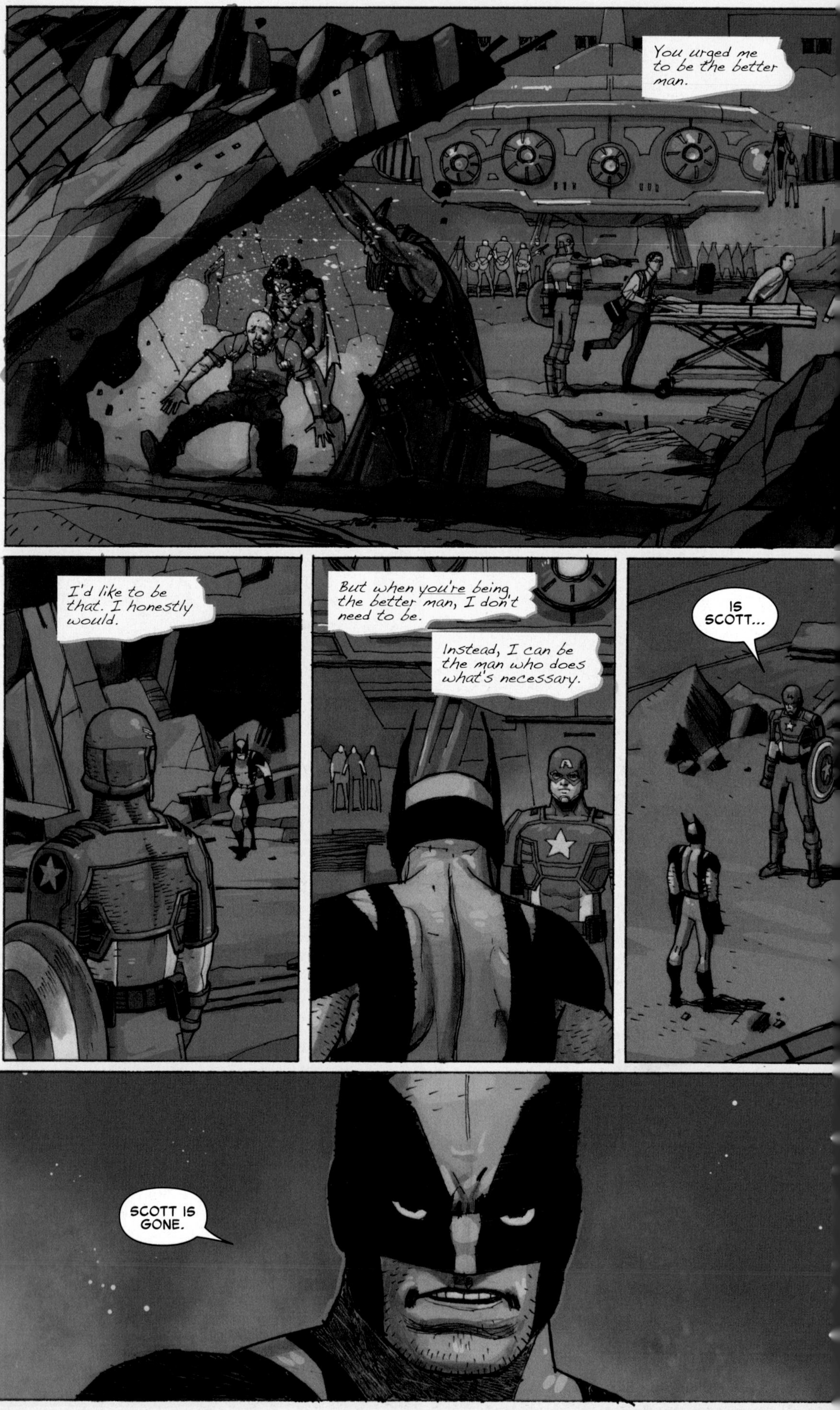
You urged me to be the better man.
I'd like to be that. I honestly would.
But when you're being the better man, I don't need to be.
Instead, I can be the man who does what's necessary.
IS SCOTT...
SCOTT IS GONE.

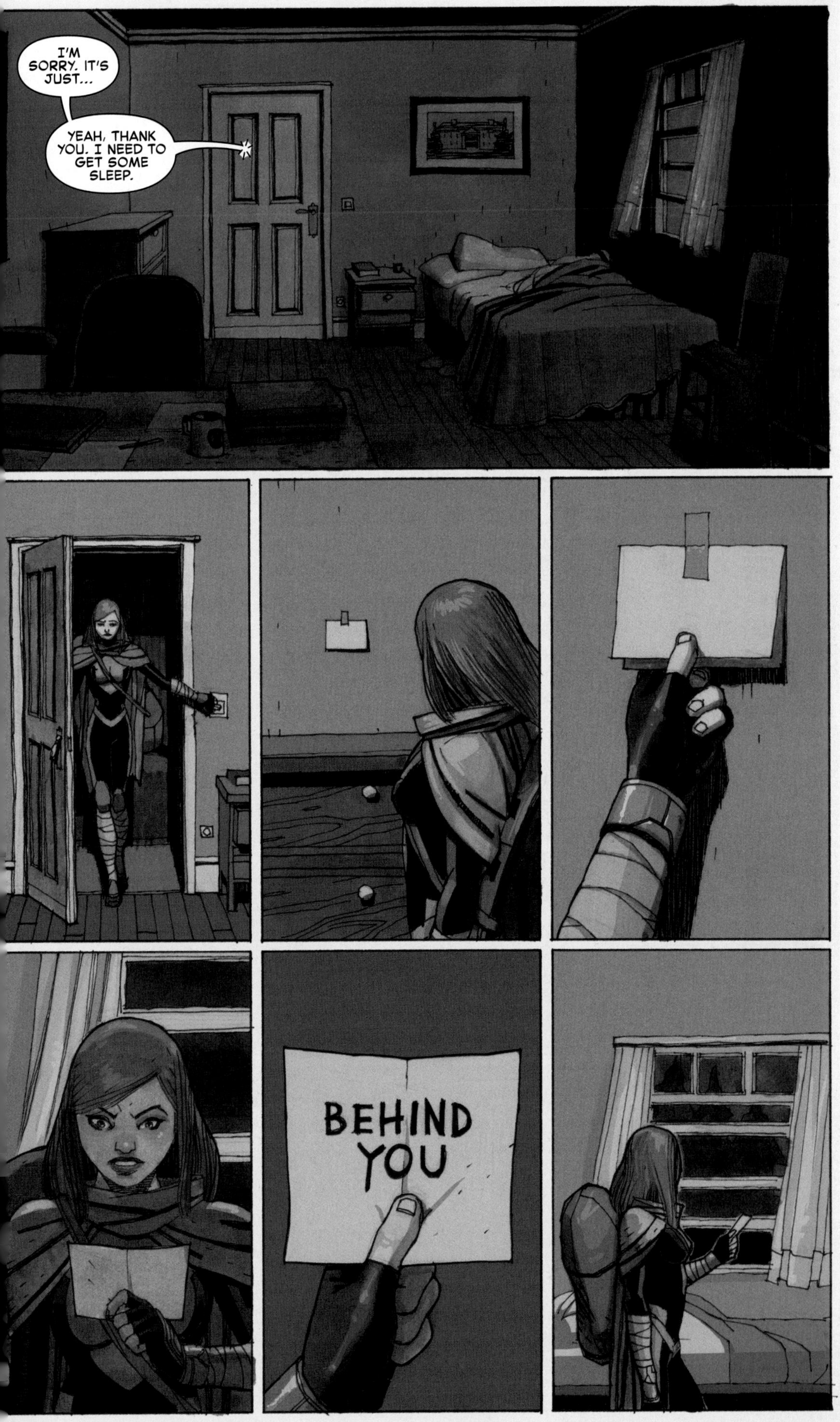
I'M SORRY. IT'S JUST...
YEAH, THANK YOU. I NEED TO GET SOME SLEEP.
BEHIND YOU

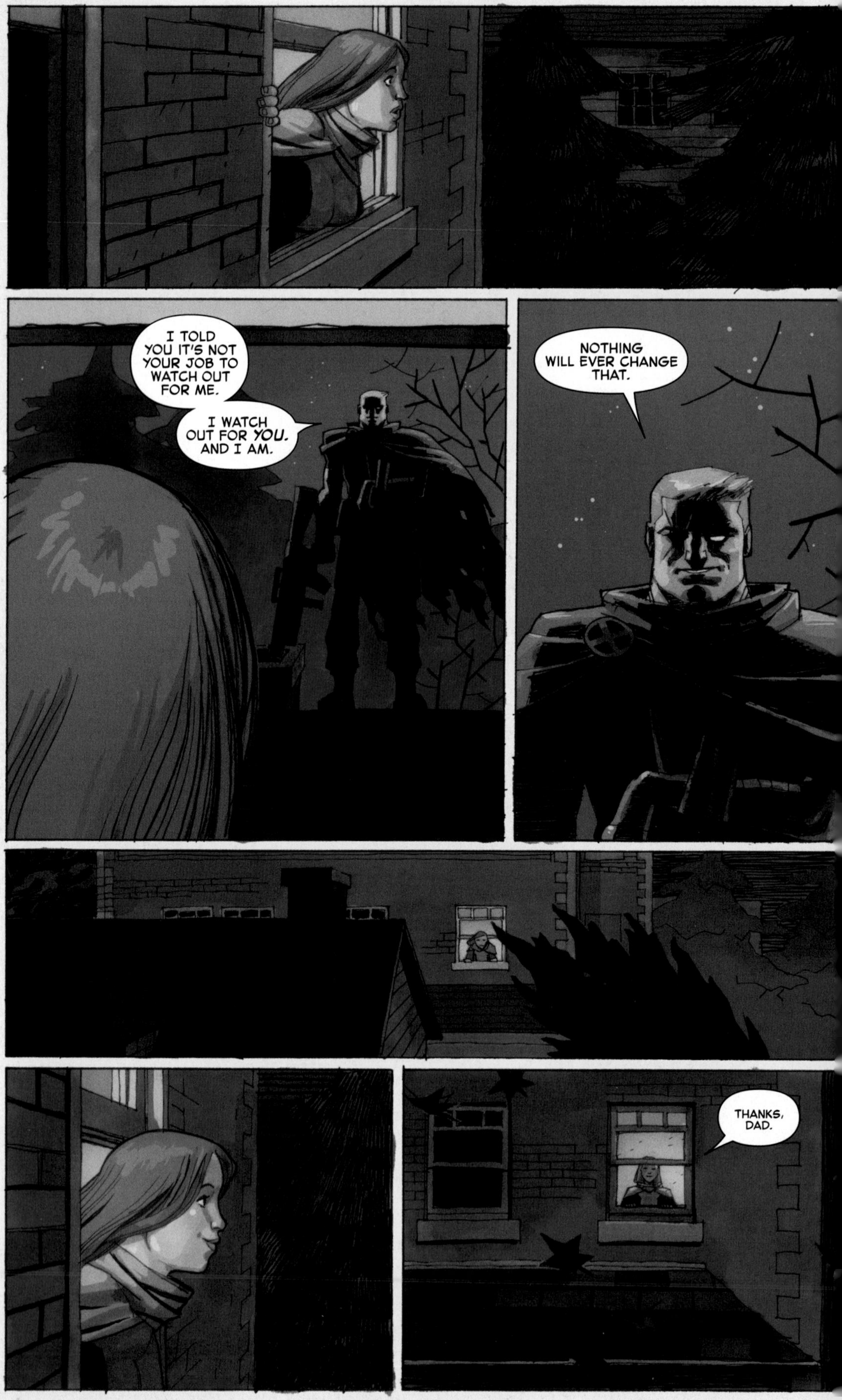
I TOLD YOU IT'S NOT YOUR JOB TO WATCH OUT FOR ME.
I WATCH OUT FOR *YOU.* AND I AM.
NOTHING WILL EVER CHANGE THAT.
THANKS, DAD.

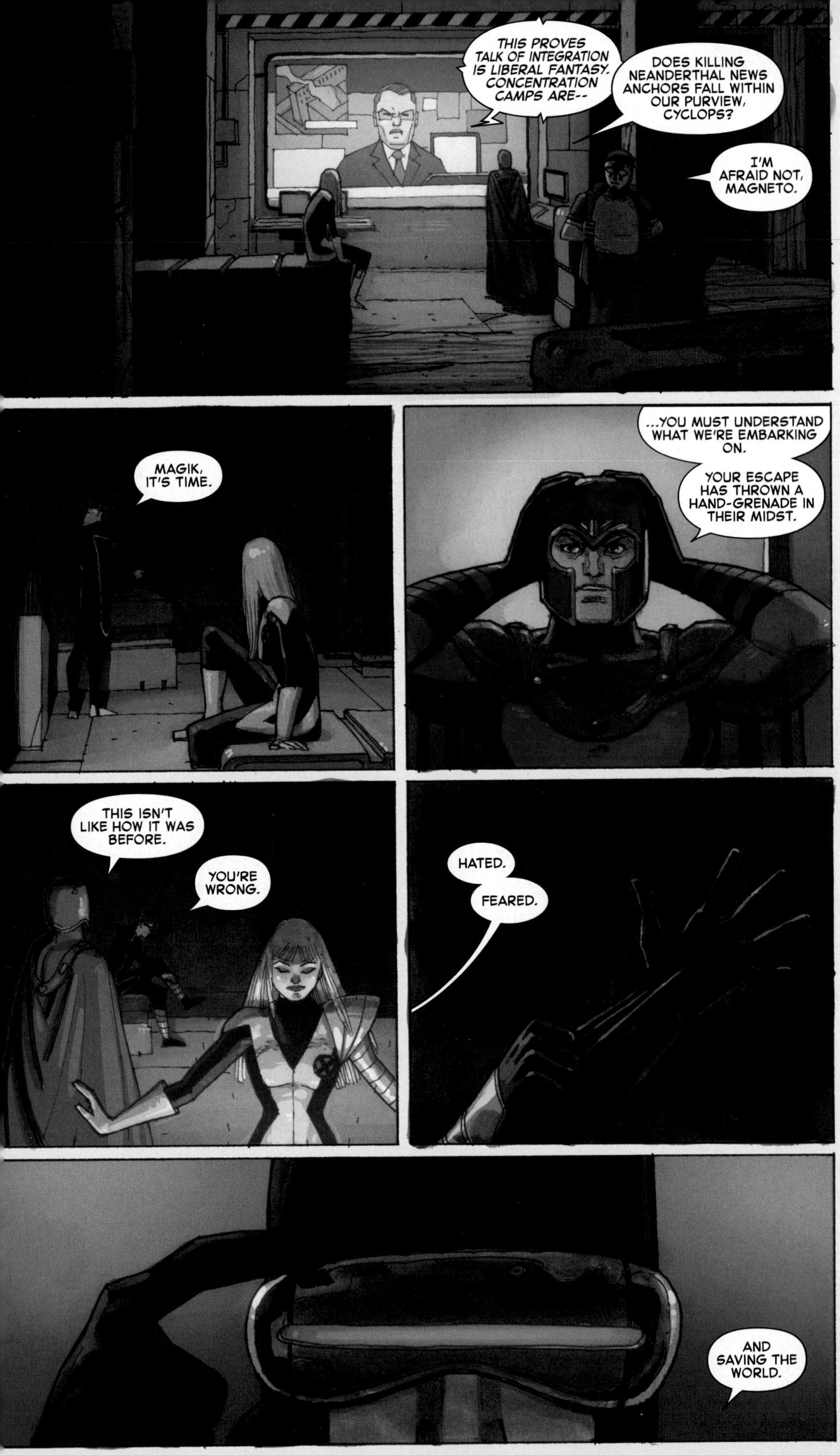
THIS PROVES TALK OF INTEGRATION IS LIBERAL FANTASY. CONCENTRATION CAMPS ARE--
DOES KILLING NEANDERTHAL NEWS ANCHORS FALL WITHIN OUR PURVIEW, CYCLOPS?
I'M AFRAID NOT, MAGNETO.
MAGIK, IT'S TIME.
...YOU MUST UNDERSTAND WHAT WE'RE EMBARKING ON.
YOUR ESCAPE HAS THROWN A HAND-GRENADE IN THEIR MIDST.
THIS ISN'T LIKE HOW IT WAS BEFORE.
YOU'RE WRONG.
HATED.
FEARED.
AND SAVING THE WORLD.

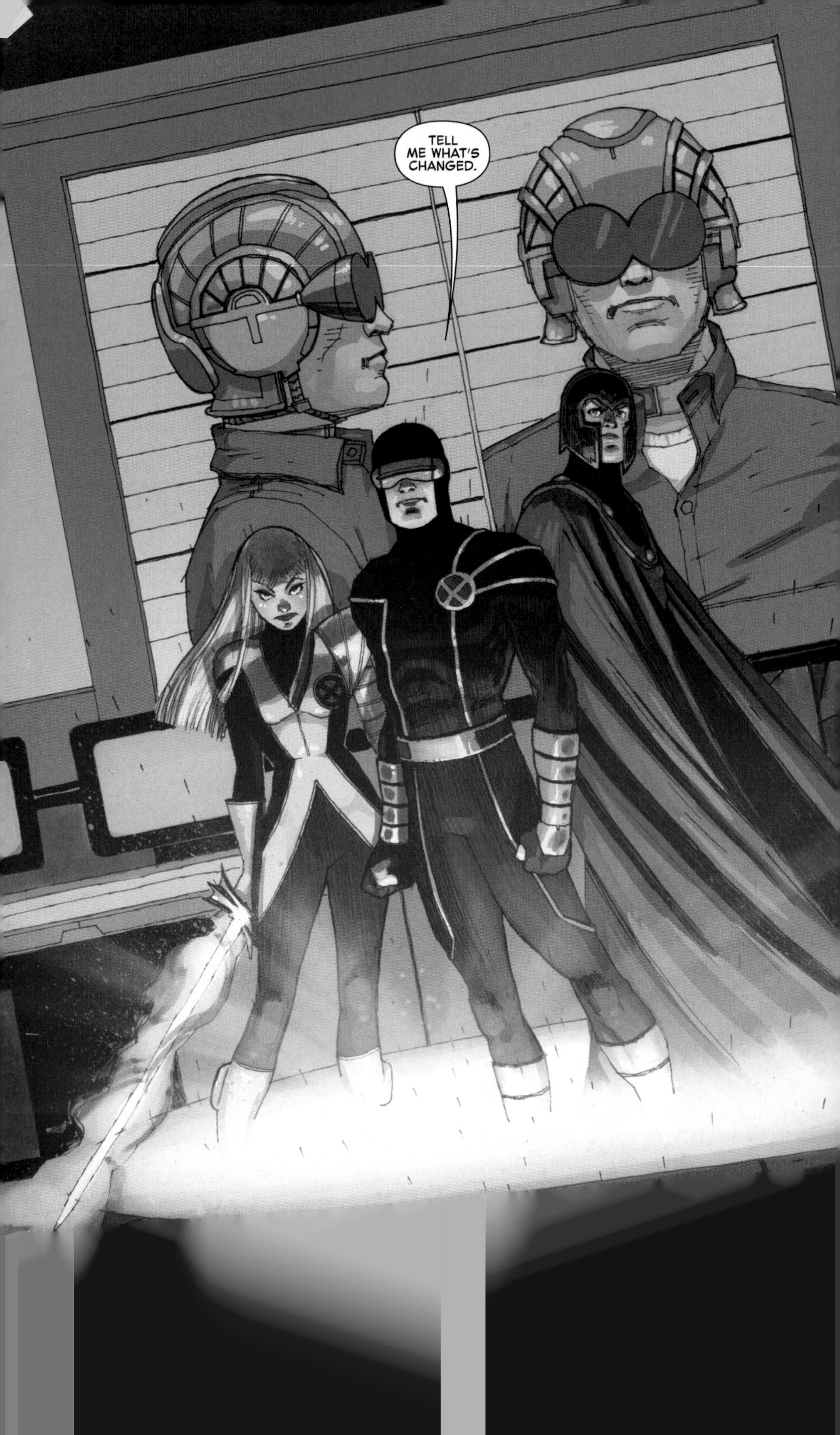
TELL ME WHAT'S CHANGED.

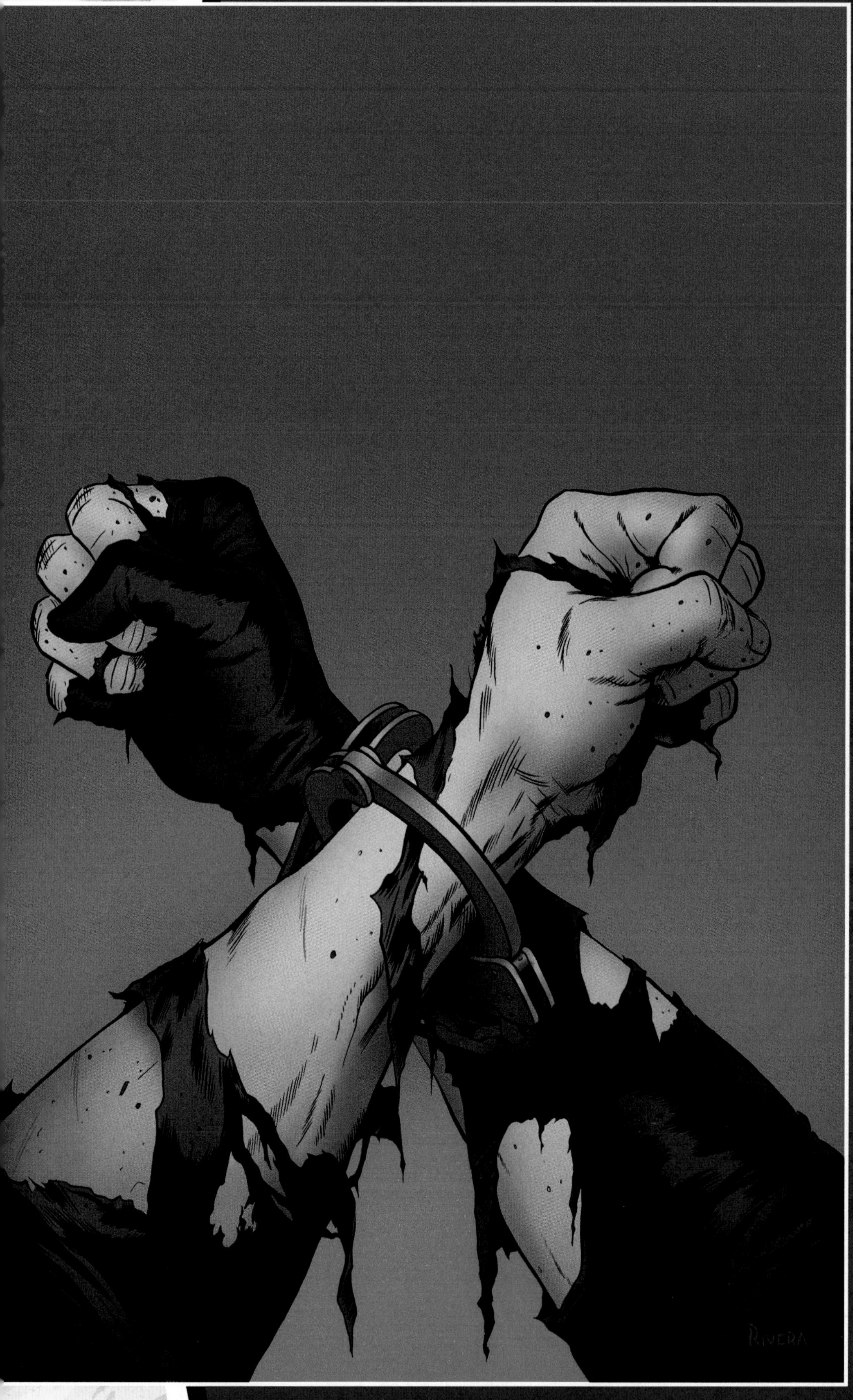
RIVERA

#1 VARIANT
BY **PAOLO RIVERA**

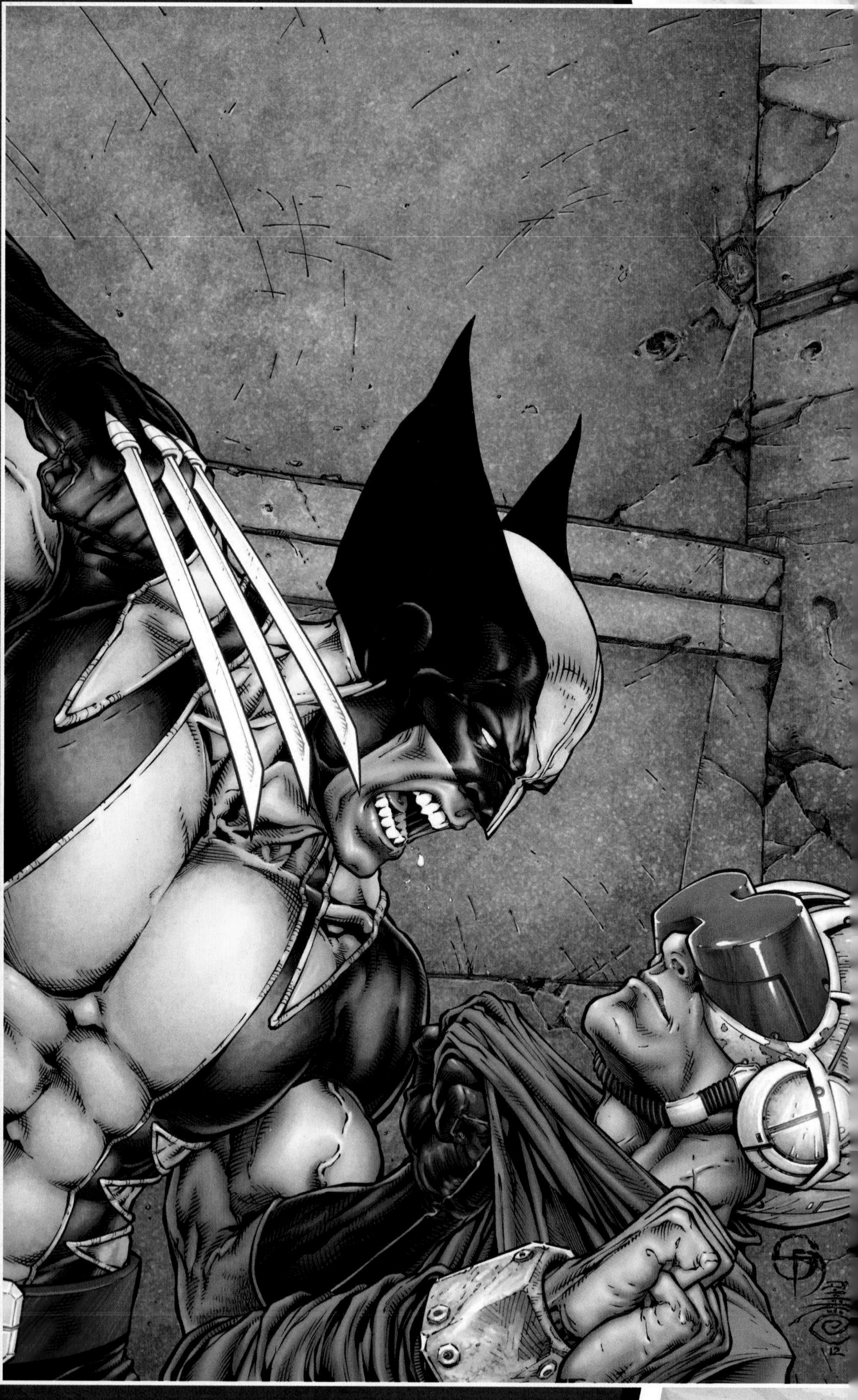

#2 VARIANT

BY **SHANE DAVIS, DANNY MIKI & MORRY HOLLOWELL**

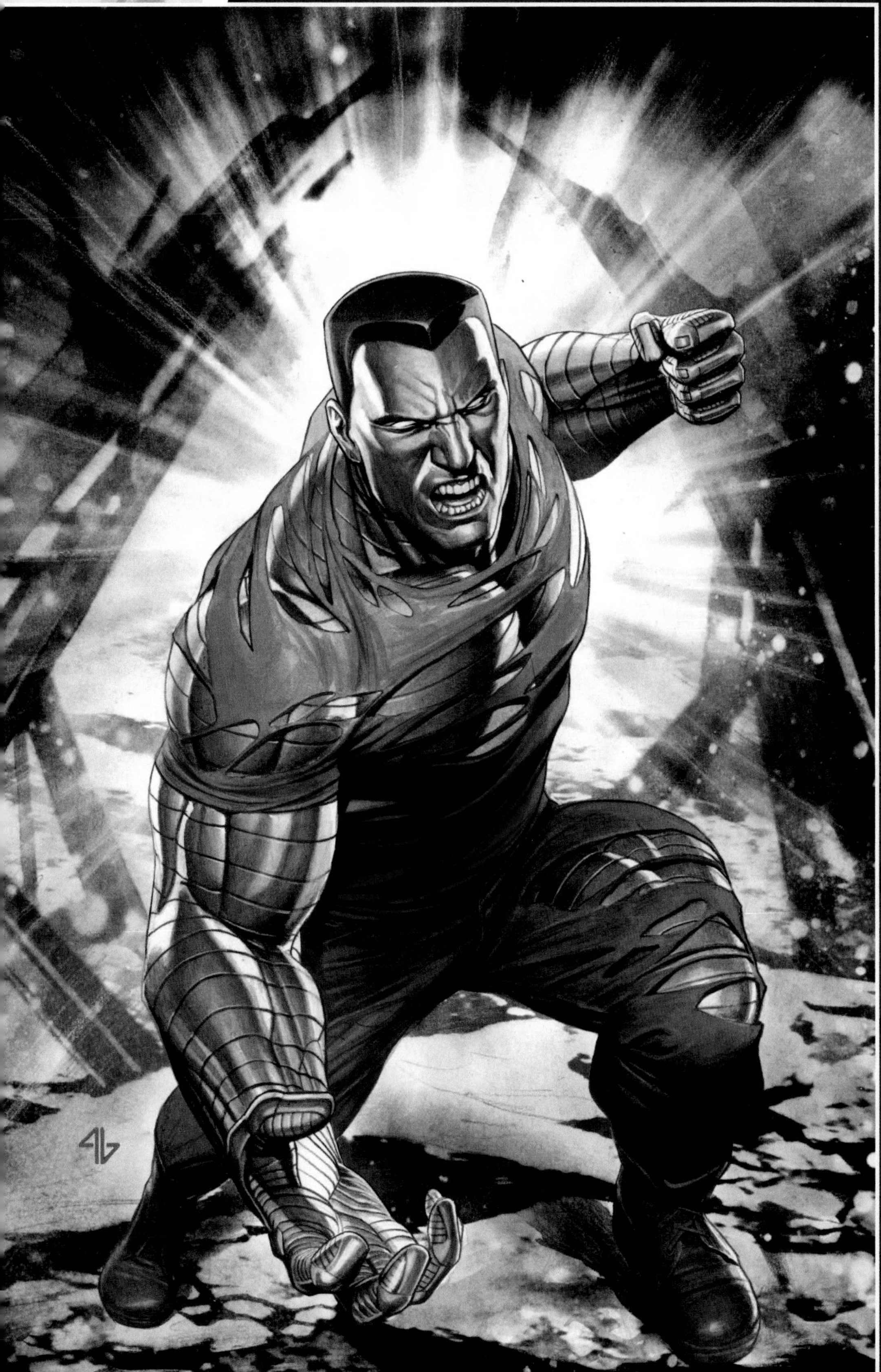

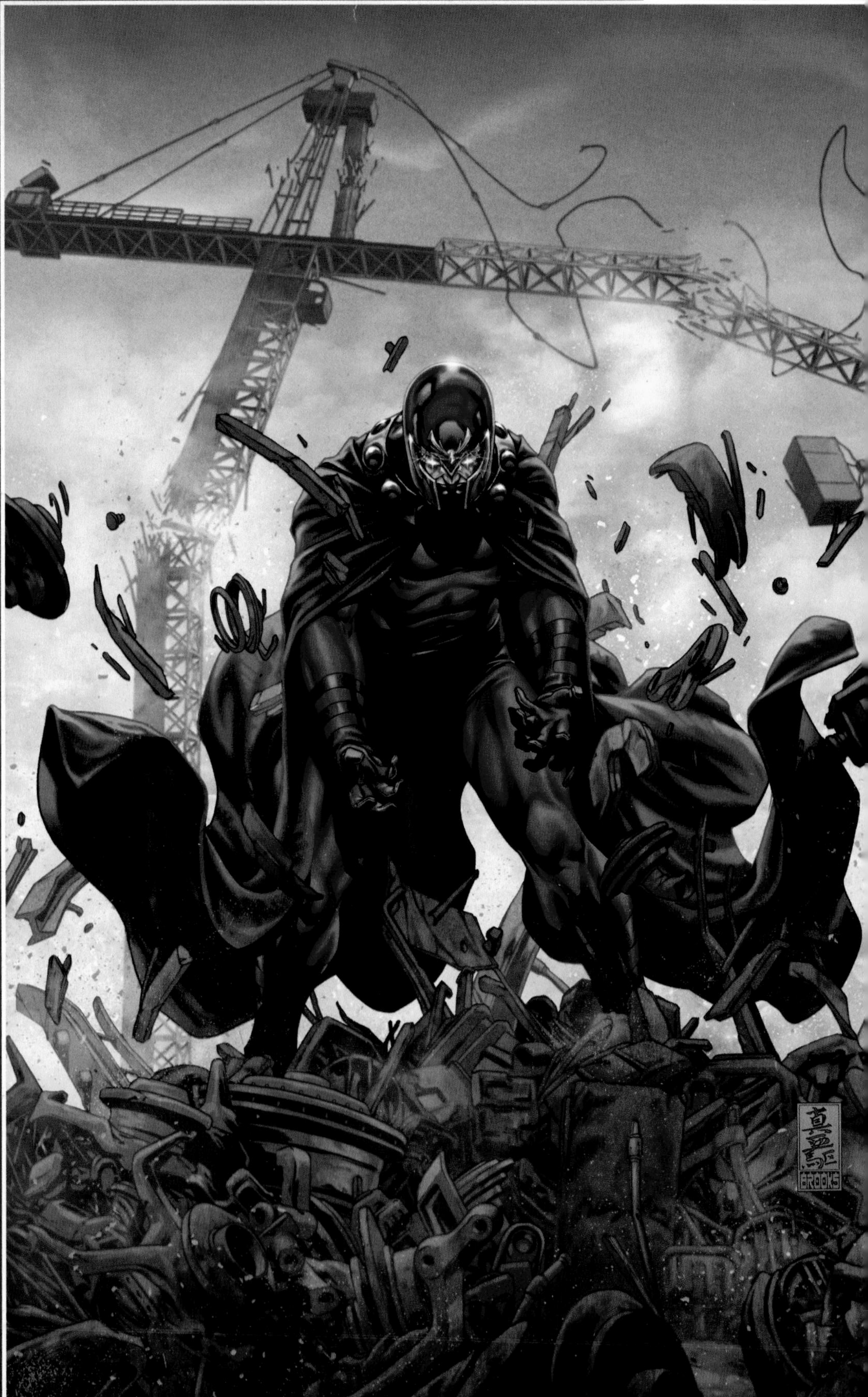
BROOKS

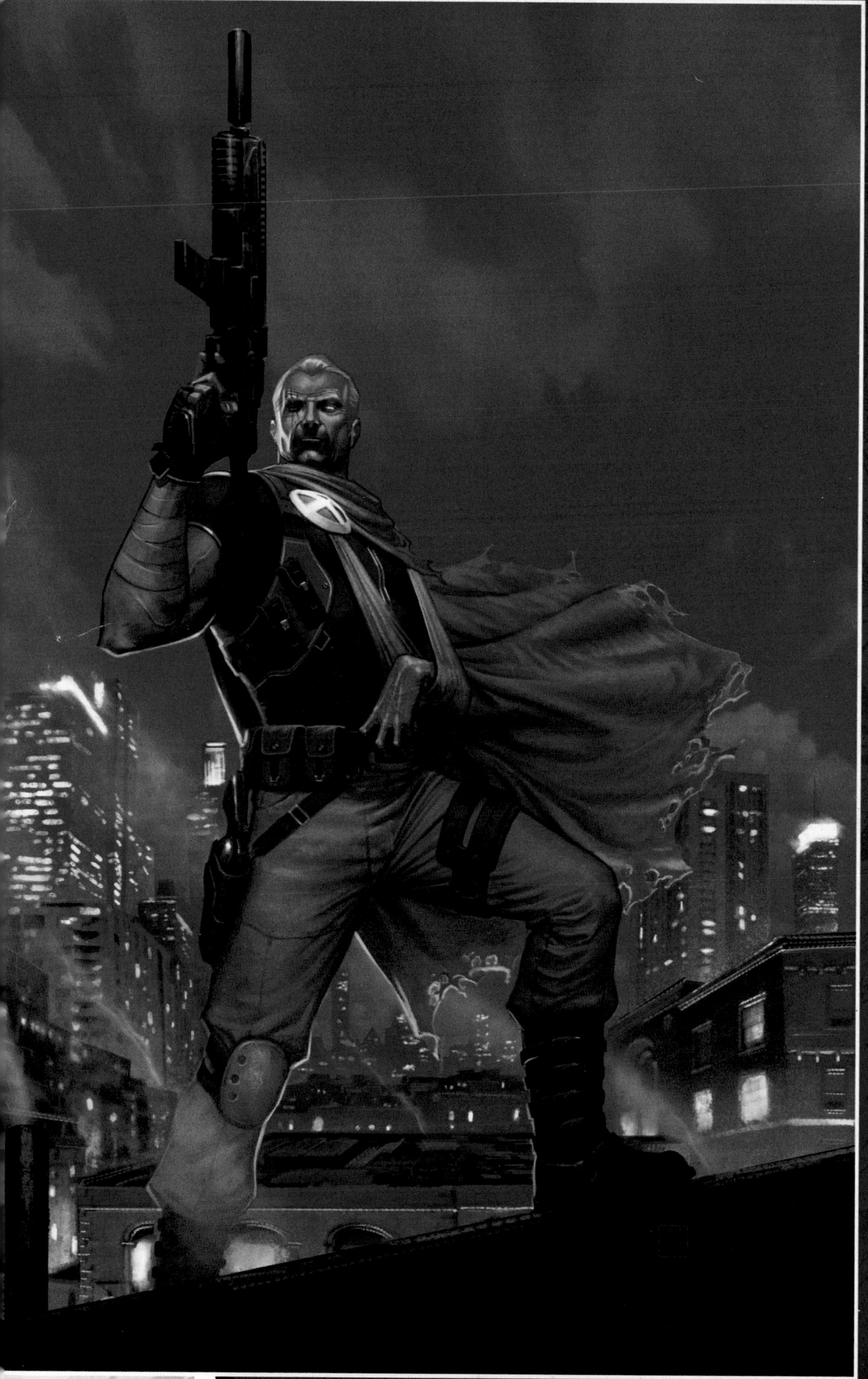

#5 VARIANT
BY **JORGE MOLINA**

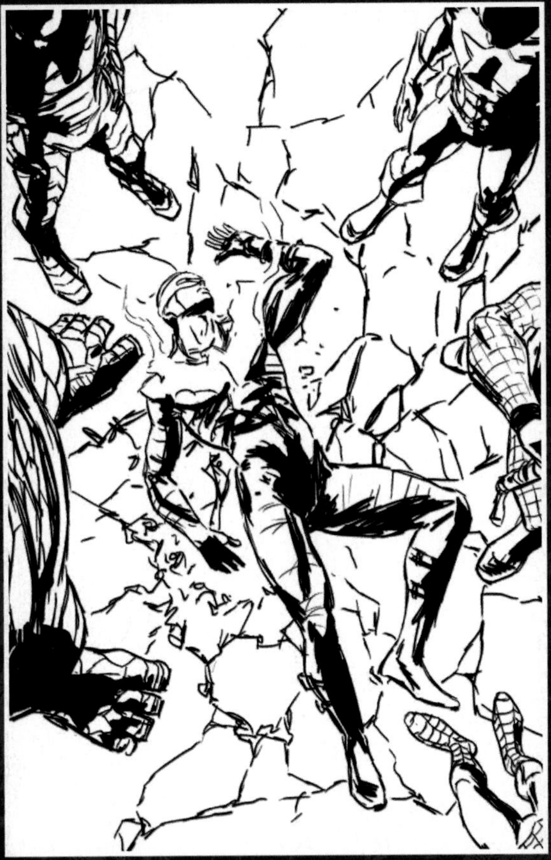

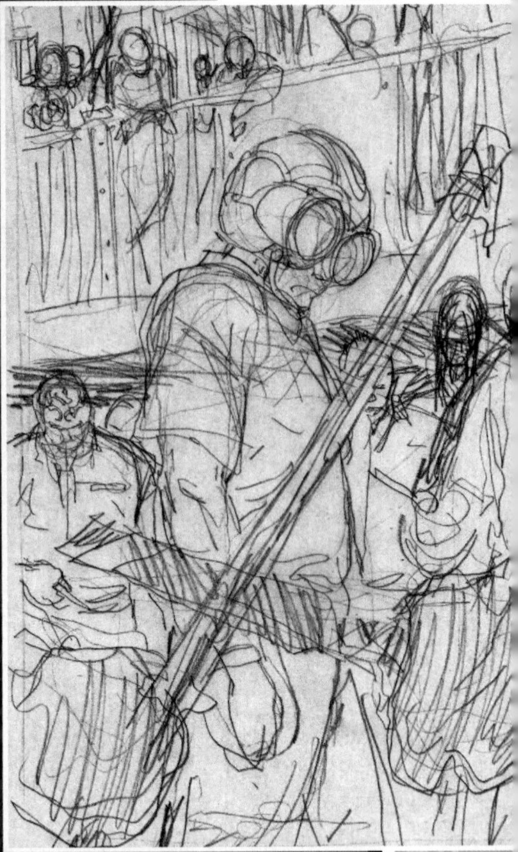

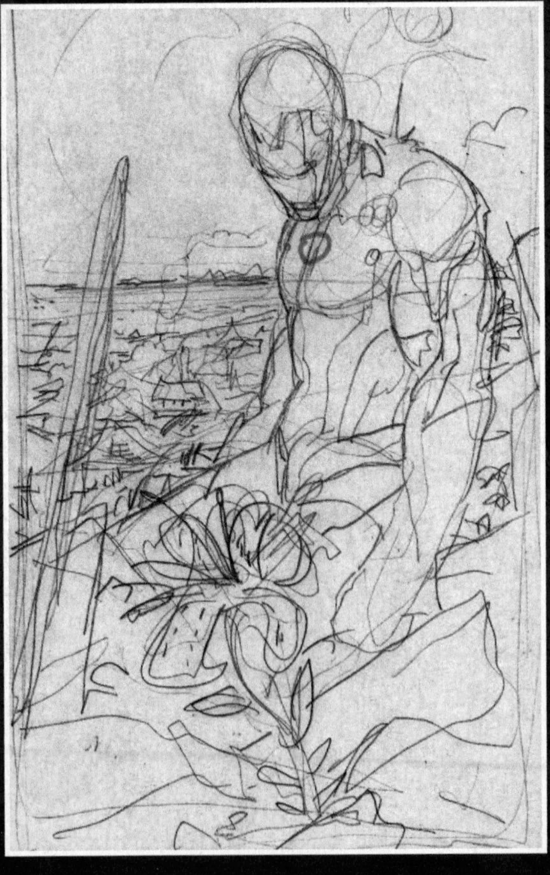

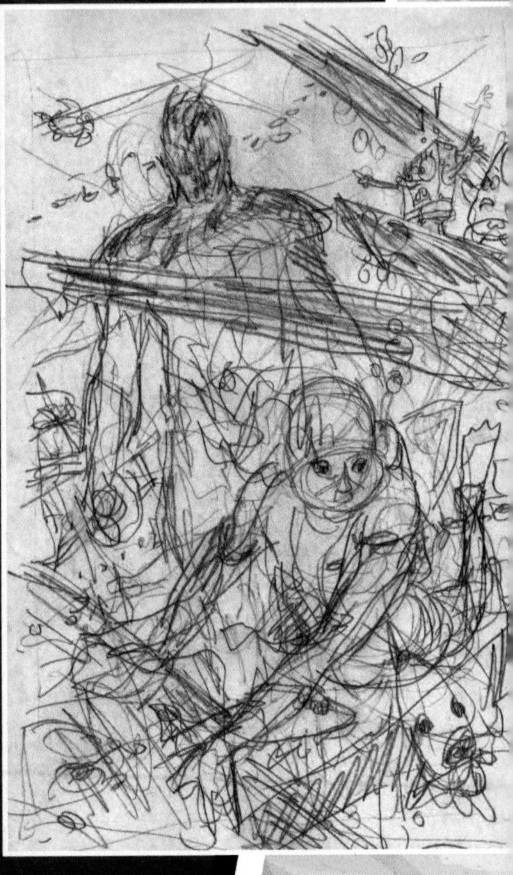

COVER SKETCH GALLERY

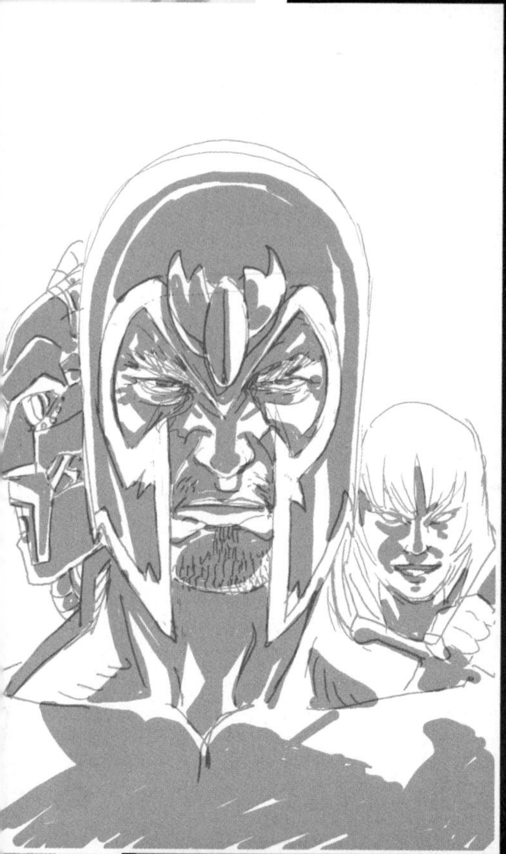

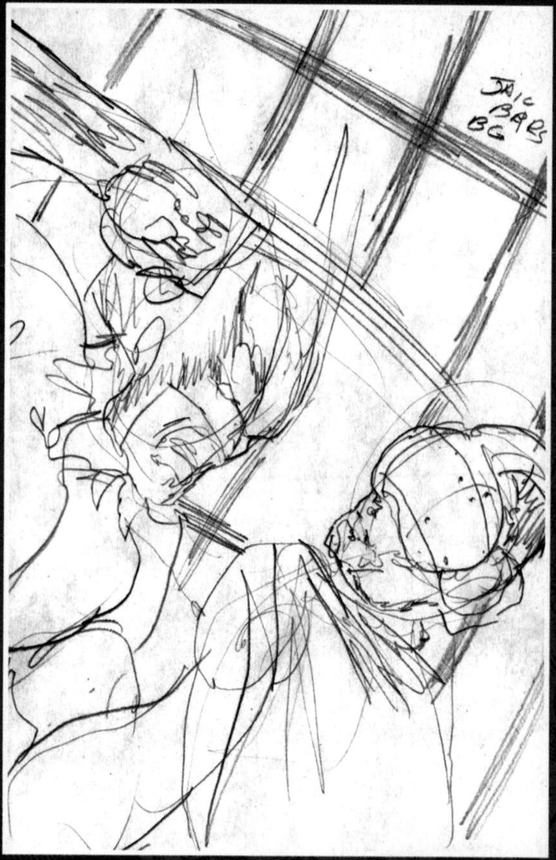

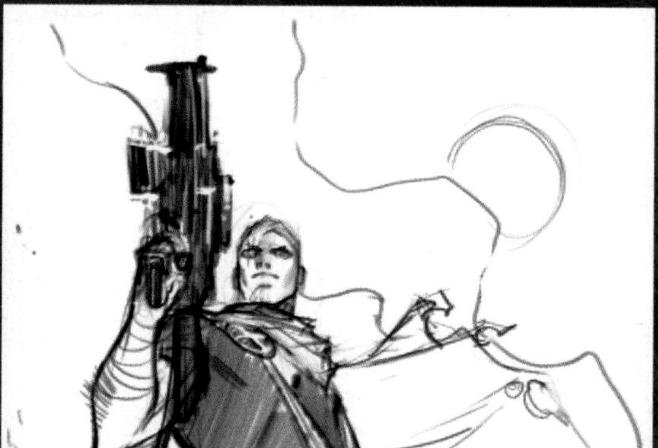

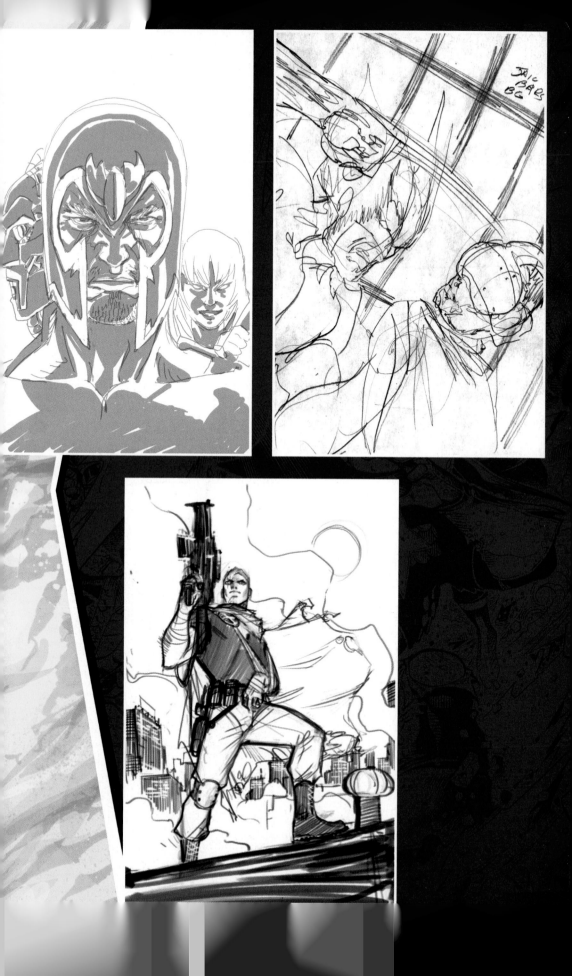

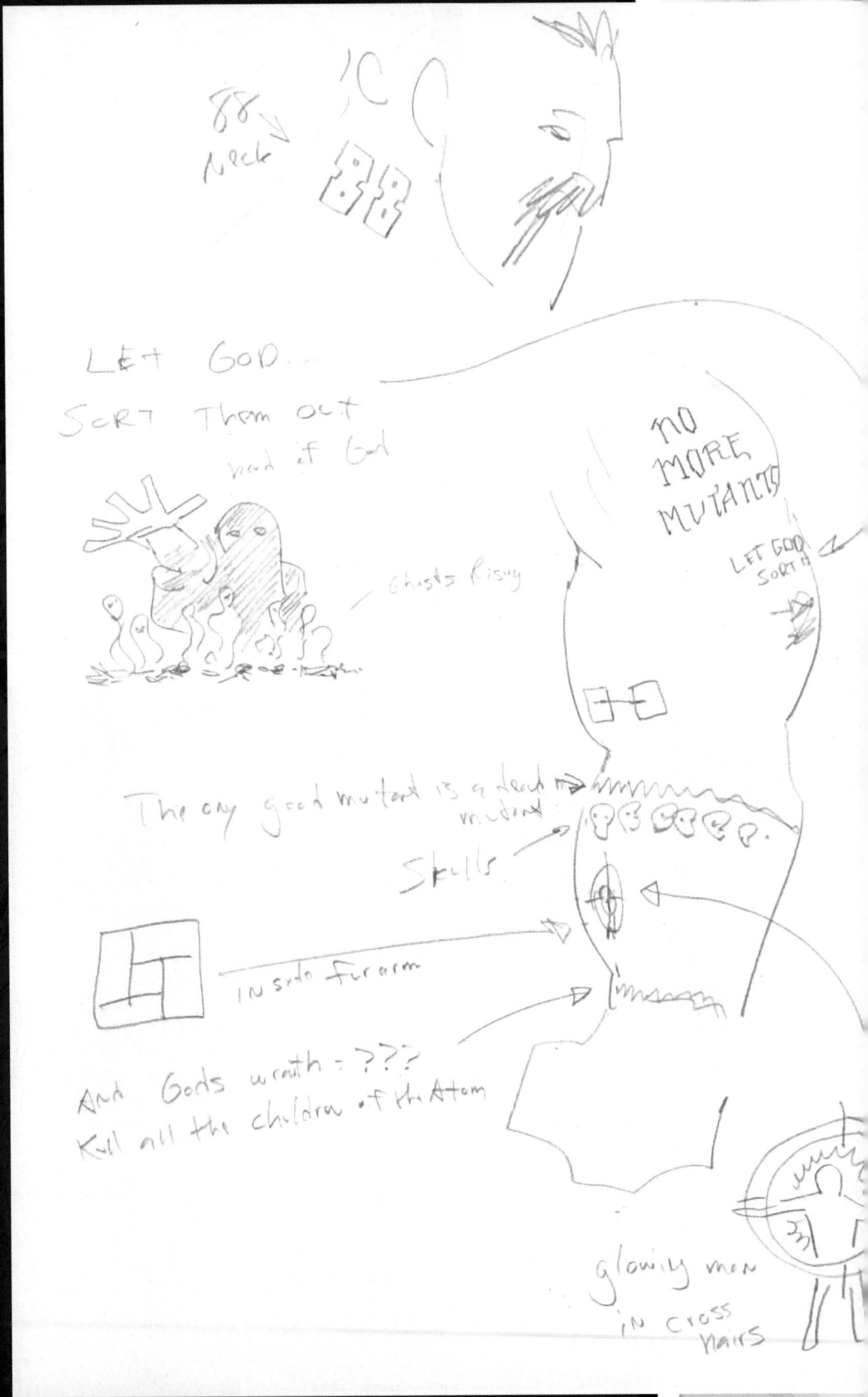
88
Neck
88
LET GOD...
SORT Them out
hand of God
Ghosts Rising
NO
MORE
MUTANTS
LET GOD
SORT
The only good mutant is a dead
mutant
Skulls
IN side forearm
And Gods wrath = ???
Kill all the children of the Atom
glowing man
IN CROSS
hairs

INMATE'S ANTI-MUTANT TATTOO GUIDE

BY STEVE KURTH

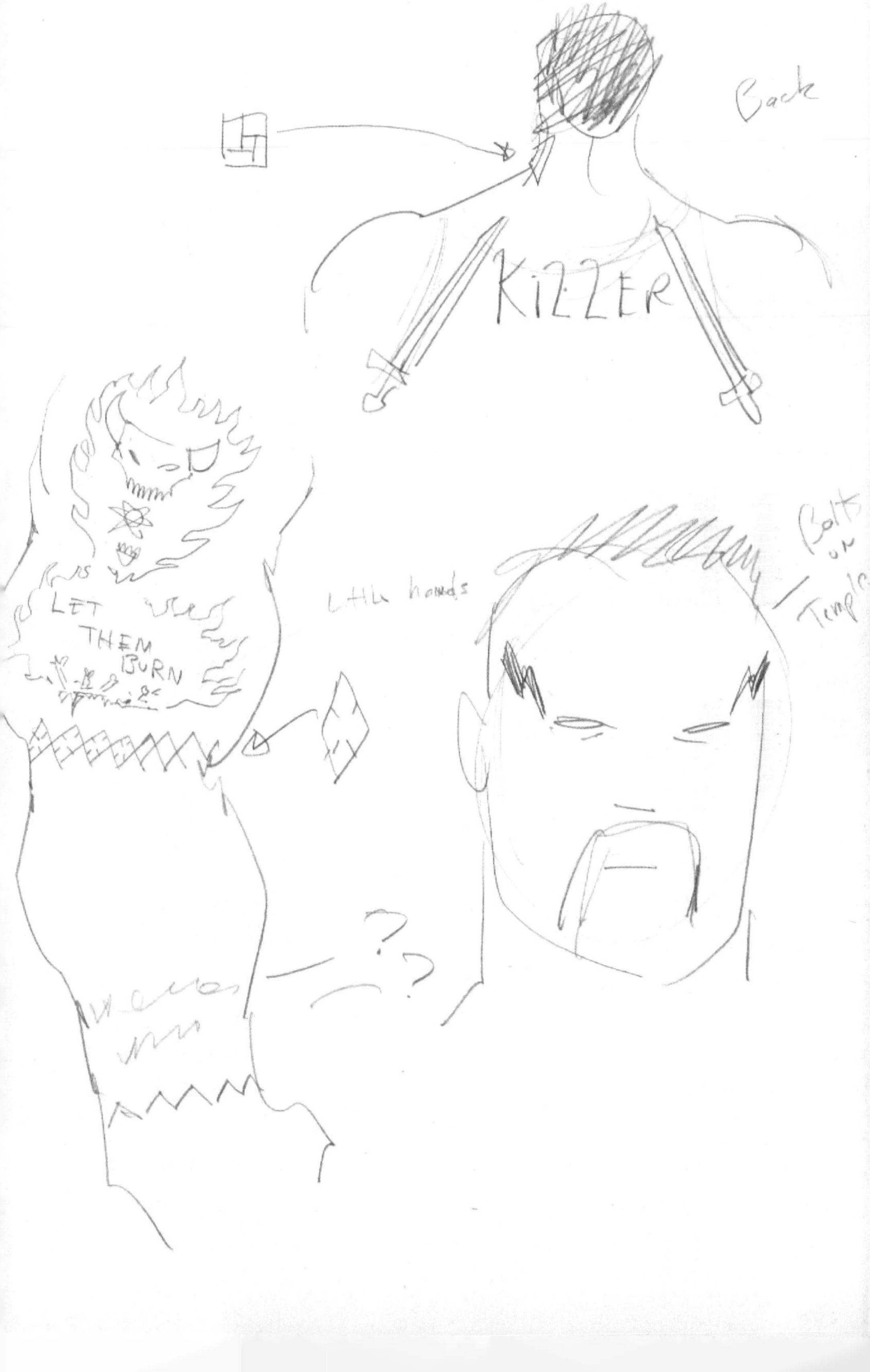

Back
KIZZER
LET THEM BURN
Little hands
Bolts on Temple
??

#1 NEW YORK COMIC CON VARIANT
BY STEVE McNIVEN, JOHN DELL & JUSTIN PONSOR